Human Authors of the New Testament

Volume 2

PAUL AND JOHN

Warren Dicharry, C.M.

St Paul Publications

This printing of *Human Authors of the New Testament*, volume 2, copyright © 1992 by The Order of St Benedict, Inc., Collegeville, Minnesota, United States of America, is published by licence of The Liturgical Press. All rights reserved.

Cover woodcut by Robert F. McGovern; design by Don Bruno

Maps on pages 19 and 99 used with permission. Copyright © United Bible Societies 1978.

St Paul Publications
Middlegreen, Slough SL3 6BT, United Kingdom
Moyglare Road, Maynooth, Co. Kildare, Ireland

ISBN 085439 412 5
Printed in United States of America

St Paul Publications is an activity of the priests and brothers of the Society of St Paul who proclaim the Gospel through the media of social communication

To my superiors and confreres of the Congregation of the Mission (Vincentian Fathers and Brothers), of the Southern Province, U.S.A., who have freed me from administration to take the Word of God to the people of God in biblical missions, retreats, workshops, and the writing of books and articles.

ILLUSTRATIONS

MAPS

CONTENTS

ABBREVIATIONS

CBC	*Collegeville Bible Commentary*
HBC	*Harper's Bible Commentary*
HBD	*Harper's Bible Dictionary*
IBC	*International Bible Commentary*
NAB	New American Bible
NCE	*New Catholic Encyclopedia*
NIV	New International Version
NJB	New Jerusalem Bible
NJBC	*New Jerome Biblical Commentary*
NRSV	New Revised Standard Version
REB	Revised English Bible
TEV	Today's English Version
WFD	Warren F. Dicharry translation

Introduction

"Just as the incarnate Word of God is human in all things except sin, so is the inspired Word of God human in all things except error." This free quotation from Pope Pius XII in his encyclical *Divino Afflante Spiritu,* the Magna Carta of modern Catholic biblical studies,[1] sums up the importance of the human authorship of the Bible. Written in 1943, that extraordinary encyclical will reach its fiftieth anniversary in 1993. Fifty years! Yet the truth contained in that landmark statement is as valid in our day as it ever was. With an economy of words, it admirably describes the mystery of inspiration, the reality of divine and human authorship on which any theory or method of biblical interpretation must be based if it is to do justice to the Scriptures. Anything less actually distorts and even abuses the Word of God. That is why Fundamentalism, which largely ignores the human authorship, and secular humanism, which largely ignores the divine authorship, do violence to one of God's greatest gifts, the Holy Bible.[2]

But enough! In my introduction to the first volume of this work,[3] I have already sufficiently discussed this basic truth. There is no further need to repeat that treatment here. Instead, I want to focus on the individual human authors who were inspired by God to write the books of the New Testament, for that is the specific subject matter of this study. We scripturists generally mention the Bible reader's need of keeping in mind the human as well as the divine authorship, but then we fail to add anything further about the individual human authors except in general, tentative, and often bookish terms, providing the reader with little or no feel for the particular human authors. Who were they? Why and how did they write what they did? If only the reader had some concrete information about the human authors, couched in such a way that he or she could actually visualize them and even identify with them, how much more real and alive would the reading of the Bible become! In the past several years, with the deaths of some rather famous authors,[4] the public has been treated to various portrayals of their lives and analyses of their writings, moving many a reader to read or reread them. Is it not the same with the Bible? Every insight into the particular human authorship not only motivates one to read his inspired work but even offers an entirely new light in which to read and understand it.

At this point, however, I must freely acknowledge that many if not most Scripture scholars today question the necessity and even the possibility of offering anything more than a vague notion of the identification and personality of the individual human authors.[5] Even for the New Testament, they maintain, we simply cannot be sure about the identity of most authors and the circumstances of their writings. Therefore, they conclude, it is best to impart only general information and even to consider the works anonymous or pseudonymous,[6] lest the reader be misled. After all, they add, anonymous and pseudonymous authorship take nothing away from biblical inspiration and canonicity.[7] And besides, they are quick to point out, the concern today is not so much with the meaning of the Scriptures to the human authors, or even to their immediate readers, as with their meaning to us, the modern readers.[8]

All of that may be true, but to me it should not be a question of either . . . or, but of both . . . and. We need to know what we can about the human authors and their intended meaning in the context of their circumstances, culture, and readership, and then we need to understand the importance and significance of their inspired writings for ourselves today. In other words, "The Word of God in Words of Men"[9] requires and deserves both an objective and a subjective approach.[10]

As a matter of fact, that is exactly what I am trying to provide in this two volume work on the five main human authors of the New Testament. Using the Bible itself as well as biblical geography, archaeology, history, and my own imagination, I attempt to give the writings of Mark, Matthew, Luke, Paul and John "a local habitation and a name."[11] Then, I try to analyze their works as objectively as possible, especially in terms of purposes, sources, literary forms, structures, and unique characteristics. Finally, I invite the reader to reflect with me on some relevant doctrinal, moral, and, above all, spiritual applications to our personal and communal lives today.

In the previous volume, I presented the first three of the New Testament's five principal human authors: Mark, "Matthew," and Luke, including his Acts of Apostles. In this second volume, I will focus on the final two authors, namely Paul and John, but with two chapters devoted to each, thus completing the appropriate biblical number of seven[12] chapters altogether. This will be accomplished by dividing the Pauline letters into his earlier and later ones and by treating separately the Gospel and Apocalypse of John. In choosing to treat Paul and John in this way, I fully realize that I am confronting a growing number of scholars who disclaim Pauline authorship for several of what I call his later letters[13] and who maintain categorically that the so-called Gospel of John and the Book of Revelation could not possibly have had the same author.[14] In addition to what I have stated above regarding such questions, let me add that I will attempt to show how the traditional attributions of authorship may not be so farfetched after all. Besides, unless the traditional authorship has been disproved "beyond a reasonable doubt"[15] (as I do believe is the case, for example, with the so-called Gospel of Matthew[16] and the Epistle to the Hebrews),[17] then I feel perfectly justified in retaining and explaining that authorship. "Possession," after all, "is nine points of the law!"[18]

Chronologically, of course, most of the letters attributed to Paul (excluding Hebrews) antedate all the Gospels as well as Acts.[19] However, there is an advantage to treating Paul after Acts because the reader will already be familiar with his life from that second work of Luke, who was one of his companions.[20] The chronological problem can, I believe, be handled effectively by the use of flashbacks, which are already familiar to the reader from their extensive use in today's media. In fact, one way to view this second volume is simply as a set of bookends to the first volume. With Paul representing the left bookend, we flash back to a time before the writings of the three synoptists, Mark, "Matthew," and Luke (with Acts), the subjects of our first volume. With John representing the right bookend, we flash forward to a time after that of the Synoptists. This also gives us something of a parallel[21] because, just as we ended the first volume with the Acts of Apostles, the first Church history, so we will conclude the second volume with the Apocalypse, the first theology of Church history.

Before the conclusion of the introduction to the first volume, I indicated that the translation of the Bible that I would use would be the *New American Bible,* which seems to be the most familiar to Catholics, for whom this work is principally but not exclusively intended, but that I would not hesitate to use whatever translation best captured the meaning of the original Greek, even providing my own translation[22] whenever necessary. Then I added that I would show which translation I would use by the following designations, listed alphabetically: JB for the *Jerusalem Bible,*[23] NAB for the *New American Bible,*[24] NEB for the *New English Bible,*[25] NIV for the *New International Version,*[26] RSV for the *Revised Standard Version,*[27] and WFD for my own translation.

In this second volume, I intend to continue the same system of identification, but with certain changes and understandings brought about by the publication of new or revised translations. Thus, the letters NAB will continue to indicate the *New American Bible,*[28] but in its revised form (at least regarding exclusive language in the New Testament) and especially in the new *Catholic Study Bible.*[29] Likewise, the letters NIV for the *New International Version* and WFD for my own translation will remain the same. However, NEB for the *New English Bible* will be changed to REB for the *Revised English Bible,*[30] while both JB for the *Jerusalem Bible* and RSV for the *Revised Standard Version* will expand to NJB for the *New Jerusalem Bible*[31] and NRSV for the *New Revised Standard Version*[32] respectively. To this list, I would like to add one more translation, *Today's English Version*[33] (TEV), especially as found in the *New Catholic Study Bible.*

While on the subject of new editions, I would like to call the reader's attention to some recent publications in the area of biblical reference works which I will cite from time to time according to their respective initials. Among these, the most important by far, especially among Roman Catholics, are the *New Jerome Biblical Commentary*[34] (NJBC) and, on a somewhat more popular level, the *Collegeville Bible Commentary*[35] (CBC). In addition, I will make use in this volume of the *International Bible Commentary*[36] (IBC) as well as the twin volumes. *Harper's Bible Commentary*[37] (HBC) and *Harper's Bible Dictionary*[38] (HBD), both of them published in conjunction with the Society of Biblical Literature.[39]

Again, as in the first introduction, I want to express my very deep gratitude to the administration, staff, and especially the librarians of Saint Thomas Seminary in Denver, Colorado for their hospitality, encouragement, and gracious help, to my superiors and confreres of our Southern Province of the Congregation of the Mission (Vincentian Fathers and Brothers) for giving me the opportunity to write, and finally to Mark Twomey and Bette Montgomery of The Liturgical Press for their indispensable assistance in enabling this complex two-volume work to reach publication.

Warren F. Dicharry, C.M.
Vincentian Evangelization[40]
Saint Stephen's Rectory,
New Orleans, Louisiana

NOTES

1. See *Rome and the Study of Scripture*, 6th ed. (St. Meinrad, Ind: Grail, 1958) 98.

2. The abuse of a sacred thing is, at least objectively, a sacrilege, but presumably there is no subjective guilt, because of lack of awareness. "Father, forgive them, for they know not what they do!" (Luke 23:34, WFD).

3. *See* the introduction to vol. 1, pp. 8–10.

4. In 1989 alone, for example, there died Samuel Beckett, Daphne du Maurier, Mary McCarthy, Georges Simenon, Irving Stone, Barbara Tuchman, and Robert Penn Warren.

5. *See* Raymond Brown, "Canonicity," *NJBC*, art. 66, par. 87.

6. Anonymity refers to unknown authorship; pseudonymity, to fictitious authorship. See *Webster's Ninth New Collegiate Dictionary*.

7. *See* Brown, "Canonicity," *NJBC*, art. 66, par. 87.

8. *See* Sandra Schneiders, "Hermeneutics," *NJBC*, art. 71, pars. 53–70; *see also* Dianne Bergant, "Introduction to the Bible," *CBC*, 31–33.

9. *See* Jean Levie, *The Bible, Word of God in Words of Men*, trans. S. H. Treman (New York: Kenedy, 1961).

10. *See* Bergant, "Introduction," *CBC*, 33–34; *see also* Raymond Brown, "Hermeneutics," *NJBC*, art. 71, par. 77.

11. *A Midsummer Night's Dream*, V.i.17, in William Shakespeare, *The Complete Works*, ed. Alfred Harbage (Baltimore: Penguin Books, 1969) 169.

12. In the Bible, numbers are often used symbolically, particularly the number seven, symbolic of completeness and perfection. See *HBD*, 711.

13. *See* Raymond Collins, *Letters That Paul Did Not Write* (Wilmington, Del: Michael Glazier, 1988); *see also* Brown, "Canonicity," *NJBC*, art. 66, pars. 56–59.

14. *See* Adela Collins, "The Apocalypse (Revelation)," *NJBC*, art. 63, pars. 7–9; *see also* Pheme Perkins, "Revelation," *CBC*, 1267.

15. Henry Black, *Black's Law Dictionary*, rev. 4th ed. (St. Paul West Publishing, 1968) 578–80.

16. *See* Benedict Vivian, "The Gospel According to Matthew" *NJBC*, art. 42, par. 2; *see also* Daniel Harrington, "Matthew" *CBC*, 862–63.

17. *See* Myles Bourke, "The Epistle to the Hebrews" *NJBC*, art. 60, pars. 2–3; *see also* George McRae, "Hebrews," *CBC*, 1246.

18. An old English proverb, familiar since the seventeenth century. *See* H. L. Mencken, *A New Dictionary of Quotations* (New York: Alfred Knopf, 1942) 946.

19. *See* Brown, "Canonicity," *NJBC*, art. 66, par. 56.

20. *See Acts* 16:10-17; 20:5–22:19; 27:1–28:28; Col 4:14.

21. The structure of parallels is frequently found in the New Testament, e.g., between Luke's Gospel and Acts and, within Acts, between the acts of Peter and the acts of Paul.

22. As credentials for offering my own translation, let me refer the reader to my work *Greek Without Grief: An Outline Guide to New Testament Greek* (Chicago: Loyola University Press, 1989).

23. Alexander Jones, ed., *The Jerusalem Bible* (Garden City, N.Y.: Doubleday, 1966).

24. *The New American Bible* (Camden, N.J.: Nelson, 1971).

25. Sandmel, Suggs, and Tkacik, eds., *The New English Bible* (New York: Oxford University Press, 1976).

26. *The Holy Bible: New International Version* (Grand Rapids: Zondervan, 1978).

27. Bernard Orchard and Reginald Fuller, eds., *The Holy Bible* (Revised Standard Version / Catholic Edition) (Collegeville: The Liturgical Press, 1966).

28. *The New American Bible* (St. Joseph Edition) with the revised New Testament (New York: Catholic Book, 1987).

29. Donald Senior and others, eds., *The Catholic Study Bible* (Revised New American Bible) (New York: Oxford University Press, 1990).

30. *The Revised English Bible* (England: Oxford and Cambridge University Presses, 1989).

31. Henry Wansbrough, ed., *The New Jerusalem Bible* (New York: Doubleday, 1985).

32. *The New Revised Standard Version* (Nashville: Nelson, 1990).

33. *The New Catholic Study Bible (Today's English Version)* (St. Jerome Edition) (New York: Catholic Bible Press, 1985).

34. Raymond Brown, Joseph Fitzmyer, and Roland Murphy, eds., *The New Jerome Biblical Commentary* (Englewood Cliffs, N.J.: Prentice Hall, 1990).

35. Dianne Bergant and Robert Karris, eds., *The Collegeville Bible Commentary* (Collegeville: The Liturgical Press, 1989).

36. F. F. Bruce, ed., *The International Bible Commentary, rev. ed.* (New York: Guideposts, 1986).

37. James Mays, ed., *Harper's Bible Commentary* (San Francisco: Harper & Row, 1988).

38. Paul Achtemeier, ed., *Harper's Bible Dictionary,* (San Francisco: Harper & Row, 1985).

39. A prestigious ecumenical and interfaith organization devoted to bib-

lical studies which publishes the *Journal of Biblical Literature* as well as numerous monographs.

40. For those who may wonder, evangelization, especially in the form of parish missions, is the first apostolate of the Congregation of the Mission, founded by St. Vincent de Paul in 1625. I use the term "Vincentian Evangelization" to designate primarily my apostolate of biblical missions, retreats, and workshops. And just as my book on biblical spirituality, *To Live the Word, Inspired and Incarnate* (Staten Island, N.Y.: Alba, 1985), serves in part as a follow-up to my biblical missions and retreats, so also this work on the human authors of the New Testament will serve in part as a follow-up to my biblical workshops.

CORINTH IN THE FIRST CENTURY A.D.

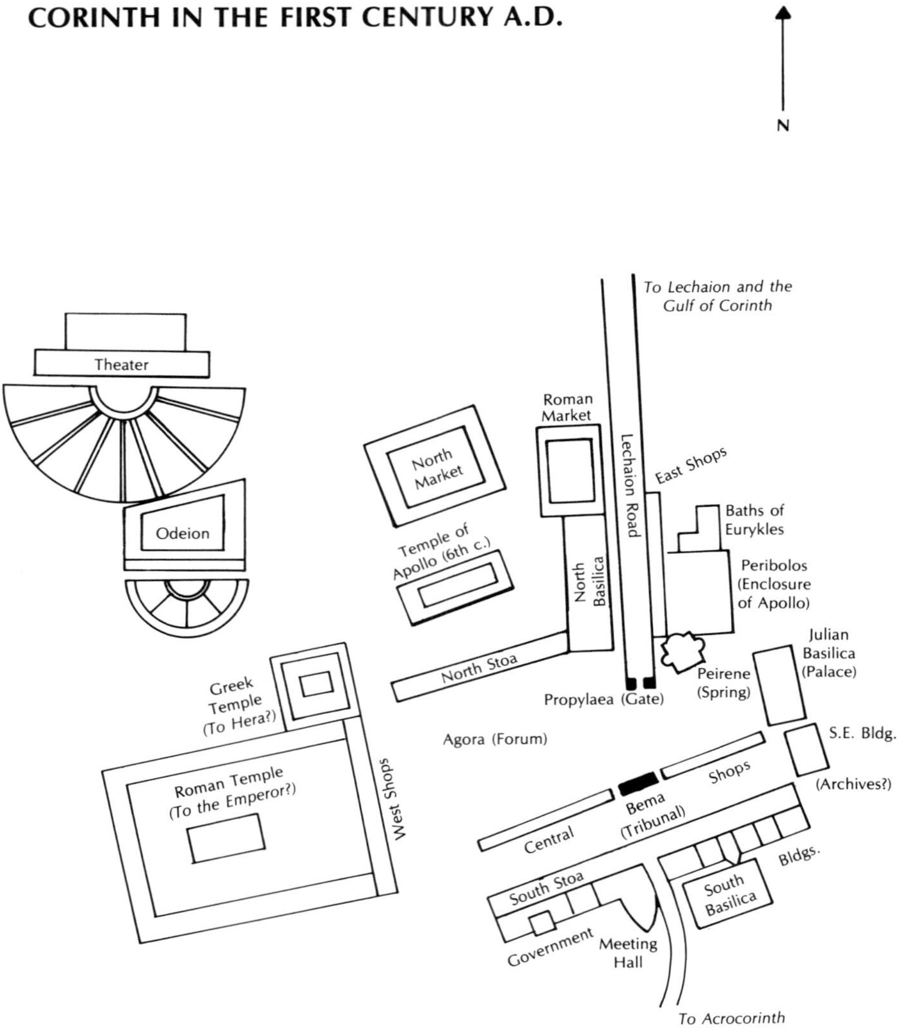

N

To Lechaion and the
Gulf of Corinth

Theater

Roman
Market

North
Market

Odeion

Temple of
Apollo (6th c.)

Lechaion Road

East Shops

Baths of
Eurykles

Peribolos
(Enclosure
of Apollo)

North
Basilica

North Stoa

Propylaea (Gate)

Peirene
(Spring)

Julian
Basilica
(Palace)

Greek
Temple
(To Hera?)

Agora (Forum)

S.E. Bldg.

(Archives?)

Roman Temple
(To the Emperor?)

West Shops

Shops

Central

Bema
(Tribunal)

South Stoa

South
Basilica

Bldgs.

Government

Meeting
Hall

To Acrocorinth

1

Passionate Paul[1] and the Early Letters[2]

Christ is living in me![3] (Gal 2:20)

THE EARLY STORY OF PAUL

He strolled alone down the Lechaion Road,[4] serene yet searching. Paul, also called Saul,[5] sensed that he had reached a crucial milestone in his life, that he was in a kind of quiet valley between the mountainous achievements of the past and the colossal challenges of the future. Guided by the Spirit, he knew that he needed to pause and review what Christ had so far accomplished through him in order to discern, if possible, how and where the Lord was calling him to minister for the remainder of his life. And what more appropriate place to do just that than here at Corinth,[6] the gateway between east and west, north and south, in strategic Greece,[7] the very city that had figured so prominently in his own past agonies and ecstasies?

In some ways, Corinth was a mirror of Paul himself. As he had spiritually died to his past prominence as a Pharisee and risen again with Christ, so had Corinth, destroyed by the Romans in 146 B.C., risen phoenix-like[8] from its ashes in 44 B.C. to become again not only flourishing and prominent but even the seat of Roman government in Achaia,[9] the principal area of Greece. And the passionate energy of Corinth in commerce, industry, athletics, and even religion[10] (albeit misguided) seemed to mirror the passionate energy of Paul, impelled[11] as he was by the inexhaustible love of the risen Christ.

As Paul continued his pensive promenade down the Lechaion Road toward the western harbor, leaving farther and farther behind the

Corinth and Acrocorinth from the Lechaion Road.

gleaming city with its impressive government buildings, temples, porticoes, offices, markets, baths, theater, and odeon,[12] his mind quickly traveled backward in time, finally coming to rest with the happy remembrance of his childhood. How providentially had God prepared him for his future apostolate! Born at Tarsus[13] in Cilicia, "no mean city"[14] in southern Asia Minor, he had grown up tricultural. Steeped in the Greek language, philosophy, and culture[15] for which the city prided itself, he had also received a thorough Jewish education from his Pharisaic parents and the local synagogue,[16] and in addition he had enjoyed all the privileges and advantages of Roman citizenship.[17] With a smile, he recalled that although (or perhaps because) he had been small for his age, his determination and boundless energy had enabled him to excel not only in his studies, but also in athletics, theater, and declamations.[18] In a much later age he would have been categorized as an overachiever.

Quickly, Saul's reverie advanced to the next stage of his life, namely his unforgettable years of rabbinical study in Jerusalem "at the feet of Gamaliel,"[19] a worthy grandson of the famous Rabbi Hillel himself.

It was also during this time, Paul recalled, that he had perfected his skill of tentmaking,[20] a useful and remunerative trade, especially in a pilgrimage city like Jerusalem.

Painfully, Saul relived that short period of his fanatic persecution[21] of those determined devotees whom he then knew only as followers of the disgraced Nazarene carpenter who had been condemned as a false messiah by the highest Jewish authorities and crucified by orders of the Roman governor. How could they accept their sufferings so patiently, even cheerfully? He vividly recalled becoming increasingly troubled by that phenomenon even while he redoubled his zeal in order to drown out his growing misgivings.

It had all begun with the powerful preaching of a young Hellenist orator named Stephen.[22] Brilliant in open debate, he had first silenced the Synagogue of Roman Freedmen (including some of Saul's fellow Cilicians)[23] and then held the great Sanhedrin itself spellbound, until he dared to taunt them as stiffnecked, uncircumcised in mind and heart, always opposing the Holy Spirit, killing the prophets, and finally betraying and murdering the Just One himself, Jesus of Nazareth, the messianic Son of Man whom he, Stephen, claimed to see in a vision standing at the right hand of the Almighty.[24] This was too much! Horrified, the Sanhedrin had summarily condemned him to stoning, and Saul had concurred in the justice of the sentence by personally watching the garments of those who were stoning Stephen to death.[25] But what actually began the process of unsettling Saul was the sight and sound of the dying Stephen praying, "Lord Jesus, receive my spirit!" And, even more disturbingly, "Lord, do not hold this sin against them!" (Acts 7:59-60, NAB).

Saul found himself torn between the attraction of Stephen's faith and forgiveness on the one hand and his own Pharisaic convictions on the other, and he clearly recalled that sleepless night when he finally decided that the only safe and sane course was to remain true to his Jewish roots as interpreted by the Sanhedrin.[26] And when that same Sanhedrin recruited him to lead the persecution of Stephen's coreligionists, what could he do but comply with the same energy that had driven him his entire life? In his zeal he even sought permission to go as far as Damascus, capital of another country and under Nabatean[27] rule, to arrest there the followers of the Nazarene sect. He did not even question the legality or justice of such an incursion. In fact, as he later came to realize, the only thing that would have made him hesitate might have been some kind of proof that the crucified Nazarene had indeed done the impossible, as his followers claimed, by actually rising from the dead on the third day. But how could he even consider such a preposterous notion? Never! No, never, until that day when the impossible truly happened and he encountered the risen Christ himself on the road to Damascus![28]

The more Paul reminisced about that unforgettable event, the more astonished and grateful he became. To think that the risen Christ himself would actually appear to him and commission him, of all people, to be an apostle to the nations![29] Not only that, but the Lord's very words in his self-revelation were to become the cornerstone of his, Paul's, entire thinking and living. "I am Jesus whom you are persecuting!" (Acts 9:5, NAB). Not only had he risen from the dead, but he continued to live in his followers! And he wanted to continue to live, to serve, to suffer even in him, Saul or Paul! How that encounter had revolutionized and shaped the rest of his life!

But, Paul remembered, while the cornerstone was there, the rest of the edifice of his new life had taken time to develop. With his life threatened by the Damascus Jews as a traitor to their cause, he had first fled to the desert of Arabia,[30] where he found the solitude and quiet he needed to rethink his Jewish background, to reinterpret the Holy Scriptures in the light of Jesus Christ, now recognized both as the Jewish Messiah and as the unique Son of God!

Every time Paul recalled the hatred that he had evoked among his fellow Jews, his whole being was filled with dismay. Just as at Damascus, so also in Jerusalem, where he had gone after three years to meet with the apostles and assist the Church there, his Jewish brothers had marked him for death, and so the Christian leaders there sent him home to Tarsus to await a more favorable time.[31] But this too was providential, for Paul now recognized and admitted to himself that he had needed more quiet time, especially for two reasons: first, to grow in his union with Christ, letting the Lord take full possession of him so that He could continue his life and ministry through him; and secondly, so that, under the guidance of the Holy Spirit, he could develop that whole Christian theology that was needed as the basis of his preaching, teaching, and pastoral guidance. Only after those years at Tarsus was he truly ready for his mission to the Gentiles.

Ready, yes, but not yet perfect, for Paul remembered with sadness how, after that first exhilarating thrust through Cyprus and southern

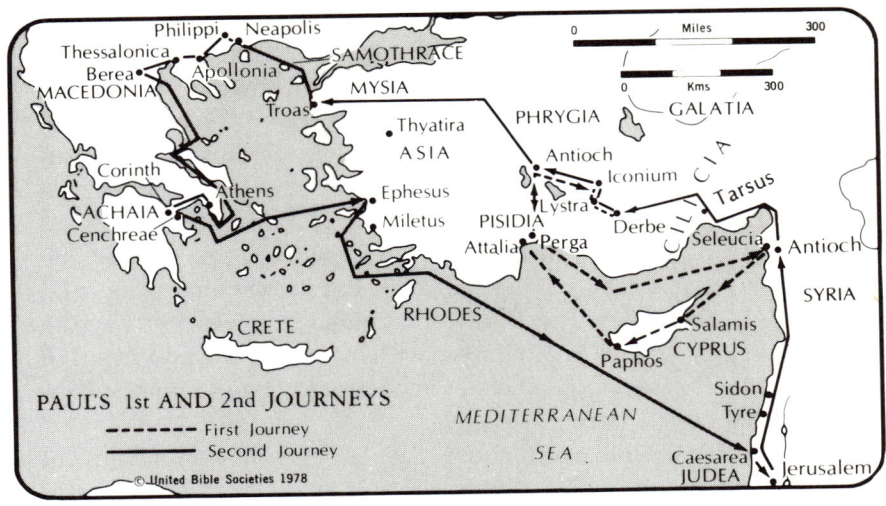

PAUL'S 1st AND 2nd JOURNEYS
- - - - - First Journey
————— Second Journey
© United Bible Societies 1978

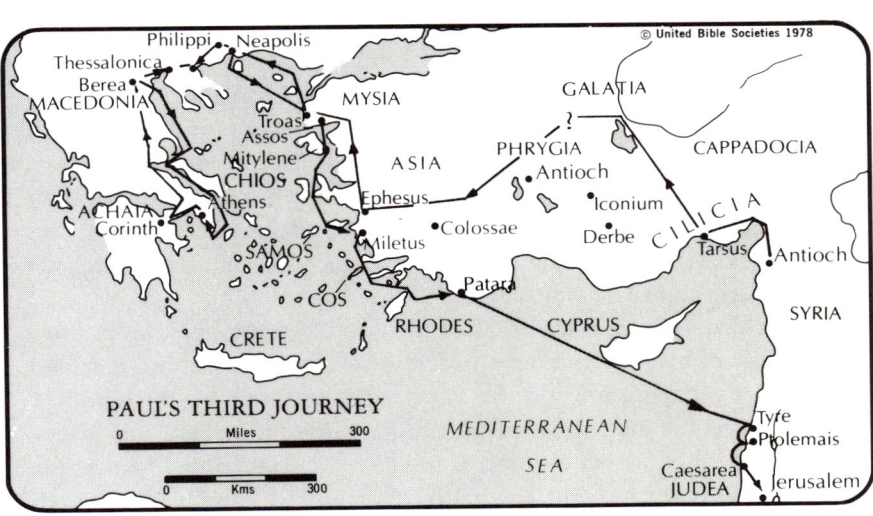

PAUL'S THIRD JOURNEY
© United Bible Societies 1978

Asia Minor,[32] and after the heady victory against the Judaizers[33] at the Council of Jerusalem,[34] he had angrily parted with his friend, Barnabas over the latter's cousin, John Mark.[35] How could he have behaved in such a way with Barnabas of all people: the "son of encouragement"[36] who had introduced him to the apostles,[37] who had traveled over the Amanus mountains from Antioch to Tarsus to enable him to begin his work among the Gentiles,[38] and who had selflessly played a second-

19

ary role to his own on that first missionary journey.[39] Someday, he hoped, he would see Barnabas again, yes and Mark too, so that he might seek their forgiveness and friendship. Meanwhile, Paul could not help but rejoice and thank God as he reviewed the even greater success of his second missionary journey. Accompanied by the erudite Silas,[40] he had first revisited overland the sites of his earlier missionary preaching in southern Asia Minor,[41] recruiting the young but very promising Timothy at Lystra.[42] Then, swinging northward, he and his two companions had found surprising success among the wild Galatians.[43] From there they had been guided due westward by the Spirit to Troas[44] on the Anatolian[45]coast, where his beloved physician friend, Luke,[46] eagerly joined his little missionary band for its first incursion into fabled Greece.

How unforgettable were those days at the military colony of Philippi,[47] at the sparkling commercial and political capital of northern Greece, Thessalonica,[48] at beautiful and receptive Beroea,[49] and at proud, dilettantish Athens.[50] Almost as if it had all happened just the day before, Paul could vividly remember the pain and humiliation of his illegal scourging and imprisonment at Philippi, but also the joy of his miraculous release and consequent conversion of the jailer and all his family.[51] Equally vivid was his enthusiastic reception in Thessalonica, especially by the Gentiles, followed by the usual rejection on the part of his fellow Jews, both there and at Beroea.[52] Then, finally, there was his disappointing failure at Athens,[53] the cultural capital not only of Greece but of the world.

After dispatching Silas and Timothy to Thessalonica to check on the fidelity of his new converts there, he had waited for them at fabled Athens, wandering around the agora and discussing with whoever would listen the story of Jesus and his resurrection. How his hopes had soared when he was invited to speak at the Areopagus![54] And how carefully he had prepared a suitably philosophical and rhetorical address that he had felt sure would win over his audience of intellectual Athenians. What a shattering experience! As soon as it dawned on his listeners that *Iesoûs* and *Anástasis* were not a new god and goddess but a man named Jesus and his resurrection from the dead, they had summarily dismissed him as a fool.[55] No matter! God had, as usual, turned the experience to good for Paul and his apostolate, since he had learned the hard way never again to preach according to Greek philosophy and rhetoric, but simply to present "Jesus Christ and him crucified."[56]

The Galatian capital Ancyra from the modern Turkish capital Ankara.

Thessalonica, capital of Northern Greece then and now.

21

Such was Paul's determination as he moved on to Corinth, but he undoubtedly had little stomach for preaching there. Overwhelmed with a sense of failure after his Athenian experience and of loneliness without Silas and Timothy, and faced with the proverbial Corinthian decadence,[57] Paul needed nothing less than an encouraging vision from Jesus himself to continue the task of evangelization. But what a pleasant surprise was in store for him! So receptive were the Corinthians that he ended up spending a year and a half there,[58] not only receiving many Jewish and even more Gentile converts but also making some very special friends[59] for life. Among these friends were a cherished Jewish couple named Aquila and Priscilla with whom Paul lodged and plied his trade as tentmaker, a leading member of the synagogue named Crispus and his whole family, and a Gentile called Titius Justus, whose ample home next to the synagogue became the first house-church of Corinth.

Meanwhile, Paul's "lost" companions, Silas and Timothy, had finally rejoined him[60] with the cheering news that his Thessalonian converts were persevering admirably in spite of Jewish opposition. They were forced to add, however, that certain matters were troubling the converts, a concern for their deceased loved ones who, they feared, would not be able to welcome Christ with them at his return in triumph. Silas and Timothy had prolonged their stay among them, trying in every way possible to relieve their fears but with no success. They would accept no reassurances except from Paul himself in person.

What to do? Paul clearly remembered that he had seen no solution at first. It would have been foolhardy for him to attempt a return to Thessalonica at that time, in the face of death threats from his fellow Jews. Still, something had to be done to calm the fears of his faithful Thessalonians. Yes, something had to be done, and done fast, but what? It was the perceptive Priscilla[61] who had the answer. "Why not write them a letter?" What an inspiration from God! Of course! A letter would be just the answer, and Paul was already well acquainted with the accepted format of letter writing in the Greek world,[62] so he could quickly visualize how, with a few changes, that format could be Christianized and personalized. "Thus, out of sheer necessity," mused Paul, "began my so-called career as a letter writer!"

Well did he remember that first of his letters: very brief indeed, but filled with expressions of his tender love for his long-suffering Thessalonian Christians. How else could he possibly convince them of his fatherly and even motherly care for them,[63] even though he could not return to them at this time as they desired? In regard to their pressing concern about their loved ones, he tried as clearly as possible to assure them that all, living and dead, would indeed participate in the Lord's second coming.[64] At the same time, and probably because he was writing out of the decadent atmosphere of Corinth, he decided to include (along with other recommendations regarding good conduct)[65] an urgent exhortation to holiness, especially in regard to sexual morality.[66]

This, Paul humbly recalled, was but the first of several letters. The second was also addressed to the Thessalonians, but at a time near the end of his sojourn in Corinth. Once again, the neophyte Christian community at Thessalonica was preoccupied with the second coming of the Lord, even expecting it momentarily, basing this expectation on a letter purportedly written by Paul himself and, in the case of a good number of the community, ceasing work and normal lives to await the parousia. This time, Paul's pastoral remedy was bitter but healthful medicine indeed, categorically disavowing the letter in question,[67] warning that the second coming would occur only after a great apostasy[68] (requiring first of all a great spread of Christianity), and finally stipulating that those who would not work should not eat![69]

His next letter, Paul reminisced, had been written on his third missionary journey from the great city of Ephesus to this very Church of Corinth. Actually, he well remembered, it was a double letter, partly containing his pastoral solutions to the problems brought to his attention by members of Chloe's household,[70] and partly offering his pastoral responses to a number of questions posed to him by letter.[71] What stuck in his mind, above all, was the opportunity that both parts of the letter had given him to develop and clarify his thoughts on a wide variety of pastoral matters, thoughts he continued to develop and apply when similar problems and questions arose among the various Churches that he had established.

His second letter to his dear Corinthian Christians had been quite different from the first. By turns consoling, self-revealing, hard hitting, and calmly directive, it was not so much a letter as a collection of letters.[72] Standing out most vividly in Paul's mind was the primary occasion of the letter, namely the dangerous challenge to him and to his apostolic authority that had been promoted in Corinth by his erstwhile opponents within Christianity, the Judaizers,[73] who had refused to accept the decision of the Council of Jerusalem against the requirement that Gentile converts should become Jews as well as Christians. In response to this threat to the very foundations of the Church at Corinth, Paul had first made a quick return trip from Ephesus, only to meet nothing but opposition and humiliation.[74] Then, on return to Ephesus, he had dispatched a newly recruited companion named Titus[75] to Corinth with a brief letter, written "with many tears,"[76] and awaited Titus' return, hopefully with good news, first in Ephesus, then in Troas. Finally, when he had gone on to Philippi, he had the overwhelming joy not only of welcoming Titus again but above all of learning from him that all was well again at Corinth.[77] How his relief and consolation had poured out in that letter, sent back to Corinth with Titus! And how his entire heart had poured out in the most self-revealing of all his letters!

Paul clearly recalled that, in his joy, he had fully intended to follow closely on the heels of Titus, both to embrace anew his repentant Corinthians and to receive the results of the collection that he had suggested for the Judean Christians suffering from famine and oppression.[78] That had indeed been his desire, but, alas, before he could put it into effect, he had been informed of new inroads of the Judaizers, this time among the Christians of Galatia in northern Asia Minor. Not again! Paul's face flushed as he remembered his anger at the news. In retrospect, he had to admit that the vehement letter he had dashed off to the Galatians upbraiding them for departing from his teaching[79] had been fueled by his anger at the Judaizers, not only in Galatia but in Corinth as well.

As always, however, God had once more turned things to his own good,[80] that of the Galatians, and, in fact, that of the Church at large. For in the process of responding to the position of the Judaizers, he had clarified and presented a theology of justification by faith[81] rather than by works, which he had neglected to do in the Corinthian crisis. Better late than never! Now he felt fully prepared to dispute with any pesky Judaizers whom he might encounter in the future. He also felt that the contrast that he had drawn in his letter to the Galatians between life in the Spirit and life in the flesh[82] would also be extremely useful in future exhortations to his flock, as would his landmark declaration in Gal 3:28 about unity and equality of all people in Christ: Jew and Gentile, slave and free, male and female.

Now here he was, back in Corinth. For the time being, all was calm. In fact, Paul felt very much like a boxer[83] with no more opponents to battle. What was the Lord asking of him now? That was the question whose answer he had hoped would rise out of his review of his life, work, and letters until now. No longer was he the athlete and orator that he had once fancied himself. In his middle fifties,[84] short and somewhat bowlegged from his long journeys on foot and animals, almost totally bald, with a rather long pointed beard, Paul fully realized that he did not present a very prepossessing figure,[85] but he was also aware that when he fixed people with his large luminous eyes, he had their full attention.

Perhaps therein lay the answer to his question. What did he see with those eyes of his? Of course! At the end of the Lechaion Road lay the Gulf of Corinth, leading to the Adriatic Sea and on to Italy and the Eternal City of Rome! Now it all made sense and he could see his future clearly! He had already, in a sense, conquered Asia Minor and Greece for the Lord; now it was time to go to the very heart of the Roman Empire with the good news of Jesus Christ!

But how? He could not just show up there one day without any prior announcement. There was already a Church in Rome, even dating back to the return from Jerusalem of some of those first Christians converted on the day of Pentecost. Out of protocol if nothing else, he really should send someone on ahead to announce his coming, for he never wanted to encroach on anyone else's missionary territory.[86] But wait! From his experience in letter writing, why not have his emissary deliver a letter to the Church of Rome, a letter that would contain his primary theological ideas and pastoral convictions, developed in his years of solitude, from his multitude of missionary and pastoral experiences, and even from his letter-writing apostolate, and presented in an orderly fashion worthy of the Church in the principal city of the civilized world?

"What a challenge," thought Paul to himself, "to draw together into one coherent whole all that I've been preaching and teaching and writing over these past several years, and to present it in a way that will be helpful to the noble Church of Rome and, who knows, perhaps to others as well! But, of course, I mustn't make the mistake of trying to say too much, otherwise the letter will be too long and then who will read it? No, I must pick and choose.

"Central to the letter must be what I learned from my risen Lord himself, namely that he himself is the core of our Christian life, and that our whole justification and salvation come, not through our own human efforts nor by our observance of the Mosaic Law but through acceptance of our crucified and risen Lord by faith[87] and living out that faith in love. He it is who frees us from our sinfulness, our earthbound life of the flesh, so that we may continue his risen life, the life of the Spirit.[88] Without him, all of us, whether Jews or Gentiles, are simply mired in sin and lacking that relationship with God for which we were created.

"To present this as effectively as possible, it would be helpful to use some of what I've learned about rhetoric when I was growing up in Tarsus. But the last thing in the world I want to do is make a philosophical presentation such as I tried with the proud Athenians. True, the Romans aren't Athenians, but, even so, the message of Christ must be based on his revelation and not on philosophy. However, there's no reason why I can't combine the Word of God and message of Christ with an effective form of Greek presentation such as a dia-tribe, a question and answer mode of development.[89]

"One thing in particular I want to grapple with is the fact that the Church, which Jesus founded among Jews, is rapidly becoming a predominantly Gentile Church.[90] In fact, that phenomenon is largely due to my own missionary efforts. I feel responsible! But what else could I do? In all my work of evangelization, I've always been careful to preach first to my fellow Jews, God's chosen people, and only when they rejected my message have I turned to the Gentiles, fulfilling my commission from the risen Christ himself. I need to make it abundantly clear to both Jews and Gentiles alike that I haven't abandoned my people any more than God himself has, that this temporary blindness of the Jews has worked to the advantage of the Gentiles, but that the latter must never forget that the Jews are still God's chosen people, for 'God's gifts and call are irrevocable.'[91]

"Then, what shall I say about conduct? For all the knowledge about God and the things of God won't be worth anything if we don't live it! Yes, I'll try to summarize for the church of Rome the highlights of Christian conduct that I've developed in my other letters, especially the ones to this very Church of Corinth.[92] But, instead of weaving doc-trine and conduct together throughout the letter as I did, especially in my longer letter to Corinth, I'm going to try and present all the doc-trine first and then the moral exhortation. In that way, I can make it perfectly clear that Christian morality is drawn, not primarily from the commandments, but from our very makeup as people united with Christ.[93] We are, therefore we act! And, in fact, our whole Christian conduct is a kind of sacrificial worship offered to God.[94]

"There! I've found what I came searching for, thanks be to God! And now that I know what Christ Jesus wants of me, I just can't wait to get started! It's so refreshing to be able to write a letter like this in which I can pick and choose the subject matter under the guidance of the Holy Spirit instead of having it always dictated by the pressing needs and crises of individual Churches.

"I want to hurry back now to the city so that I can share this exciting development with my friends and missionary companions. For they've been a large part of my preaching and writing apostolate, and I'm sure they'll have an important role to play in this climactic letter to the Romans. Come to think of it, I'm truly blessed in having a number of companions who make ideal secretaries,[95] thus saving me the tedious work of personally writing on wax tablets and then transcribing onto papyrus.[96]

"Thank you, my dear Lord Jesus, for guiding me this far through your Holy Spirit, for showing me the challenging possibilities of the future, and for favoring me with wonderful friends and helpers who can assist me in fulfilling those possibilities according to your holy will and that of your heavenly Father. Amen!"

ANALYSIS OF PAUL'S EARLY LETTERS

As in the first volume treating Mark, "Matthew," and Luke-Acts, so also in this volume treating Paul and John, I shall, in the interests of time and space, couch the analyses of their works in summary outline form. Also, each analysis will be divided into two parts, namely, an overview of the works and an outline or outlines of those same works. Specifically in the treatment of Paul's letters, the overview will treat his letters in general while the outline portion will include both a particular analysis and an outline (if necessary) of each letter or group of letters. This, I trust, will become clearer as we proceed.

I. Overview: The Letters of Paul in General

    A. Nature of Paul's writings

        1. It is generally agreed among Scripture scholars that Paul's

writings are true letters rather than epistles, whereas Hebrews and the General Epistles are normally epistles rather than letters.

2. The distinction is simply this: A letter is written to a particular person or group, usually in reply to a letter or special situation; an epistle is a discourse, exhortation, or essay addressed to readers at large and possibly couched in letter form, such as an open letter in today's society.

B. Format of Paul's letters

1. In general, Paul follows the normal format for letters in the world of his day, as confirmed by the discovery of numerous personal and business papyrus letters in *koinê*, or common, Greek. Paul, however, does not hesitate to adapt the usual format to his own needs and purposes.

2. Thus, Paul's letters normally contain these parts:

   a) An identification of the writer and the one(s) addressed, together with a salutation (greeting)

   b) A thanksgiving and prayer (or vice versa). When the thanksgiving is deliberately omitted, as in the case of Galatians, the omission is dramatic. Often, this section provides a preview of the general tone and content of the letter.[97]

   c) The body or content of the letter, consisting in general of doctrinal teaching and moral exhortation, sometimes interwoven throughout the letter, sometimes in clear succession[98]

   d) Final greetings to and from individuals, together with final blessings and farewells

C. Process of Paul's letter writing

1. Paul, like many letter writers of his time, or any time, normally used an amanuensis, or secretary, to whom he dictated the contents of his many letters.

   a) Differences in the style and vocabulary of his letters can be explained, at least in part, by his use of different secretaries and the amount of freedom he allowed each to use his own words. An example of this kind of freedom in today's world is found in executive secretaries, who often have wide latitude in expressing their employers' thoughts.

b) Paul's secretaries would have written his words with a metal stylus on wax tablets, and then, especially when the available tablets were all covered with writing, a halt was needed to allow the secretaries to transcribe the material from the wax tablets to papyrus with reed pen and primitive ink, after which the wax tablets would be smoothed out and prepared for more dictation.[99]

c) Paul's occasional inconcinnity (inelegance due to a break in thought) may well have occurred because of an interruption of his dictation, whether from the appearance of some visitor or the necessary break for transcription or perhaps just because his thought may have run ahead of his dictation and his secretary's ability to write it on the wax tablets.

D. Sources of Paul's letters

1. In general, the content of Paul's letters derives from his conversion experience, his years of contemplation and reflection on the Hebrew Scriptures, his missionary and pastoral experience, and sometimes Christian tradition as learned from others, particularly the original apostles.[100]

2. In particular

a) The content is tailored to the needs of the Church or person to whom Paul is writing or, as with Romans, represents a self-introduction.

b) Illustrations are usually from the Old Testament, either from the Hebrew text or the Septuagint.[101]

c) It is thought that certain hymns and sayings in Paul's letters were not original with him but borrowed from the Christian community.[102]

d) Like Jesus, Paul sometimes used examples from construction, farming, or horticulture,[103] but unlike Jesus, he also used athletics, theater, or even terminology from mystery religions.[104]

E. Arrangement of Paul's letters

1. In the New Testament, Paul's letters are usually arranged

according to length and importance, with letters to churches preceding those to persons.

2. Thus, Romans, 1 and 2 Corinthians, and Galatians, considered Paul's "Great Letters," head the list, followed by "Ephesians," Philippians, Colossians, 1 and 2 Thessalonians, 1 and 2 Timothy, Titus, and Philemon. (The fact that Hebrews follows all of these clearly indicates that it belongs with the General Epistles rather than with the Pauline Letters.)

F. Authenticity (authorship) of the letters

1. In recent years, this has been the subject of much debate among Scripture scholars, Catholics and conservative Protestants generally maintaining the traditional authorship, while liberal Protestants have tended to question or deny the Pauline authorship of such letters as Colossians and "Ephesians," the Pastorals (1 and 2 Timothy and Titus), as well as 2 Thessalonians.

2. Today, judging by the most recent commentaries,[105] Catholic and some conservative Protestant scholars tend to agree with the liberal Protestant position, denying or at least questioning the Pauline authorship of the above-named letters, generally attributing them to the first or second generation after Paul. All agree, however, that lack of Pauline authorship does not in any way affect the inspiration and canonicity of the letters in question.

3. As indicated in my introduction to this volume, I have chosen to follow the more traditional position, both because it fits better with the purpose of this work, namely to give the reader a feel for the human authors, and because to me the case for the more liberal position has not been proven beyond a reasonable doubt.

G. The chronology of Paul's letters:

1. Obviously, theories about the chronology of the Pauline letters will depend to some extent upon theories regarding their authorship.

2. Even among traditional opinions of Pauline authorship, there is generally no agreement regarding the chronology of Paul's letters.

3. My own theory of the chronology of Paul's letters normally follows my ideas about their setting and content, as I hope is evident from the story parts of this work.

H. The division of Paul's letters

1. Here again, different authors divide Paul's letters according to their own theories about authorship, chronology, and setting.

2. In my presentation, following a more conservative theory of authorship, I am dividing Paul's letters according to their content (and what I perceive to be their setting) in the following way:

End of world

a) Eschatological[106] Letters: 1 and 2 Thessalonians

b) General Pastoral Letters: 1 and 2 Corinthians

Salvation

c) Soteriological[107] Letters: Galatians and Romans

d) Captivity Letters: Philippians and Philemon; Colossians and "Ephesians"

e) Personal Pastoral Letters: 1 Timothy, Titus, and 2 Timothy

II. Analyses and Outlines of Paul's Early Letters

A. Eschatological Letters: 1 and 2 Thessalonians

1. General impression: Very brief letters written to allay fears in a time of crisis

2. Circumstances: Paul's first letters and the first writings of the New Testament, written to the persecuted Christians at Thessalonica from Corinth on his second missionary journey around A.D. 51 or 52.

3. Purposes: To correct misconceptions and allay fears of the Thessalonian Christians regarding the parousia, or second coming of Christ

a) In 1 Thessalonians, Thessalonian fears that their deceased loved ones would miss the parousia

b) In 2 Thessalonians, Thessalonian conviction that the parousia was about to occur, resulting in the quitting of jobs to await Jesus' coming

4. Characteristics

a) Tender expressions, especially in 1 Thessalonians, Paul referring to the Thessalonians as his brothers about twenty times and to himself as their father (1 Thess 2:11), even their mother (1 Thess 2:7)

b) Pauline use of highly figurative language in regard to the parousia, language that should not be interpreted too literally (1 Thess 4:13-18; 2 Thess 2:1-12)

c) Important references to the theological virtues of faith, hope, charity (1 Thess 1:3), to holiness of life, especially in regard to sexual morality (1 Thess 4:3-8) and, notably, tradition (2 Thess 2:15; 3:6)

5. Authorship

a) Pauline authorship undisputed for 1 Thessalonians

b) Pauline authorship disputed and widely denied for 2 Thessalonians, principally because of apparent change of thought regarding the parousia, but not proven beyond a reasonable doubt

6. Outlines: 1 and 2 Thessalonians too brief and relatively uncomplicated to require outlines.

B. General Pastoral Letters: 1 and 2 Corinthians

1. General Impression

a) 1 Corinthians: The most pastorally rich of all Paul's letters, full of teachings for us today

b) 2 Corinthians: The most personally self-revealing of all Paul's letters, full of teachings for our personal spiritual lives

2. Circumstances

a) 1 Corinthians: Originally, Paul's second letter to Corinth, written from Ephesus on Paul's third missionary journey, around A.D. 54

b) 2 Corinthians: Perhaps a combination of Paul's first, third, and fourth letters to Corinth (see below under purposes), written on Paul's third missionary journey, from Ephesus and Philippi around A.D. 53–56

3. Purposes

a) 1 Corinthians

(1) Part one (chs. 1–6): to solve problems reported by Chloe's household (1:11)

(2) Part two (chs. 7–16): to answer questions posed to Paul by letter (7:1)

   b) 2 Corinthians

     (1) Brief letter one: to prevent Christians from marrying pagans (1 Cor 5:9; 2 Cor 6:14–7:1)

     (2) Letter three ''with many tears'': to counter Judaizers and uphold authority as an apostle (2 Cor 2:4; 10:1–13:13)

     (3) Letter four: the rest of 2 Corinthians, mainly to console the Corinthians, complete reconciliation with them, and direct the collection

4. Characteristics

   a) 1 and 2 Corinthians

     (1) Extremely pastoral, showing Paul's profound personal concern for a local Church at once lovable and troublesome

     (2) Some of Paul's most important teachings about ministry (1 Cor 1–4; 2 Cor 2–6)

   b) 1 Corinthians

     (1) Important solutions to problems of disunity, the scandal of incestuous conduct, lawsuits before pagan judges, and sexual immorality

     (2) Important answers to questions about marriage and celibacy, idol offerings, liturgy, spiritual gifts, and bodily resurrection

5. Authorship: There seems to be no doubt or debate about the Pauline authorship of 1–2 Corinthians.

6. Outlines:

   a) 1 Corinthians

     (1) Introduction: greeting and thanksgiving (1:1–9)

     (2) Part I: Corinthian problems (1:10–6:20)

       (a) Factions[108] in the Church (1:10–4:21)

         i) Nature of the dissension (1:10–17)

           a. Competitive allegiances to leaders

           b. Attachment to philosophy, rhetoric

         ii) Solution to the situation (1:18–4:21)

           a. The cross above philosophy, rhetoric

b. Christian wisdom based on revelation

c. Preachers, leaders, are but servants

(b) Moral disorders in the Church (5:1–6:20)

    i) Scandal of the incestuous man (5:1-13)

      a. Problem: Christian sexual scandal[109]

      b. Solution: excommunication[110]

    ii) Christian lawsuits before pagans (6:1-11)

      a. Problem: scandal of Christian greed

      b. Solution: detachment and charity

    iii) Sexual immorality in Corinth (6:12-20)

      a. Problem: tempting "sexual religion"

      b. Solution: personal union with Christ

(3) Part II: Corinthian questions (7:1–15:58)

(a) On marriage and celibacy (7:1-40)

    i) On marriage (7:1-16)

      a. Marriage rights; celibacy preferred

      b. Indissolubility; Pauline Privilege[111]

    ii) Remain in state as called (7:17-24)

    iii) Celibacy, virginity, widowhood (7:25-40)

      a. Free to marry; freedom of celibacy

      b. Virgins, widows advised to remain so

(b) On meats offered to idols (8:1–11:1)

    i) General rule: no idols exist, so eat with a clear conscience (8:1-8)

    ii) But two special cautions[112] (8:9–10:22)

      a. Avoid scandal (8:9–9:27)

      b. Avoid overconfidence (10:1-22)

    iii) Conclusion: Eat with caution, concern for others, and God's glory (10:23–11:1)

(c) On conduct at Christian assemblies (11:2-34)

    i) Directive on women's headdress (11:2-16)

    ii) Directives on good order and charity at the agape and Eucharist (11:17-34)

      a. Scandal of divisions and intemperance

      b. Proper dispositions for the Eucharist[113]

(d) On the use of spiritual gifts[114] (12:1-14:40)

    i) Unity in variety means community (12:1-31)

         a. One Spirit, many gifts, common good

         b. One Christ, many members, one body[115]

      ii) The greatest gift: agape love[116] (13:1-13)

      iii) Directives on spiritual gifts (14:1-40)

         a. Prophecy superior to tongues

         b. Good order necessary with gifts

   (e) On resurrection from the dead (15:1-58)

      i) The truth of the resurrection[117] (15:1-34)

         a. Christ is risen; we also will rise

         b. "Baptism for the dead" and witnesses

      ii) The manner of the resurrection (15:35-58)

         a. What kind of body? Analogies (15:35-49)

         b. How do the dead rise? Christ (15:50-58)

(4) Conclusion: various particulars (16:1–16:24)

   (a) Collection for the Judean poor[118] (16:1-4)

   (b) Paul's plans for the future (16:5-12)

   (c) Directives, commendations, greetings, and final blessing (16:13-24)

b) 2 Corinthians (structured according to relationships and visits)

  (1) Greetings and thanksgiving, filled with joy and consolation (1:1-11)

  (2) Part I: past relationship (1:12–7:16)

   (a) Paul sincere in deferring visit (1:12–2:11)

   (b) Paul's sublime ministry[119] (2:12–7:16)

      i) Relationship with Corinthians (2:12–3:3)

      ii) Sublime new covenant[120] ministry (3:4–5:10)

      iii) One of love, reconciliation[121] (5:11–7:4)

      iv) Paul's joy at news from Corinth (7:5-16)

  (3) Part II: present relationship (8:1–9:15)

   (a) Exhortation to generosity (8:1-15)

   (b) Exhortation to welcome Titus (8:16–9:5)

   (c) Assurance of great rewards (9:6-15)

  (4) Part III: future relationship (10:1–13:10)

   (a) Warning of power in next visit (10:1-17)

   (b) Comparison with Judaizers (11:1–12:13)

      i) Constant Church concern (11:1-15)

    ii) Extraordinary sufferings (11:16-33)

    iii) Visions and revelations (12:1-6)

    iv) Strength in weakness[122] (12:7-10)

    v) Reprise: Church concern (12:11-13)

  (c) Renewed warnings and pleadings in view of Paul's third visit (12:14–13:10)

(5) Appeals, salutations, blessings (13:11-13)

Please note: The above outline of 2 Corinthians is only a feeble attempt to bring some order out of what is, I am convinced, a combination of two or three letters.

C. Soteriological Letters: Galatians and Romans
  1. General impression
    a) Galatians: Paul's most vehement, polemic letter, with the possible exception of parts of 2 Corinthians and parts of Philippians
    b) Romans: Paul's most carefully thought out, structured, and worded letter, coming closest to being an epistle rather than a letter
  2. Circumstances
    a) Galatians: Written to the Christians of Galatia in northern Asia Minor (present day Ankara)[123] from Philippi during Paul's third missionary journey, around A.D. 56.
    b) Romans: Written to the Christians of Rome, Italy, from Corinth during Paul's third missionary journey, around A.D. 56-57.
  3. Purposes
    a) Galatians: To establish that justification and salvation come through faith in Christ and not by observance of the Mosaic Law, as insisted on by the troublesome Judaizers
    b) Romans: To establish that justification comes through faith in Christ and salvation through life in Christ, written as Paul's self-introduction prior to visiting Rome
  4. Characteristics
    a) Galatians: Clear and forceful, especially concerning justification by faith, life in the Spirit rather than the

flesh, unity and equality of all in Christ, and Paul's own life in Christ crucified

b) Romans: Profound but clear to one understanding the development, for which the outline should help; magnificent description of life in Christ and the Holy Spirit

5. Authorship: There is no question among scholars about the Pauline authorship of both letters, though there is question about the time and place of Paul's Letter to the Galatians.

6. Outlines

a) Galatians (hard to outline but worth a try)

   (1) Introduction (1:1-10)

      (a) Greetings and salutations (1:1-5)

      (b) Amazement and anathema (1:6-10)

   (2) Personal and biographical (1:11–2:21):

      (a) Paul's gospel is from God (1:11-24)

      (b) Approved by the apostles (2:1-10)

      (c) Defended against Peter[124] (2:11-14)

      (d) Paul's resumé of his gospel (2:15-21)

   (3) Scriptural and theological (3:1–4:31)

      (a) Justification by faith, not Law (3:1-22)

      (b) Faith's fruits: sonship, equality,[125] and freedom (3:23–4:31)

   (4) Moral and hortatory (5:1–6:10)

      (a) Warning against loss of freedom (5:1-12)

      (b) Instructions on proper use of freedom . . . love and humility, responsibility and perseverance (5:13–6:10)

   (5) Conclusion

      (a) Personal signature (6:11)

      (b) Resumé and blessing (6:12-18)

b) Letter to the Romans

   (1) Introduction (1:1-15)

      (a) Extended address and greeting[126] (1:1-7)

      (b) Thanksgiving and prayer (1:8-10)

      (c) Desire to visit Rome (1:11-15)

   (2) Part I: Doctrine—gospel of Christ (1:16–11:36)

(a) Through the gospel, the holiness of God justifies the person of faith (1:16–4:25)

   i) Theme announced: salvation through the gospel, revealing God's holiness (1:16-17)

   ii) Theme negatively explained: without the gospel, God's wrath against all[127] (1:18–3:20)

   iii) Theme positively developed: God's holiness in Christ received by faith (3:21-31)

   iv) Theme illustrated: Abraham justified by faith[128] (4:1-25; small doxology, 4:25)

(b) The love of God assures salvation to those justified by faith (5:1–11:36).

   i) Theme announced: Once justified, we can now hope for salvation[129] (5:1-11).

   ii) Theme negatively explained: Christ's life in us brings freedom (5:12–7:25)

     a. from sin[130] and death (5:12-21),

     b. from self through Christ[131] (6:1-23),

     c. from the Law through grace[132] (7:1-25); small doxology, 7:25).

   iii) Theme positively developed: Christ's life in us is lived in the Spirit and destined for glory[133] (8:1-39). We are

     a. empowered by the Spirit (8:1-13),

     b. children of God and glory (8:14-18),

     c. groaning with all creation[134] (8:19-25),

     d. praying in the Spirit (8:26-27),

     e. inseparable from Christ (8:28-39).

   iv) Theme illustrated: God is not contradicting promises to Israel (9:1–11:36).

     a. Israel's infidelity not contrary to God's direction of history[135] (9:1-33)

     b. Israel's failure due to her own culpable refusal (10:1-21)

     c. Israel's failure partial, temporary, for sake of the Gentiles (11:1-32; great doxology, extolling God's mysterious wisdom, 11:33-36)

(3) Part II: Conduct—the demands of our new life in the Spirit (12:1–15:13)

    (a) Life in Christ is sacrificial worship of God and transformation into Christ[136] (12:1-2).

    (b) We are all members of Christ's body, united by his love (12:3-21; 13:8-10; 14:1-23).

    (c) We must obey lawful authority,[137] make good use of time, and put on Christ[138] (13:1-14).

    (d) We must live in peace and joy, patience and self-denial in Christ (14:1–15:13; brief doxologies, 15:5-6, 13).

(4) Conclusion (15:14–16:27)

    (a) Paul's apostolic vision, plans,[139] and need of prayers (15:14-33)

    (b) Personal commendations, e.g. Phoebe the deaconess,[140] and greetings (16:1-16)

    (c) Avoid disunity, disobedience (16:17-20)

    (d) Greetings from Corinthians (16:21-24)

    (e) Doxologies (15:33; 16:20) and great concluding doxology (16:25-27)

REFLECTIONS ON PAUL'S EARLY LETTERS AND OUR LIFE

So far I have attempted to reconstruct the life and letters of St. Paul up to and including his missive to the Roman Christians prior to his intended visit to that all-important Church. I have also analyzed and discussed the letters of Paul in general and then, in analyses and outlines, the Eschatological, Early Pastoral, and Soteriological Letters in turn. All of this was for the purpose of understanding Paul himself and of discovering what he intended to say in his writings. Now we have the opportunity to reflect on and apply to our personal and communal lives the lessons we have learned so that we may come to know what meaning they may hold for us in our own time. Before beginning our reflections, however, it would be well to remember two facts in particular: (1) that in his life and writings Paul was concerned almost exclusively with the risen Christ,[141] principally living on in his Church and its members, especially in Paul himself, and (2) that Paul never attempted to construct a system of theology or spirituality, and therefore his teachings must be gleaned piecemeal from his various letters.

At this time, I will normally confine our reflections to the letters of Paul that we have so far examined, but on occasion it may be helpful to flash forward to what he has to say in one or more of what I am categorizing as his later letters. I am referring above all to Philippians, which, like 2 Corinthians, is so self-revealing. In this regard, it may be well to remember that many authors tend to list both Philippians and Philemon among Paul's earlier writings.

Our reflection in this segment on Paul and his letters will consider in turn (1) Paul the mystic, (2) Paul the theologian, and (3) Paul the missionary and pastor. Under these headings, we will hardly be able to consider exhaustively all the ramifications of Paul's life and thought, but we will, I trust, succeed in touching the highlights.

Paul the Mystic

It must appear to some that in referring to Paul as a mystic we are contradicting much if not all of our story about the great apostle. How could this fiery, almost frantic missionary be called a mystic by any stretch of the imagination? Is not a mystic someone who lives the life of a hermit, away from people, totally absorbed in contemplation of God, and favored with visions, divine locutions, levitations, or similar mystical phenomena? Sometimes, yes, but certainly not always. Nor is that notion of a mystic central to mysticism. What is central is that the mystic is one who surrenders his whole being and life to God, one who is in a sense possessed and driven by God, one who therefore lives, thinks, loves, works, and suffers, no longer by his mere human initiative and energy, but by the initiative and energy of God.[142]

The perfect example of the true mystic, of course, was Jesus Christ in his human nature and during his earthly life. As I explained in reflecting on Mark's Gospel, Jesus was as human as it was possible for him to be, living by faith, needing those many years at Nazareth to grow in "wisdom, maturity, and grace before God and men" (Luke 2:52, WFD), and reaching the heights of the mystical life, as confirmed by God at his baptism by John: "You are my son, my beloved! In you I am well pleased" (Mark 1:11, WFD). And his mysticism, far from hindering his almost constant activity during the three years of his public ministry, actually fueled, energized, and directed that activity. As we see in Mark 1:35 and Luke 6:12, Jesus sometimes prayed alone in the early morning or even spent whole nights in prayer, but immediately afterward he resumed his tireless activity of preaching and teaching, explaining, "Let us go elsewhere, into the neighboring towns, so that I may preach there also, for that is why I have come forth" (Mark 1:38, WFD). And was it not his persevering prayer in the Garden of Gethsemane (Mark 14:32-42) that gave him the superhuman courage and patience to bear his unspeakable sufferings and even the feeling of abandonment by God himself (Mark 15:34)?

In the same way, though of course to a lesser degree, Paul was able to combine the highest mysticism with the most energetic activity and most acute sufferings. To be more accurate, it was precisely his mystical union with the risen Christ that enabled him to accomplish so much in his activity and sufferings. From his blinding but eye-opening encounter with Christ on the Damascus Road[143] when Jesus identified himself with his followers (Acts 9:5), from his solitary years in Arabia and Tarsus (Gal 1:17; Acts 9:30; 11:25), and from the "dark nights" and "deserts" of his very missionary and pastoral experience, Paul grew in mystical union with the risen Christ throughout his Christian life, achieving like Christ a glorious martyrdom at the end.

Both from the account in Acts of Paul's conversion and from his letters, it seems obvious that the crucial truth that drove Paul throughout his Christian life and letters was the basic, all-encompassing conviction that the risen Christ himself was continuing to live, minister, and suffer in him and in his fellow Christians. "I am Jesus whom you are persecuting" (Acts 9:5, NAB, etc.). But let Paul himself tell us about it in his own words, culled mainly from his earlier letters.

Paul's principal references to union with Christ can be rather evenly divided between seven (the perfect biblical number), which are expressed in the first person singular where Paul is speaking of himself, and the rest of his references, which also add up to seven. Let us look first at those pertaining to Paul himself, since that is our principal focus.

In Gal 2:20, WFD, Paul vividly describes Christ's life in him: "I live, no longer I, but Christ is living in me; what I now live in the flesh, I live in the faith of the Son of God, who loved me and delivered himself up for me." Because of this intimate union with Christ, he can assure his beloved Philippians that he yearns for them all with the very affections of Christ himself (Phil 1:8). And to the same Philippians, Paul rhapsodizes about his rejection of his past life in order to gain Christ and find himself in union with him (Phil 3:8-9) who has taken possession of him (Phil 3:12). Having already suffered even stoning in and for Christ, Paul does not hesitate to conclude his letter to his troublesome Galatians with these powerful words: "Henceforth, let no one give me any trouble, for I bear the scars of Jesus in my body" (Gal 6:17, WFD). And, contemplating the prospect of death, he declares to the Philippians, "To me, to live is Christ and to die is gain!" (Phil 1:21, WFD). In his self-introduction to the Romans, he declares: "In Christ Jesus, then, I have reason to boast of my work for God. For I will not venture to speak of anything except what Christ has accomplished through me to win obedience from the Gentiles" (Rom 15:17-18, NRSV). And finally, in a preview of the letter of Paul to the Colossians we find a rather long and very remarkable Pauline statement, which seems to sum up all that we have seen in the previous references:

> It is now my joy to suffer for you; for the sake of Christ's body, the church, I am completing what still remains for Christ to suffer in my own person. I became a servant of the church by virtue of the task assigned to me by God for your benefit: to put God's word into full effect, that secret purpose hidden for long ages and through many generations, but now disclosed to God's people. To them he chose to make known what a wealth of glory is offered to the Gentiles in this secret purpose: Christ in you, the hope of glory.
>
> He it is whom we proclaim. We teach everyone and instruct everyone in all the ways of wisdom, so as to present each one of you as a mature member of Christ's body. To this end I am toiling strenuously with all the energy and power of Christ at work in me. (Col 1:24-29, REB).

Equally impressive are the seven statements in which Paul speaks of union with Christ in all ways except the first person singular. And, interestingly, almost all of these references are from my list of early letters. For example, in 1 Cor 6:16-17, WFD, Paul combats the sexual immorality so rampant in Corinth by going right to the crux of the matter. "Do you not know that your bodies are members of Christ? Will you take the members of Christ and make them members of a prostitute? No indeed! Do you not know that one who is united with a prostitute is one body (with her)? For it says, 'The two will be one flesh.' But one who is united with the Lord is one spirit (with him)."

This union with Christ Paul celebrates as not only possible but even unbreakable, at least by outside forces. "Who will separate us from the love of Christ?" he asks defiantly in Rom 8:35, WFD, and answers his own question by listing all the possible external threats, dismissing them all in turn. But we humans are destined for more than an indissoluble spiritual union with Christ. We are called to identification with him, to being transformed into his very image! Is this not the clear import of Rom 8:29, WFD, "For those whom he foreknew he also set apart beforehand to be conformed to the image of his Son, so that he, the Son, might be the firstborn among many brothers"?

Elsewhere, however, Paul clearly indicates that our transformation into Christ is not a sudden, once-for-all happening but rather a gradual process that consumes our entire lifetime. "All of us," exults Paul in 2 Cor 3:18, NAB, "gazing with unveiled faces on the glory of the Lord, are being transformed into the same image from glory to glory, as from the Lord who is the Spirit." This same idea of the gradual accomplishment of something that is stated elsewhere as a *fait accompli* can be found in a comparison between Gal 3:27, WFD, "All of you who have been baptized into Christ have clothed yourselves with Christ," and Rom 13:14, WFD, "But clothe yourselves with the Lord Jesus Christ, and pay no attention to the desires of the flesh." The expression, "to clothe oneself" or "to put on" Christ, I believe, is a theatrical figure, reflecting Paul's facile use of symbols from Greek culture. In Greek theater, one who was to portray a famous historical or mythical personage would "put on" or "clothe himself with" the mask and costume of that personage.[144] Here, of course, Paul is not simply referring to playacting. The Greek word for an actor is *hypócritēs*, from which we have the term "hypocrite." No, he is referring to living the role of Christ throughout our life, which is another way of speaking of our union and identification with him. To that total union and identification with Christ, Paul challenges all of us, no matter what our life situation may be, just as he challenges and prays for the Ephesians in Eph 3:14-19, WFD:

> For this reason I bend my knees before the Father, from whom every family in the heavens and on earth is named, that he may grant you, according to the richness of his glory, to be strengthened in power through his Spirit with respect to the inner man, to have Christ abide through faith in your hearts, to be firmly rooted and established in love, so that you may be able to comprehend with all the saints what is the breadth and length and height and depth, to know also the love of Christ which surpasses knowledge, so that you may be filled with all the fullness of God.

It should be evident by now that the truth that Paul recognized as central, not only for him in his own life and ministry but for all Christians regardless of their state of life, is that the risen Christ chooses to continue his life and ministry in and through each of us. In this he may also have recognized that he was but reflecting a possible spiritual meaning of those mysterious verses in Gen 1:26-27, NRSV, "Let us make humankind in our image, according to our likeness. . . . So God created humankind in his image, in the image of God he created them, male and female he created them." Could this not be what Paul had in mind when, in Rom 8:29, he made that thought-provoking statement about God's predestination of us "to be conformed to the image of the Son?" Is not the Son, Jesus Christ, "the image of the invisible God" (Col 1:15, NAB) and in Heb 1:3, NAB, "the refulgence of his glory, the very imprint of his being"?

If it is of our very nature to be not only united with but transformed into Christ, how can we possibly be happy unless we are seriously striving, with the grace of God, to fulfill our sublime destiny? If any confirmation is required, we need only look at Gen 2:7, where God is described as making us in three dimensions, which come to be expressed throughout the Bible as flesh, person, and spirit[145] As spirit, we are naturally oriented to union with God, who is spirit, a truth that is confirmed by numerous biblical texts as well as by the lyrical words of St. Augustine: "You have made us for yourself, O Lord, and our hearts are restless until they rest in you!"[146]

Paul the Theologian

Whole books, in fact whole sets of books, have been written on the theology of St. Paul. Obviously, time and space prevent anything approaching an exhaustive treatment of this fascinating subject. Our reflection, therefore, will be confined to Paul's most carefully ordered theological presentation, to be found in his great Letter to the Romans, and even there to only a limited number of subjects, notably those that have been sources of misunderstanding, controversy, and division among Christians.

However, before we begin our theological reflections, it will be well for us to keep always in mind that the source of Paul's theology was not Greek philosophy but a combination of his own experience of Christ, beginning with his conversion encounter on the Damascus Road; his careful study of the Hebrew Scriptures in the light of Christ, especially during his quiet years in Arabia and Tarsus, his missionary and pastoral experiences, and the ongoing guidance of the Holy Spirit, illuminating him with that supernatural wisdom he describes so lyrically in 1 Cor 2:6-16, NAB:

> Yet we do speak a wisdom to those who are mature, but not a wisdom of this age. . . . Rather we speak God's wisdom, mysterious, hidden, which God predetermined before the ages for our glory. . . . This [wisdom] God has revealed to us through the Spirit.
>
> For the Spirit scrutinizes everything, even the depths of God. Among human beings, who knows what pertains to a person except the spirit of the person that is within? Similarly, no one knows what pertains to God except the Spirit of God. We have not received the spirit of the world but the Spirit that is from God, so that we may understand the things freely given us by God. And we speak about them not with words taught by human wisdom, but with words taught by the Spirit, describing spiritual realities in spiritual terms.
>
> Now the natural person does not accept what pertains to the Spirit of God, for to him it is foolishness, and he cannot understand it, because it is judged spiritually. The spiritual person, however, can judge everything but is not subject to judgment by anyone.
>
> For "who has known the mind of the Lord, so as to counsel him?"[147] But we have the mind of Christ.

The moral of this is that, if we wish to understand the theology of Paul, we must rely not on Greek philosophy, "the wisdom of this age" referred to by Paul, but on revelation found in the Scriptures and the living tradition of the Church, and on the guidance of the Holy Spirit. For, as we read in 2 Pet 3:15-16, NAB: "And consider the patience of our Lord as salvation, as our beloved brother Paul, according to the wisdom given to him, also wrote to you, speaking of these things as he does in all his letters. In them there are some things hard to understand that the ignorant and unstable distort to their own destruction, just as they do the other scriptures."

First and foremost among Paul's teachings that have been the occasion of Christian divisions is his most central doctrine, namely that concerning justification and salvation. Even before Paul wrote his great letters on this subject to the Galatians and Romans, it had already been the crucial question dividing Christians roughly along Jewish and Gentile lines. In Acts 15, Luke relates how the controversy had come to a head at the end of the first missionary journey of Paul and Barnabas among the Gentiles, when some Christians from Judea objected to the missionaries' practice of receiving Gentiles directly into the Church through faith and baptism without requiring circumcision and the observance of the Mosaic Law. Without the fulfillment of these requirements, they cried, there could be no salvation for Jews or Gentiles.

In the same chapter, we read the dramatic description of the Council of Jerusalem, in which Peter, as leader of the Church, settled the issue, arguing from his own divinely directed reception, without circumcision, of the centurion Cornelius and his entire household at Caesarea, chiding his fellow Jewish Christians for trying to burden Gentiles with the yoke of the Mosaic Law, which they themselves had been unable to bear, and concluding that "we believe that we will be saved through the grace of the Lord Jesus, just as they will" (Acts 15:11, NRSV). Even James, the recognized leader of Jewish Christianity, had to agree with Peter, simply adding some recommendations for Gentile observance to avoid scandalizing the Jews.[148]

With this decision or dogma,[149] formalized in a letter sent to Antioch in Syria, the center for mission activity among the Gentiles, the matter seemed to be settled. But unfortunately, it was far from settled for some of the Jewish Christians, who simply refused to accept the decision. Obviously, their centuries-long Jewish heritage kept them from recognizing in Judaism only a preparation for the universal religion of Christianity. Coming to be known as Judaizers, that is, people who insisted on everyone becoming in effect Jews before they could be Christians, they proceeded to hound Paul's steps throughout his missionary activity, most notably in Galatia, Philippi, and Corinth. And it was in his angry response to them in his letter to the Galatians that Paul first laid out his theology concerning justification and salvation. Later, as we have seen, he drew up his theology on this subject in a more carefully arranged fashion as a self-introduction to the Christians of Rome.

Succinctly worded, Paul's theology of justification and salvation insists that Jews and Gentiles alike can be justified and saved, not by observance of the Mosaic Law but by faith and baptism. Simple enough! This is really nothing more than an explanation of the decision of the Council of Jerusalem. It was only centuries later that new controversy arose over Paul's theology. By this time, the Church being human as well as divine, a great number of abuses had proliferated among Catholics, abuses the Fifth Lateran Council[150] was convened in 1512 to correct, but without notable success. It seemed almost inevitable that, if the Church would not or could not reform herself, someone or some movement would arise to do so, but in such a way that great divisions would result.

Sure enough, just five short years later, an Augustinian monk named Martin Luther,[151] brilliant but undisciplined, thought he discovered a fundamental error in the teaching and practice of the Catholic Church. Contrary to her insistence on good works, including the works involved in the gaining of indulgences,[152] justification, according to St. Paul in his Letter to the Romans, was possible only by an act of faith. In fact, he insisted, Paul's example of Abram's justification in Gen 15:6 clearly indicated that the patriarch was only declared just or righteous because of his belief. In other words, justification is a juridical declaration that one receives if he or she believes in the death and resurrection of Jesus Christ for the salvation of all, without the need or efficacy of any good works.[153]

The Catholic response was swift. Quoting the Epistle of James, Catholic theologians countered that "faith if it does not have works is dead" (Jas 2:17, WFD), "faith without works is useless" (Jas 2:20, WFD), even that "a person is justified from works and not from faith alone" (Jas 2:24, WFD). Then there ensued a fixing and hardening of positions. Luther's followers insisting on justification solely by faith and Catholics insisting just as strongly on justification by good works. Perhaps if they had been able to dialogue and examine the Scriptures together, this monumental confrontation might never have gotten out of hand. Today, through joint study and dialogue, it is generally agreed among Catholic and Protestant scholars alike that the sword of division has largely been sheathed.[154] Unfortunately, however, that agreement has not always filtered down to the rank and file among Christians.

The best way to understand today's general agreement among Christian scholars is to evoke the example of Abram in Gen 15:6, which is quoted by Paul in Gal 3:6 and Rom 4:3 as well as by James in Jas 2:23: "Abram believed God, and it was credited to him as righteousness" (NIV, NAB). Looking first at the all-important context, it is generally agreed that in Genesis Abram's faith was credited before any covenant (Gen 15:18) or circumcision (Gen 17:10) or obedience in offering to sacrifice Isaac (Gen 22); also that Paul, in both Galatians and Romans, is contrasting the faith of Abram to the works of the Mosaic

Law insisted on by the Judaizers. Then, regarding the text, which Paul quotes from the Septuagint Greek translation,[155] it is agreed that "believed" is the correct translation of the Hebrew *he'emin*,[156] as evidenced by the Jews' own Greek translation, *epísteusen*, rather than "was faithful," as many Jewish scholars continue to render it into English. It is also agreed, however, that the faith or belief involved here and in Scripture generally is not just an intellectual acceptance of truths but a total acceptance of God and his promises with a total surrender of oneself.[157]

It is also generally agreed among Christian scholars that the final word, "righteousness" or "justice" is a fair translation of the Hebrew *se'daqah* and the Greek *dikaiosúne* and that it describes a state of holiness or right relationship with God. It is the middle term, "was credited" or "was reckoned," that in times past, beginning with Martin Luther, has been the bone of contention. Today, however, scholars have reached a virtual consensus that while the Hebrew *ya'she'beah* and Greek *elogísthe* do contain the idea of a judgment or juridical statement, they represent a typical Eastern type of circumlocution. In other words, Abram's faith was credited as righteousness in the sense that he was justified or received into a right relationship with God. No kind of artificial acceptance of Abram as righteous, if in fact he were not, could possibly be attributed to the all holy God. Another and perhaps clearer example of such typical circumlocution occurs in the annunciation account when the angel Gabriel says of the child to be conceived and born, "He will be great and will be called the Son of the Most High" (Luke 1:32, NIV), which is a circumlocution or roundabout way of saying, "He will be the Son of the Most High."

Finally, in what seems to be a contradiction between the teaching of Paul and James, we need to look above all at their different contexts and purposes. Paul is countering the Judaizers and emphasizing that justification comes by faith because, until we are in what we Catholics call the state of grace,[158] no prior works of ours, whether of the Mosaic Law or otherwise, can possibly merit justification. The natural cannot merit the supernatural. However, James may be countering an extreme interpretation of Paul and insisting that the faith that justifies must be one that is truly alive and results in good and charitable works. For us Catholics, with our traditional insistence on good works, it is important to remember, as I have just stated, that our natural works cannot possibly merit justification, but that once we are justified, once Christ lives in us, then our good works are really his, our virtues are truly his and therefore meritorious[159] of more grace in this life and glory hereafter.

Before leaving these early chapters of Romans, I would like to attempt three clarifications. First, there is a well-known tendency among some Protestants to equate justification and salvation, as if once a person is justified by faith he or she is also saved for life and for eternity. However, Paul himself makes a clear distinction between justification and salvation when he explains without any equivocation to the Roman Christians,

> Therefore, since we have been justified through faith [past tense], we have peace [present tense] with God through our Lord Jesus Christ, through whom we have gained access [past tense] by faith into the grace in which we now stand [present tense]. And we rejoice in the hope of the [future] glory of God (Rom 5:1-2, NIV).

> Since we have now been justified [past tense] by his blood, how much more shall we be saved [future tense] from God's wrath through him! For if, when we were God's enemies, we were reconciled to him [past tense] through the death of his Son, how much more, having been reconciled [past tense] shall we be saved [future tense] through his life! (Rom 5:9-10, NIV).

In other words, we are justified by faith, yes, but once justified we must live in Christ according to God's will and let Christ live in us so that, dying in that state of right relationship with God, we will be saved and attain an eternity of glory in heaven, as Paul himself emphasizes in Rom 2:6, NRSV: "He will repay according to each one's deeds"; and Phil 2:12, NRSV: "Work out your own salvation with fear and trembling."

A second clarification that may be helpful concerns the manner of our salvation through Jesus Christ. First of all, we traditionally place most of our emphasis on his saving death, giving a lesser emphasis to his saving resurrection. The truth of the matter is that if Jesus had died but had not risen from the dead, we would not be saved. Paul makes this abundantly clear in 1 Cor 15:16-17, NIV: "For if the dead are not raised, then Christ has not been raised either. And if Christ has not been raised, your faith is futile; you are still in your sins." And in Rom 4:25, NIV: "He [Christ] was delivered over to death for our sins and was raised to life for our justification."

A third clarification also involves the question, How did Christ achieve our justification and salvation? Was it by substitution, satisfaction, or solidarity? In fact, it seems to have been by all three, but especially by the third. Jesus did indeed suffer and die vicariously for our sins, the innocent for the guilty, when he "was handed over for our transgressions" (Isa 53:5; Rom 4:25, NAB). He also satisfied or paid the ransom for our sins, for "Christ ransomed us from the curse of the law by becoming a curse for us, for it is written, 'Cursed be everyone who hangs on a tree' " (Gal 3:13, NAB). But, above all, Jesus saved us through solidarity by uniting himself to our sinful human nature and thereby enabling us to die to our sins by his death and to rise to a new life, his life, by his resurrection, because "for our sake he made him to be sin who knew no sin, so that in him we might become the righteousness of God" (2 Cor 5:21, NRSV). And, of course, we for our part unite ourselves with him primarily by means of baptism, which Paul beautifully describes in Rom 6:1-11 as a death and resurrection with Christ.

Finally, turning to Rom 9–11, where Paul agonizes over the mystery of the rejection of Israel and call of the Gentiles, we discover those enigmatic passages from which John Calvin[160] derived his doctrine of predestination and prereprobation, for example: "Even before they had been born or had done any thing good or bad (so that God's purpose of election might continue, not by works but by his call) she [Rebecca] was told 'The elder shall serve the younger.' As it is written, 'I have loved Jacob but I have hated Esau' " (Rom 9:11-13, NRSV). Then, after citing the example of Pharaoh, about whom Paul says, "He [God] has mercy on whomever he chooses and he hardens the heart of whomever he chooses" (Rom 9:18, NRSV), he then proceeds to use the example of pottery (possibly an allusion to Wis 15:7-8). "Has the potter no right over the clay, to make out of the same lump one object for special use and another for ordinary use? What if God, desiring to show his wrath and to make known his power, has endured with much patience the objects of wrath that are made for destruction; and what if he has done so in order to make known the riches of his glory for the objects of mercy, which he has prepared beforehand for glory?" (Rom 9:21-23, NRSV).

When read without regard to Paul's purpose and context, it would certainly seem that Paul is teaching not only predestination but prereprobation, that is, that God makes some people for glory in heaven and others for eternal punishments in hell. But is that really what Paul is trying to say? Not at all! He is not referring to any individual persons but to peoples, namely to God's choice of Israel (the descendants of Jacob), whom he loves, instead of Edom (the descendants of Esau), whom he loves less,[161] and then to his mysterious use of Israel's rejection of Christ to call the Gentiles to salvation. Even in the case of . . . pharaoh, he is not considered here as a certain individual but as the embodiment of Egypt.[162] Nor did God really harden his heart. Rather, he hardened his own heart, as becomes abundantly clear in the account of the ten plagues in Exod 7–12, even though sometimes, to emphasize God's control of nature and history, he is described as hardening the heart of Pharaoh.[163]

It is clear, then, that Calvin was totally mistaken in applying Paul's words to individuals rather than peoples. Fortunately, even among the Presbyterians, followers of Calvin today, it is virtually impossible to find anyone who accepts his frightening doctrine of prereprobation, principally because it would be totally unjust of God to bring some people into the world to suffer eternal punishment no matter what they did. Predestination is perfectly orthodox,[164] as we see in Rom 8:29, for God has destined all of us beforehand for transformation into his Son and for eternal glory, but prereprobation[165] is utterly foreign to the very nature of God, who is love itself.[166]

Paul the Missionary and Pastor

The terms "missionary" and "pastor" usually designate two different kinds of ministry; the former referring to those who, as "fishers of men,"[167] engage primarily in evangelizing those who are not yet members of the Church; the latter describing those who, as "shepherds of souls,"[168] are concerned with helping the members of the Church to live and grow in their Christian faith. In Paul, however, the two terms are marvelously combined, since, throughout his extraordinary missionary career, he is also the caring shepherd of souls, bearing the "daily pressure of anxious concern for all the churches," which he paints in vivid colors: "Who is weak, and I am not weak? Who is led into sin, and I am not infuriated?" (2 Cor 11:28-29, WFD). For this reason, we shall reflect on both facets of Paul's ministry simultaneously. In doing so, we shall attempt to delineate the principal features of Paul, missionary and pastor, principally from Luke's portrait in Acts and from Paul's letters, primarily 1 and 2 Corinthians. Our purpose, of course, is not simply to know Paul better but to learn from him how we too can and should fulfill our own call to ministry as missionaries and shepherds of souls. And, while our reflection will, I trust, be helpful above all for those ordained to ministry or preparing for it, I hope that, in these days of universal ministry, it will be useful also to religious and laypeople.

In our consideration of this important subject, we shall focus on two aspects in particular: (1) the dimensions of Paul's and our Christian ministry, and (2) the qualities that characterized Paul's and should characterize our Christian ministry. Needless to say, the great model of Paul's missionary and pastoral ministry was Jesus Christ, the incomparable evangelizer of the poor[169] and shepherd of souls,[170] and we can do no better than imitate Paul in letting Christ continue his life and ministry in us as well.

The Dimensions of Paul's Ministry. It is clear that Paul considered his first duty to be that of preaching the good news of Jesus Christ, as he clearly indicates in 1 Cor 9:16-17, NIV: "Yet when I preach the gospel, I cannot boast, for I am compelled to preach. Woe to me if I do not preach the gospel! If I preach voluntarily, I have a reward; if not voluntarily, I am simply discharging the trust committed to me." Referring to his and his fellow apostles' commission to preach, Paul provides the reason for its necessity and importance in Rom 10:14-15, NIV: "How, then, can they call on the one they have not believed in? And how can they believe in the one of whom they have not heard? And how can they hear without someone preaching to them? And how can they preach unless they are sent? As it is written, 'How beautiful are the feet of those who bring good news!' "[171]

And in Rom 15:15-16, NIV, Paul alludes to his duty of preaching the good news as nothing less than priestly. "I have written you quite boldly on some points, as if to remind you of them again, because of the grace God gave me to be a minister of Christ Jesus to the Gentiles with the priestly duty of proclaiming the gospel of God, so that the Gentiles might become an offering acceptable to God, sanctified by the Holy Spirit." However, that preaching was not confined to missionary activity but was also needed and exercised in the established churches, as we see in 2 Cor 5:20, NIV: "We are therefore God's ambassadors, as though God were making his appeal through us. We implore you on God's behalf: be reconciled to God."

But while officially preaching the good news is the duty and prerogative of those who are sent, teaching or instruction can be carried on much more widely, as Paul seems to indicate in Rom 15:14, NIV: "I myself am convinced, my brothers, that you yourselves are full of goodness, complete in knowledge and competent to instruct one another." And that the expression "brothers" does not exclude women is indicated by the beautiful story in Acts 18:24-26, NIV of Aquila and Priscilla with Apollos at Ephesus: "Meanwhile a Jew named Apollos, a native of Alexandria, came to Ephesus. He was a learned man, with a thorough knowledge of the Scriptures. He had been instructed in the way of the Lord, and he spoke with great fervor and taught about Jesus accurately, though he knew only the baptism of John. He began to speak boldly in the synagogue. When Priscilla and Aquila heard him, they invited him to their home and explained to him the way of God more adequately."

In the Church today, preaching the word of God is the first duty of bishops and priests, and one of the duties of permanent deacons. This is abundantly clear from all the Church documents[172] and ceremonies of ordination.[173] It is no secret, however, that many of the laity, notably the large number of educated laity, feel neglected in this very important area of Church life. Part of the problem, in my personal opinion, is the lack of in-depth knowledge of the Scriptures, both because of the many other requirements in today's seminaries and because of the lack of requirements regarding the biblical languages of Hebrew and particularly Greek.[174] "Everything suffers in translation,"[175] hence if one really wants to plumb the Bible's riches, at least a basic knowledge of biblical languages is necessary. Also, a priest's or permanent deacon's preparation for orders needs to be augmented and updated by continuing education throughout one's life and ministry.

Along with the preaching apostolate, however, Paul and his missionary companions also had to be involved in the duties of Church administration, such as the appointment of presbyters (elders, priests) in each Church (Acts 14:23), the solving of problems (1 Cor 1-6), the answering of questions (1 Cor 7-15), the collection for the poor of Judea (2 Cor 8-9), and the administration of sacraments, particularly baptism (Acts 19:1-6) and the Holy Eucharist (1 Cor 11:23-34). In all of this, Paul and his companions were allowing Christ the Good Shepherd (John 10:11-18) to continue through them his loving concern for his flock. Paul himself equivalently reminded his Ephesian presbyters of this in his farewell at Miletus[176] in Acts 20:28, NRSV: "Keep watch over yourselves and over all the flock, of which the Holy Spirit has made you overseers,[177] to shepherd the Church of God that he obtained with the blood of his own Son."

This was also the reason why Paul so painstakingly instructed his Churches not only in true doctrine but also in the totality of Christian conduct. Most revealing is the beginning of his moral section in Rom 12:1-2, REB: "Therefore, my friends, I implore you by God's mercy, to offer your very selves to him: a living sacrifice, dedicated and fit for his acceptance, the worship offered by mind and heart. Conform no longer to the pattern of this present world, but be transformed by the renewal of your minds. Then you will be able to discern the will of God, and to know what is good, acceptable, and perfect."

In the Church today, with all the brokenness in the world, there is greater need than ever for shepherds who will care for the flock instead of themselves (Ezek 34:2, 8), who have the loving sensitivity and compassion of Christ himself. If theirs is only the human concern that we naturally feel for people in their needs and not the concern of Christ himself, then it will either burn out[178] in a few years or lead into dangerously emotional relationships.

Finally, an important but often overlooked dimension of the missionary and pastoral ministry of Paul, as of Christ himself, was that of suffering. It is clear from all the gospels that Jesus saved the world not by his preaching, teaching, or miracles but by his suffering, death, and resurrection. And, when Ananias of Damascus balked at receiving Saul or Paul into the Church, Jesus' reply in Acts 9:15-16, NIV was, "Go! This man is my chosen instrument to carry my name before the Gentiles and their kings and before the people of Israel. I will show him how much he must suffer for my name." And it was clearly as proof of the authenticity of his apostolate that Paul recounted in detail his many sufferings in 1 Cor 4:9-13; 2 Cor 4:7-18; 6:3-10; 11:21-12:10; Gal 2:19; 6:17; Phil 1:20-26; 2:17, summing up his theology of suffering in Rom 8:16-18, NAB: "The Spirit itself bears witness with our spirit that we are children of God, and if children, then heirs, heirs of God and joint heirs with Christ, if only we suffer with him so that we may be glorified with him. I consider that the sufferings of this present time are as nothing compared with the glory to be revealed for us." And, if I may anticipate one of the later letters, Paul in Col 1:24-25, NAB, provides the ultimate reason for the patient, even cheerful acceptance of suffering. "Now I rejoice in my sufferings for your sake, and in my flesh I am filling up what is lacking[179] in the afflictions of Christ on behalf of his body, which is the Church, of which I am a minister in accordance with God's stewardship given to me to bring to completion the word of God."

In our day, it is bad enough for the world about us, particularly through advertisements and commercials,[180] to conspire with our basic instinct of self-preservation in moving us to abhor suffering in any shape or form. What is really sad, however, is to hear preachers from the pulpit or more often from the television screen decry suffering of any kind as an unmitigated evil condemned by God. To a large extent, they revert to a Deuteronomic theology[181] of rewards and punishments in this life, as if this life were all there is and Jesus' sufferings were at most salvific phenomena belonging to the past and having no connection with our own inevitable sufferings today. Does not Jesus himself challenge us in all the Gospels to take up our cross (daily) and follow him? (Mark 8:34; Matt 16:24; Luke 9:23; John 12:26).

Whole generations of elderly and ailing people, as well as younger but ill or injured persons, have passed out of this life without being instructed and therefore generally without realizing the priceless value of suffering in union with Christ for their own sanctification, for the good of their loved ones, for peace and justice on the earth, and for the ongoing salvation of the whole world! If "a mind is a terrible thing to waste,"[182] what must we say about such a treasure as sharing Jesus' sufferings being left hidden in a field,[183] unbought and unclaimed?

The Qualities of Paul's Ministry. Obviously, under this heading, we could eventually list, at the very least, all the theological and moral virtues.[184] Time and space, however, do not permit such a lengthy treatment, and so we shall confine our reflections to two principal considerations: (1) the mutual virtues of humility and love and (2) the missionary and pastoral virtues of availability, adaptability, and affability.[185]

I have referred to humility and love as mutual virtues because only to the extent that we are emptied of self by genuine humility can we be filled with the love of Christ, which alone enables us to carry on an effective Christian ministry in the face of all odds and for years on end, as Paul so clearly exemplified.

That Paul was humbly conscious of the basic fact that all he was, all he had, all he accomplished, was due to the graciousness of God and specifically to the love and choice of Jesus Christ is evident in innumerable expressions to that effect in his letters. When faced with the problem of factions in the Corinthian Church, based on personal allegiance to individual preachers, Paul hits hard at this dangerous development by reminding the Christians of the insignificance of Apollos and himself in 1 Cor 3:5-7, NIV. "What, after all, is Apollos? And what is Paul? Only servants, through whom you came to believe, as the Lord has assigned to each his task. I planted the seed, Apollos watered it, but God made it grow.[186] So neither he who plants nor he who waters is anything, but only God, who makes things grow."

The Greek word used for servant in the above quotation is *diákonos,* meaning a paid or indentured servant, whence we derive our English word "deacon." Another word, *doûlos,* signifying a slave, is used by Paul of himself, especially at the beginning of some of his letters, for example, "Paul, slave of Christ Jesus" (Rom 1:1, WFD). But there is still another word for servant or slave, which is the most graphic of all. It occurs in 1 Cor 4:1, WFD, where Paul urges the Christians, "So let a person think of us as underrowers of Christ and stewards of the mysteries of God." The Greek word here is *hypērétēs,* referring to a slave pulling an oar on the lowest bank of oars in a Roman or Greek trireme. How low can one get? In 2 Cor 4:7, NRSV, Paul says of himself and his fellow missionaries, "We have this treasure in clay jars so that it may be clear that this extraordinary power belongs to God and does not come from us."

And finally, referring to himself alone in regard to his mysterious "thorn in the flesh," he declares, "So, I will boast all the more gladly of my weaknesses, so that the power of Christ may dwell in me" (2 Cor 12:9, NRSV). And is there any doubt that Paul had long ago made his own the example of the humble Son of God, which he proposed to his beloved Philippians in Phil 2:5-11,[187] WFD? Familiar as it is, it still deserves repetition here:

> Have this attitude of mind among yourselves
>   which was also in Christ Jesus,
> Who, though he existed in the nature of God,
>   did not regard being equal to God
>   something to be desperately clung to,
> But emptied himself, taking the nature of a slave,
>   coming to be in the likeness of humans
>   and, being recognized in form as human,
> He humbled himself, becoming obedient to death,
>   even to the death of the cross.

And because of this God has raised him on high
and has bestowed on him the name
which is above every other name,
So that in Jesus' name every knee should bend
in heaven, on earth, and under the earth
and every tongue should openly profess
That Jesus Christ is Lord of all
To the glory of God the Father!

But some will say, Then why is Paul always talking about himself and his authority? That does not seem to be very humble, does it? By our standards, perhaps not. We have the idea that humility requires us never to mention ourselves except in a demeaning fashion. But true humility recognizes God's gifts as gifts and uses them in his service. It also, when necessary, upholds its authority for the good of the Church, as Paul was forced to do against the Judaizers in particular, who attempted to win over Paul's converts to the Mosaic Law by denying his apostolic authority to preach and teach.[188]

The greatest danger in ministry today is pride, that "thief of the holocaust,"[189] which, like the insidious serpent of Eden,[190] seeks to inject self-glorification into even our most zealous endeavors. And unconsciously promoting this egotism are our thoughtful laypeople, who are so quick and effusive in showing appreciation for our meager efforts. Not that I recommend a moratorium on such expressions of gratitude and even praise. We are all human and tend to need some gentle human "strokes," but through our own reflection and prayer life we need always to refer the glory to Christ, to whom it belongs. For anything we ministers of Christ do that is worthwhile is really his ministry in and through us for his people, who are in effect showing their appreciation for Christ's ministry through us. Were we to keep that glory for ourselves, it would be not only theft on our part but even a kind of prostitution of God's gifts.[191] And the more we allow ourselves to indulge our ego in this way, the more we find ourselves ministering on a purely natural level, on which we tend either to exhaust our limited energy and "burn out" or to become so addicted to human praise that we may leave our "first love,"[192] Jesus Christ, and abandon his ministry.

That Paul was an apostle of passionate Christian love, which drove him literally to spend himself and be spent in the service of Jesus Christ and his people, can hardly be overlooked in reading his letters. Significantly, in his very first letter, as we have seen earlier, he calls the Thessalonian Christians "brothers" at least fifteen times and does not hesitate to refer to himself as their "father"[193] and even their "mother."[194]

Nor is this tender manner of speaking confined to Paul's first letter. In 1 Cor 4:14-15, REB, he declares: "I am not writing this to shame you, but to bring you to reason, for you are my dear children. You may have thousands of tutors[195] in Christ, but you have only one father; for in Christ Jesus you are my offspring, and mine alone, through the preaching of the gospel." And with his obstreperous Galatians he does not hesitate to plead in these startling terms (Gal 4:19, NRSV): "My little children, for whom I am again in the pain of childbirth until Christ is formed in you."

As is well known, while in English there is only one word for love, in Greek there are at least three: *érōs* for passionate sexual love, *philía* for friendship, and, above all, *agápē* for spiritual love, divine love, the love of Christ himself shared with us. Now, while it is clear from both Acts and Paul's letters that he had a rare capacity for making and keeping friends,[196] it is just as evident that the love that controlled his life and impelled his ministry was the love of Christ himself, not just in the sense of Paul's love for Christ, which was exceptional, but above all Christ's love in Paul. Surely that is the full meaning of his statement in 2 Cor 5:14-15, WFD, in which I will translate the basic meaning of the Greek verb *synéchō* (I control) but also add the popular version: "For the love of Christ controls (and impels) us,[197] who are convinced that one died for all, hence all have died; and he died for all so that the living may no longer live for themselves but for him who died and rose again for them." And the qualities of this same *agápē* love of Christ in Christians Paul describes in detail in that classic passage in 1 Cor 13:4-7, WFD, which we can also use as an appropriate portrait of Paul's own Christian love: "Love is patient, love is kind; it is not jealous, nor conceited, nor arrogant; it does not behave improperly, does not seek its own interests; it is not easily upset, does not store up an injury, does not enjoy what is unfair, but rejoices in the truth; it silently bears all things, believes all things, hopes all things, endures all things."

But, as with humility, so also with love, especially in the above description, Paul's critics counter that he himself did not always practice what he preached. Perhaps not, for Paul had to grow in the love of Christ just as we do, but rather than stand in judgment on him, we need to remember that he often had to defend his apostolic authority and the truth about Jesus Christ, which meant that love itself required an uncompromising attitude toward those who would sow error among his Christians. Can a shepherd afford to tolerate the wolf that is endangering his sheep?

By way of application of the foregoing reflections on Paul's humility and Christian love, let us now consider how he exemplified the three missionary and pastoral virtues of availability, adaptability, and affability.

First, regarding *availability*, could anyone have given a more shining example, considering the thousands of miles that he traveled on foot or, at most, on horseback or donkey to visit and revisit the entire area from Jerusalem to Rome? Then, in the realm of *adaptability*, he himself admirably describes his practice of this virtue in 1 Cor 9:19-23, NAB:

> Although I am free in regard to all, I have made myself a slave to all so as to win over as many as possible. To the Jews I became like a Jew to win over the Jews; to those under the law I became like one under the law—though I myself am not under the law—to win over those under the law. To those outside the law I became like one outside the law— though I am not outside God's law but within the law of Christ—to win over those outside the law. To the weak I became weak, to win over the weak. I have become all things to all, to save at least some. All this I do for the sake of the gospel, so that I too may have a share in it.

Finally, while Paul comes across at times as humorless and even grim, especially when fighting to retain his converts' loyalty to Christ, he is nevertheless also a man of joy and *affability*, as indicated in many places, for example, in his letter of joy addressed to the Philippians, particularly in Phil 1:4 and 4:1-7 as well as in his famous dictum, which occurs in his directives about the collection in 2 Cor 9:7, NAB: "God loves a cheerful giver."

We have now completed our long journey with Paul, covering the earlier period of his life and letters up to and including his great Letter to the Romans. Now we will leave Paul, but only temporarily, for a kind of intermission, because in the following chapter we will consider the rest of Paul's life and letters. And just as in a musical performance the portion after the intermission is normally shorter than the previous one, so will it be also in our treatment of Paul. Our next chapter will be considerably briefer than this one, simply from the nature of Paul's life and letters. Meanwhile, let us rest in the Lord, as I trust Paul did sometimes on his long missionary journeys.

NOTES

1. I have chosen the adjective "passionate" for Paul, particularly during this earlier, more missionary part of his extraordinary life, because of his impassioned hate-love relationship with Christ and Christianity, first as the zealous persecutor and later as the loving and tireless propagator.

2. The early letters included in this first chapter on Paul will include 1 and 2 Thessalonians, 1 and 2 Corinthians, Galatians, and Romans.

3. I have chosen this statement of Paul's in Galatians as the fundamental conviction and reality that governed his entire Christian life and apostolate.

4. I prefer the Greek spelling "Lechaion" Road rather than the more common spelling of "Lechaeum" Road, derived from Latin, partly because Corinth is a Greek city and partly from reading the roadsign HODOS LECHAION when visiting Corinth. The road leads to the western port of Corinth, called Lechaion, situated on the Gulf of Corinth.

5. Saul, meaning "asked [of Yahweh]," was evidently the Jewish name given Paul from birth, probably in honor of King Saul, a fellow Benjaminite and the first king of Israel. But he was also called by the Roman name of Paul, most likely from birth as a Roman citizen. Even though Luke in Acts does not refer to him by his Roman name of Paul until the conversion of Sergius Paulus, the proconsul of Cyprus, in Acts 13:4-12, it is somewhat farfetched to think that he received his name from the proconsul. The word itself is a contraction of the Latin *parvulus*, meaning "small or little." It is quite possible that Paul received this Roman name at his birth because he was smaller than usual, and he remained so all his life. Our equivalent might be the fairly common nickname "Shorty." Was this a contributing factor in his becoming an overachiever? Quite possibly so!

6. Corinth, in Greek *kórinthos*, of unknown origin and meaning, was the principal city and capital of Achaia, which comprised the lower half of Greece, including Athens. Situated on the Isthmus of Corinth, which united the Peloponnesus to the rest of Greece, it controlled not only the land commerce north and south in Greece but also the shipping east and west between the Aegean and Adriatic Seas. Most mariners preferred to transship their cargo or even have their boats hauled on runners across the narrow isthmus rather than risk the dreaded winds and waves, not to mention the longer voyage around the Peloponnesus.

7. Greece is rightly referred to as strategic because it lay on the direct route between Rome and the eastern areas of her vast empire.

8. The phoenix (in Greek, *phoînix*) was the word used for a large legendary bird resembling the peacock or sometimes the ostrich, which was sup-

posed to have lived a minimum of five hundred years, after which it burned itself, then rose anew from the ashes. Naturally, it came, in time, to be used as a symbol of Jesus' resurrection. The word also signified a palm tree and, probably from the latter meaning, provided the origin of the name Phoenicia for northern Chanaan. See *The New Encyclopaedia Britannica* 9:393.

Corinth, as the leader of the Achaean League opposing Roman domination, was utterly destroyed in 146 B.C. by the Roman general Mummius, except for the seven simple but very magestic Doric columns of the fifth century B.C. temple of Apollo, which still dominate the ruins of Corinth today. In 44 B.C., Julius Caesar decided to rebuild Corinth as a Roman city and principal capital of Greece, but by the time of Paul, around A.D. 51–52, the population had become extremely cosmopolitan with a majority being Greeks.

9. Achaia, as explained in n. 6, comprised the lower half of Greece. The name may have been conferred on the area by Rome because of the Achaian or Achaean League, comprising many of Greece's principal cities, led by Corinth.

10. Corinth was both prosperous and popular: prosperous on account of her commercial advantages, explained in n. 6, and her industry, which included her famous pottery ware; popular because of her Isthmian Games, held every two years, as well as her famous cult of Aphrodite (Latin, Venus), the goddess of sexual love. She even gave her name to the third type of Greek architecture, featuring fluted columns holding graceful capitals decorated with acanthus leaves, which were far more ornate than the starkly simple Doric and the scroll-like Ionic types. It is ironic that one of the most famous examples of Doric architecture is that of the ancient temple of Apollo at Corinth, while one of the outstanding representatives of Corinthian architecture is the massive temple of Olympian Zeus at Athens.

11. *See* 2 Cor 5:14. Later, in our reflections, we will take a closer look at this verse in its original Greek in order to learn its correct and complete meaning.

12. Some of the many structures of ancient Corinth in gleaming white marble were such government buildings as the main place of assembly, called the *bouleutérion* in Greek and *curia* in Latin; at least three basilicas or palaces, the famous *bêma*, or tribunal, where Paul was brought before the proconsul Gallio (brother of the philosopher Seneca); several temples, principally that of Apollo in the city proper and that of Aphrodite on Acrocorinth, the mountain dominating the city; stoas or covered porticoes in almost every direction; markets in both Greek and Roman style, the former called an agora, the latter a forum; baths, especially the famous Spring of Peirene; a stadium for footraces; an amphitheater for Roman-style games; a theater for drama; an odeon for recitals and orations. Excellent maps and descriptions are found in Sonia de Neuhoff, *Ancient Corinth and its Museum* (Athens: Apollo Editions, n.d.) and in Jerome Murphy-O'Connor, *St. Paul's Corinth: Texts and Archaeology* (Wilmington, Del: Michael Glazier, 1983).

13. Tarsus, the birthplace of St. Paul, was the capital of Cilicia in southeastern Asia Minor, now Turkey. Nestling between the Taurus mountains to

the north, the Amanus mountains to the east, and the Mediterranean Sea to the south, it had been an ancient fortified Hittite stronghold and later a commercial, industrial, educational, and cultural center noted especially for its schools of Stoic philosophy, founded at Athens around 300 B.C.by Zeno of Citium (near Larnaca) in Cyprus.

14. *See* Acts 22:3. It is obvious from Paul's description of his native city that he was quite proud of hailing from what he described as "no mean city" with the implication that he was well educated and deserved a hearing from his Jewish and, to a large extent, Hellenistic (Greek-speaking Jewish) audience in Jerusalem.

15. In addition to its educational and philosophical advantages mentioned above, Tarsus, as the region's capital, would also have been a center for Greek theater as well as athletics. Good descriptions of Tarsus can be found in W. M. Ramsay, *The Cities of St. Paul: Their Influence on His Life and Thought* (Grand Rapids: Baker, 1965) 85–235, and Sherman Johnson, *Paul the Apostle and His Cities* (Wilmington, Del: Michael Glazier, 1987) 25–34.

16. Like strict observers of Jewish Law through the centuries and today, Paul's parents, above all his Pharisaic father, would have ensured both personally and through the synagogue school Saul's thorough education in Hebrew, Aramaic, and the Mosaic Law, culminating in his Bar Mitzvah at the age of thirteen.

17. After the assassination of Julius Caesar in 44 B.C., Tarsus and other eastern cities came under the rule of the conspirators Brutus and, especially, Cassius. When Tarsus resisted that domination, Cassius inflicted harsh reprisals on the inhabitants, whereupon Mark Anthony retaliated by granting them Roman citizenship, and even though they understandably sided with Anthony and Cleopatra against Octavian or Augustus, the latter wisely decided not to cancel their citizenship after his victory at the Battle of Actium in 31 B.C. As a result, Paul's father had become a Roman citizen and Paul himself was born into that status with its priceless privileges. Some idea of its unique social value can be derived by comparing it with United States citizenship today.

18. There are indications in both Acts and Paul's letters that, growing up at Tarsus, he had been actively involved in Greek athletics and perhaps also in theater and rhetoric. It is difficult to imagine anyone using athletic imagery as much as he does without his having personally engaged in athletic contests. Not only in his farewell address in Acts 20:17-38, notably 20:24, but also in many of his letters, foot races in particular seem to be a favorite form of Pauline illustration, for example in 1 Cor 9:24-27; Gal 2:2; 5:7; Phil 2:16; 3:12, 14, 16; 2 Tim 4:7. Amphitheatrical and theatrical imagery is far less evident in Paul's letters, occurring primarily in 1 Cor 4:9; Gal 3:27; Rom 13:14, to which we will return in greater detail later in our examination of Paul. Paul's training in rhetoric appears most prominently, of course, in his Athenian discourse (Acts 17:22-31), but many passages in his letters also exemplify his facility at declamation, for example in his defense of his apostolic authority in 2 Cor 10–12 and in Phil 3:2-21.

19. Gamaliel (God has repaid me), often referred to as Gamaliel I or the

Elder to distinguish him from his stern grandson, Gamaliel II (who had Jewish Christians labeled as *minim* or heretics and barred from the synagogue), was not only Paul's teacher (Acts 22:3) but also recommended leniency regarding the apostles to his fellow members of the Sanhedrin (Acts 5:34-39).

20. Tentmaking was a common occupation in Tarsus and in all Cilicia, whose Greek name *kilíkia* means "goat hair," which was widely prized in the weaving of tent cloth. It is probable, therefore, that Paul learned the trade in his native city but may well have perfected it in a pilgrimage city like Jerusalem. It was also the basis of his initial association in Corinth with Aquila and Priscilla, who became his converts and dear friends (Acts 18:1-3). Throughout his active ministry, Paul took pride in using his trade to support himself and his companions (Acts 20:33-35; 1 Cor 9:1-18; 2 Cor 11:7-11).

21. "Saul, meanwhile, was trying to destroy the church; entering house after house and dragging out men and women, he handed them over for imprisonment" (Acts 8:3, NAB).

22. Stephen, in Greek, *stéphanos*, meaning "crown," was a Hellenist, that is, a Greek-speaking Jew, converted to Christianity and chosen as a deacon to assist the apostles in material concerns so that they could give themselves to prayer and preaching (Acts 6:1-7). However, the Holy Spirit obviously had other plans and almost immediately moved Stephen and later Philip to actively engage in the apostolate of preaching, defending the faith, and baptizing (Acts 6:8-10; 8:4-7, 26-40).

23. Stephen, filled with the Holy Spirit, successfully engaged in debate his fellow Hellenists, including Cilicians, natives of Paul's own Roman province (Acts 6:8-10). Was Paul himself among them? It would seem not, since the synagogue in question was one of freedmen, that is, former slaves who had attained their liberty, whereas Paul was born a free Roman citizen. However, he may well have come to know about Stephen from his fellow Cilicians who were members of that synagogue.

24. *See* Acts 7:55-56.

25. *See* Acts 7:58. Paul is described here as a *neanías*, a young man, which could indicate anyone up to the age of forty. In those days, one did not even begin any kind of public life until the age of thirty (Luke 3:23).

26. The Sanhedrin (in Greek *synédrion*) comprised the supreme council, or deliberative body, of the Jews. First mentioned by the Jewish historian Josephus as existing during the reign of Antiochus the Great (223–187 B.C.), the council first occurs in the Bible, according to the Alexandrian Canon accepted by Catholics, in 1 Macc 11:23; 12:6; 14:28; 2 Macc 1:10; 4:44; 11:27. Composed entirely of Judean Jews, Galileans being excluded, the Sanhedrin comprised three groups of members: elders of the chief families or clans; high priests, including the current and former high priests and elders of the four high priestly families; and scribes or lawyers, most of whom were Pharisees. See John McKenzie, *Dictionary of the Bible* (Milwaukee: Bruce, 1965) 152-53.

27. It would seem to be extremely presumptuous and arrogant of Saul and the Sanhedrin to attempt to arrest Jewish Christians in Damascus, the former capital of Syria, but two facts must be noted: (1) that in 63 B.C. Pompey, the

Roman general, had united the entire area into the Roman province of Syria, of which Palestine was regarded as a part, even though in time it had its own kings and governors, and (2) that the Sanhedrin was regarded by Jews as having authority over the lives and practices of Jews everywhere in the world. Hence, later on, Gamaliel II and the Sanhedrin at Jabneh or Jamnia, now composed entirely of Pharisees, were able to expel Jewish Christians from synagogue worship in Antioch of Syria and elsewhere.

The Nabateans, with their impregnable capital at Petra in the area of ancient Seir, the traditional stronghold of the Edomites, descendants of Esau, achieved great power and wealth roughly from 300 B.C.to A.D. 300 through their control of the trade routes south of the Dead Sea, even taking Damascus in their expansion. In 2 Cor 11:32-33, Paul tells of his narrow escape from Damascus in a basket out of the clutches of the ethnarch (*ethnárchēs*), or governor, of the Nabatean king Aretas (Aretas IV), who was trying to arrest him. The site of Petra was lost from the time of the Crusades until its rediscovery by John L. Burckhardt in 1812. Since then, but especially since 1925, when access became easier, this "rose-red city half as old as time" has been enjoyed as one of the tourist wonders of the world. *See* Iain Browning: *Petra* London: Chatto & Windus, 1982).

28. *See* Acts 9:3-6; 22:6-10; 26:12-18; 1 Cor 15:8-10; Gal 1:15-16.

29. *See* Acts 9:15; 22:15; 26:12-18; cf. Matt 28:19; Mark 16:15; Luke 24:47; Acts 1:8.

30. *See* Gal 1:17. We can only speculate about the location of Paul's sojourn in Arabia.

31. *See* Acts 9:30 and Gal 1:21.

32. Read Paul's first journey, Acts 13-14.

33. Judaizers, as the name indicates, were Jewish Christians who insisted on making Gentiles Jews by circumcision and imposition of the Mosaic Law before they could become Christians. The name applies especially to those who continued in this attitude even after the Council of Jerusalem.

34. The Council of Jerusalem, held in A.D. 49 or 50, is not considered one of the ecumenical councils of the Church for the simple reason that the Church was not yet ecumenical, that is, not yet embracing the inhabited world. However, it was an extremely important council because it decided the crucial question of justification and salvation by faith and baptism or by circumcision and the Mosaic Law.

This first Church council is recounted in Acts 15:1-30. It is clear from a careful reading of the council proceedings that not only did Peter, as leader of the Church, preside at the assembly, but in effect he decided the issue, with the silent consent of all assembled. Even James, the leader of the Jewish Christians, concurred with Peter but added four recommendations to help the Gentiles to avoid scandalizing the Jews (more on this in the reflections).

35. Paul's objection to taking Barnabas' cousin, Mark, on the second missionary journey was that the young man had deserted them on the first journey (Acts 13:13). As we have seen when studying Mark, his desertion was probably due to the fact that he was very young and away from home for the

first time, so that he was homesick for his mother in Jerusalem. The disagreement did cause Paul and Barnabas never to go on another missionary journey together (Acts 15:36-39), but clearly Paul was later reconciled with them, for he speaks highly of them in 1 Cor 9:6 and 2 Tim 4:11.

36. Barnabas is highly praised and called "son of encouragement" in Acts 4:36-37.

37. After Paul's conversion, when the Church in Jerusalem was still very wary of him, it was indeed Barnabas who introduced him to the apostles. *See* Acts 9:27.

38. After several years of enforced "rest" at Tarsus, Paul was recruited by Barnabas to help in the task of converting and instructing new Christians, mainly Gentiles, at Antioch, as we read in Acts 11:25-26.

39. It was indeed humble of Barnabas to "take a back seat" to Paul because in Acts 13:2, 7 Barnabas is listed first, but after Paul's confrontation with Elymas the magician at Paphos in Cyprus, it is always Paul who is the main spokesman, as we see in Acts 13:9-13 and elsewhere.

40. Silas (another form of Saul?), or Silvanus (woodsman), was a well-educated Jew who, like Paul and Mark, bore a Roman name as well. That did not necessarily mean that he was a Roman citizen. He was obviously very open to the direct reception of Gentiles into the Church, for he was one of the bearers of the letter of the Council of Jerusalem along with Paul and Barnabas as well as one other named Judas or Barsabbas (Acts 15:22, 32). Paul probably admired Silas' combination of learning and zeal, which he considered ideal for the second missionary tour (Acts 15:40). Peter also came to admire and use Silas, the apparent writer of his First Epistle (1 Pet 5:12).

41. For the journey of Paul and Silas through southern Asia Minor, see Acts 15:41; 16:1-2, 6.

42. Timothy, whose Greek name means "one who honors God" or perhaps "one whom God honors," was, like John Mark, very young when recruited by Paul at Lystra. Perhaps Paul was already remorseful about his rejection of Mark. The relationhship of Paul and Timothy, especially as the years transpired, formed a wonderful example of a close spiritual friendship that spanned the generation gap. The recruitment of Timothy is told in Acts 16:1-3.

43. In my story of Paul, I am adhering to the so-called northern Galatian theory, which posits that Paul, after visiting Cilicia, Lycaonia, and Phrygia, then turned north to the Galatian territory proper and did not content himself with visiting the Roman province of Galatia, which included the foregoing areas (Acts 16:6).

The Galatians, as the name implies, were Gauls and hence different from the rest of the people around them in Asia Minor. "The name is derived from the Gauls who invaded Macedonia, Greece, and Asia Minor in 279 BC and the following years; they finally settled in Anatolia, where they established a kingdom. In 64 BC Galatia became a client state of Rome, and in the following years the territory of the kingdom was extended into adjoining regions" (McKenzie, "Galatia," *Dictionary of the Bible*, 292).

44. Having been forbidden by the Holy Spirit to diverge to the south toward Ephesus or toward the north to Pontus, Paul and his companions reached Troas on the Aegean coast (Acts 16:6-8). The name Troas seems to be a combination of Troy and Alexander, for it was a kind of new Troy laid out by Alexander the Great himself.

45. The westernmost area of Asia Minor was called Anatolia, especially by the Greeks in Achaia and Macedonia. The word comes from the Greek *anatolé* meaning "rising" or "dawn," because to the Greeks west of Asia Minor the sun rose to their east, that is, in western Asia Minor.

46. At Troas Paul made one more recruit, namely Luke the "dearly beloved physician" (Col 4:14), who would later be the author of the twin works, his Gospel and Acts. Some think that he may also have been the Macedonian whom Paul saw in a dream at Troas beckoning him to come over to his country. Perhaps, but we cannot be sure. What we do know is that immediately afterward we encounter the first of the three "we sections" in Acts, namely Acts 16:10. It will be noticed that this section ends at Philippi, where the next "we section" apparently takes up again.

47. On the Roman military colony of Philippi, we can read not only Acts 16:11-40 but also the description given in connection with Luke's writings in vol. 1 of this work.

48. For a description of Thessalonica, modern Salonika, Saloniki, or Thessaloniki, the capital of northern Greece, or Macedonia, *see* Johnson, *Paul and His Cities*, pp. 76–80.

49. For a description of Beroea, *see* Johnson, *Paul and His Cities*, 80.

50. For a description of Athens, *see* especially F. F. Bruce, *Jesus and Paul: Places They Knew* (London: Scripture Union, 1981) 97–100.

51. For the story of Paul at Philippi, *see* Acts 16:12-40.

52. For the story of Paul at Thessalonica and Beroea, *see* Acts 17:1-15.

53. For the story of Paul at Athens, *see* Acts 17:16-34.

54. There is some confusion about what is meant by the "Areopagus" in Acts 17:19. Is Luke speaking literally about the stone hill of Ares, or Mars, the god of war, which lies between the Acropolis above and the agora below? Or is he speaking of the court or council of the Areopagus, which is made up of leading citizens of Athens? In my own opinion, it is the former that is intended, largely because the entire affair seems so informal and spontaneous. However, one member of the council of the Areopagus named Denis must have been listening, because he became one of Paul's converts, later bishop of Athens, and today the Latin cathedral of Athens is named after him.

55. Evidently, while Paul was wandering about the agora of Athens and speaking about Jesus and the resurrection with whoever would listen, they misunderstood him, thinking that he was introducing a new divine couple, named *Iesoûs* (a masculine noun) and *Anástasis* (a feminine noun) (Acts 17:18). When it dawned on them from Paul's address at the Areopagus that he was talking about a man who, he claimed, had risen from the dead, they dismissed him with the flippant expression "We will hear you again about this another time" (Acts 17:32), which was their equivalent of our modern "Don't call us. We'll call you."

56. On Paul's determination to preach only Christ and him crucified, *see* 1 Cor 2:2.

57. So proverbial was the decadence of Corinth that prostitutes were commonly called "Corinthian girls." This, of course, was partly due to the affluence of the city, stemming from her thriving commerce and industry. But it was also due to her situation as a double port city, as host every other year to the Isthmian Games, held in the nude, and, above all, as the site of the famous temple of the goddess of sexual love, Aphrodite, or Venus.

58. For Paul's vision and success, *see* Acts 18:9-11.

59. For Paul's Corinthian friends, *see* Acts 18:2-8.

60. For the return of Silas and Timothy and their report about the situation at Thessalonica, *see* Acts 18:5 and 1 Thess 1:12; 3:1-8.

61. It is only my imaginative speculation that has Priscilla make the initial suggestion about writing a letter, but there is a reasonable basis for it. First of all, it is commonly believed that while Aquila was a tentmaking Jew from Pontus in Asia Minor (Acts 18:2-3), Priscilla, or Prisca (as Luke and Paul variously called her here and in Rom 16:3), was a highborn Roman lady whose family lived in a substantial house where the catacomb of St. Priscilla exists in Rome today. Secondly, it is worthy of note that Priscilla is usually listed before Aquila, for example, in their interesting instruction of the impressive preacher, Apollos, at Ephesus in Acts 18:26. Thirdly, is it not usually the wife, especially one as educated as Priscilla, who is the letter writer in the family and therefore more likely to think of and suggest to Paul this means of communicating with the Thessalonians?

62. The format of letters in Paul's world will be treated in the second or analytical part of this chapter.

63. Paul addresses the Thessalonians as "brothers" at least fifteen times in his first letter alone, and some twenty times in both letters. In addition, he does not hesitate to refer to himself as their father in 1 Thess 2:11-12 and even as their mother in 1 Thess 2:7-8.

64. Paul, in describing Jesus' second coming in 1 Thess 4:13-18, is using typical figurative eschatological (end time) language, which unfortunately the fundamentalists insist on interpreting literally, with trumpets blaring and all of us, living or dead, flying through the air like Superman to meet the Lord in the "great rapture." Imagery like this in 1 and 2 Thessalonians when overemphasized causes us to overlook the truly substantive riches of the letters.

65. For Paul's instructions on good conduct, *see* 1 Thess 4:1-2, 9-12; 5:12-22.

66. For Paul's caution about sexual morality, *see* 1 Thess 4:3-8. Thessalonica itself, of course, was a thoroughly pagan city, with all the loose morals implied therein, but I cannot help thinking that Paul's concern was influenced also by his writing from the morally polluted atmosphere of Corinth.

67. Paul's disavowal of the spurious letter in question is found in 2 Thess 2:2.

68. Paul's treatment of the "great apostasy" that must occur before Christ comes again is found in 2 Thess 2:3-12. As mentioned in n. 64 regarding the "rapture" in his earlier letter, the eschatological language contained in this portion should not be taken too literally. Another point to remember is that

to a Jewish mind like Paul's, corporate personality was a common concept, that is, the usage in which a single person stands for a whole group or movement. It happens to be a historical truth that atheistic communism is the first world movement based on the idea that there is no God. The fact that communism seems to be on the wane does not necessarily mean that it is not "the great apostasy." It could mean rather that the second coming of Christ is not as far in the future as we might think.

69. For Paul's blunt words about work, *see* 1 Thess 3:10.

70. Paul's reference to the report from members of Chloe's household about problems at Corinth is in 1 Cor 1:11.

71. The letter that sought Paul's answers to questions of the Corinthians is referred to in 1 Cor 7:1.

72. Paul clearly wrote at least four letters to the Corinthians. However, we havè only two, and whether those two somehow contain all four will be discussed when we take up the analysis of those letters.

73. It is not at all clear just what the opposition was at Corinth that caused Paul such personal sadness. Many believe it was an incipient form of Gnosticism, of which we will see evidences in the letters to the Colossians and Ephesians. I personally do not think so. If the whole matter was one of a movement and not just one of a personal or communal rebellion such as Moses faced in Num 16, then the most logical candidate was his old nemesis, the Judaizers. What possibly supports this is the reference to Jewish Christian preachers in 2 Cor 11:22-23. Whatever it was, it was a crucifixion for Paul.

74. Paul's painful and humiliating visit to Corinth is mentioned in 2 Cor 2:1, 5-11.

75. Paul's latest recruit, the Gentile Titus, referred to in 2 Cor 2:12-13 and 7:5-7, does not seem to be the same as the Titus, or Titius Justus, of Corinth listed in Acts 18:7, for apparently Paul needs to introduce Titus to the Church of Corinth (2 Cor 8:23).

76. The letter written "with many tears" is mentioned in 2 Cor 2:4; 7:8. As we will see, all or part of it may be contained in our present 2 Corinthians.

77. Paul's joy at Titus' arrival in Philippi with good news about Corinth is expressed in 2 Cor 2:12-13; 7:5-7, 13-16.

78. In 2 Cor 8-9, Paul encourages and directs the collection for the Christian poor of Judea, at the same time providing us with an excellent example of why and how to ask for funds when that is necessary.

79. Instead of the usual thanksgiving at the beginning of Paul's letters, his angry missive to the Galatians substitutes a ringing expression of amazement that they have so quickly abandoned his "gospel" and allowed themselves to be misled by the Judaizers (Gal 1:6-9).

80. In Rom 8:28, NAB, Paul declares, "We know that all things work for good for those who love God, who are called according to his purpose."

81. We will take up in depth Paul's teaching on justification by faith (Gal 2:15–3:29; 5:1-14) when we consider Paul the theologian in the third part of this chapter.

82. Paul's contrast between the spirit and the flesh is found in Gal 5:13-26.

For now, the important thing to remember is that in the Hebrew anthropology, spirit does not mean soul and flesh does not mean body. No, by the term "spirit" is meant our entire being aspiring to total union with God by our very nature, while "flesh" pertains to our whole being inclined to the human weakness of illness, accident, death, temptation, sin. This is confirmed by Paul's list of works of the flesh in Gal 5:19-21, many of which have nothing to do with the body.

83. Paul refers to himself as a boxer in 1 Cor 9:26.

84. We do not know just when Paul was born and therefore how old he was at this time, but a good guess would place his birth around what we call A.D. 1, which would put him in his mid-fifties at this time. That would also make him from five to eight years younger than Jesus, according to the corrected estimate of the year of Jesus' birth under Herod the Great, who died in 4 B.C.

85. This description of Paul is from the legendary *Acts of Paul*, "And he [Onesiphorus] saw Paul coming, a man little of stature, thin-haired upon the head, crooked in the legs, of good state of body, with eyebrows joining, and nose somewhat hooked, full of grace; for sometimes he appeared like a man, and sometimes he had the face of an angel." See Montague James, *The Apocryphal New Testament* (Oxford: Clarendon, 1972) 273.

86. Paul himself tells the Romans in Rom 15:20 that he does not preach where others have already done so.

87. Paul's treatment of justification by faith in his Letter to the Romans is found in Rom 3:21-4:25.

88. Paul's treatment of the contrast between spirit and flesh in his Letter to the Romans occurs in Rom 8:1-17.

89. The original meaning of "diatribe" (in Greek, *diatríbō*, meaning "I rub against, spend time, etc.,") referred to a method of development that involved asking and answering questions. The modern meaning is quite different, for a diatribe today, according to Merriam-Webster's *Ninth New Collegiate Dictionary*, signifies "a bitter and abusive speech or writing; ironical or cynical criticism." Obviously, I am using the term diatribe in its earlier meaning (see *HBD*, 763).

90. To Paul, as an heir of centuries of Judaism, the fact that his fellow Jews, God's chosen people, refused to accept Jesus as their Messiah or Christ while Gentiles of all kinds readily embraced Christianity constituted an inscrutable mystery comprehended only by God, a mystery Paul treats at some length in Rom 9-11.

91. See Rom 11:29, WFD. The Jews are still God's chosen people, the only individual people he has ever chosen. However, Christians are also chosen by God from all the peoples of the earth to be one spiritual people in the risen Christ. If ever, then, there should be two people loving each other it should be Jews and Christians, but rarely has that been true during our common history.

92. It is interesting to note in the section of Romans devoted to conduct or morality how much Paul "borrows" from prior letters, especially 1 Corin-

thians, for example, his teaching on the spiritual gifts and unity in the Church as the (mystical) body of Christ (Rom 12:3-8; 1 Cor 12:1-31); his insistence on love (Rom 12:9-21; 13:8-10; 1 Cor 13:1-13); and his practical guidance about food offered to idols (Rom 14:1-15:6, 1 Cor 8:1-11:1).

93. In Romans more than in any other letter, Paul argues persuasively that justification and salvation come through faith operating in love rather than through works of the Law. Appropriately, then, in Romans more than elsewhere, he first presents all his doctrine in Rom 1-11 and then in Rom 12-16 draws practical moral and spiritual implications.

94. It is extremely noteworthy that Paul begins his moral section with a spiritual, even mystical, exhortation to the Roman Christians to offer themselves as a living sacrifice, holy and pleasing to God, their spiritual worship, and instead of conforming their conduct to that of the world, to be transformed (into Christ) by the renewal of their thinking so that they might be able to discern the will of God, namely what is good, pleasing, and perfect in his eyes (Rom 12:1-2). This actually summarizes all of Paul's moral and spiritual doctrine, for if we truly give ourselves to God and allow ourselves to be transformed into Christ, then we live under the direction of the Holy Spirit, who guides us according to God's will. And is this not the twofold purpose of the Eucharist, namely to offer ourselves with Christ to the Father and, receiving Christ in return from the Father, to be more and more transformed into him that we may continue his life and ministry in the world today?

95. It is generally agreed among Scripture scholars that Paul, in writing his famous letters, followed the usage of his time by employing amanuenses, or secretaries, to whom he dictated sometimes verbatim but at other times quite possibly in broader terms or themes, leaving it to the secretaries to choose words and fill in details, and perhaps just adding some words of his own at the end, as we see in 2 Thess 3:17 and Gal 6:11. Of his known friends, the most likely candidates as secretaries were Silas, Luke, and Timothy, but we usually cannot know for sure because Paul, like writers of his time, does not favor us with an identification of his secretaries. In Rom 16:22, however, one "Tertius" identifies himself (perhaps on his own initiative) as the secretary for that great letter and then proceeds to greet the readers in the Lord (see *HBD*, 1130).

96. The laborious process of writing will be more fully described in the following section, the analysis of Paul's early letters.

97. Examples of the prayer and thanksgiving providing a preview of the general tone and content of the letter can be readily seen in 1 and 2 Thessalonians, 1 and 2 Corinthians, and Romans, while in Galatians Paul's startling expression of amazement rather than thanksgiving immediately rivets his readers' attention.

98. For example, doctrine and conduct are interwoven all through 1 Corinthians but treated successively in Romans.

99. See *HBD*, 1149.

100. The Greek word for "tradition" is *parádosis* from the verb *paradídomi*, meaning "I give or hand along." The correlative term is *paralambáno*, mean-

ing "I receive or take along." Paul uses this very terminology especially in 1 Thess 4:1; 2 Thess 2:15; 3:6; 1 Cor 11:23; 15:1-3; Rom 6:17. An objective reading of these texts will underline the importance of oral tradition in the life and ministry of the Apostle Paul. Confirmation of this can be found in *Theological Dictionary of the New Testament*, 2:172–73: "For Paul Christian teaching is tradition . . . and he demands that the churches should keep it since salvation depends on it (1 Cor 15:2). He sees no antithesis between pneumatic piety and the high estimation of tradition. The essential point for Paul is that it has been handed down (1 Cor 15:3) and that it derives from the Lord (1 Cor 11:23) . . . [meaning] that the Lord's supper, its celebration and the appropriate words come from the Lord (through the apostles), not that Paul received the formula in visionary instruction by the ascended Lord."

101. Paul, like the other New Testament writers, usually cited the Hebrew Testament in its Greek translation, made by Jewish scholars in Alexandria some two centuries before Christ. It is commonly called the Septuagint from the tradition or legend that seventy scholars in all were involved and is commonly designated in biblical circles by the Roman numeral for seventy, LXX. Christian writers seemed to use the Septuagint for three principal reasons: (1) They were writing in Greek and therefore it was easier and more natural to refer to the Greek translation of the Old Testament; (2) for Gentiles and even for Jews outside of Israel, Greek was the primary language, and therefore it was a virtual necessity for Paul and other New Testament writers addressing an extra-Palestinian readership to use the Hebrew Testament in Greek translation; (3) in the providence of God and the development of Jewish messianic expectations, the Septuagint prepared the way for Christ and Christianity, for example, in its translation of the Hebrew *ha almah* meaning "the young woman" in Isa 7:14, into the Greek *hē parthénos* meaning "the virgin."

102. An example of a hymn in a Pauline letter commonly thought to be a community hymn is the famous *Carmen Christi*, or "Hymn of Christ," in Phil 2:5-11, but see the penetrating study of R. P. Martin, *Carmen Christi* (Cambridge, England: University Press, 1967), which seems to indicate, in ch. 13, pp. 42–62, that the arguments for and against Pauline authorship are fairly evenly balanced and therefore inconclusive.

103. The best example of Paul's use of figures from farming and construction occurs in 1 Cor 3:5-17, particularly 1 Cor 3:9, NAB: "For we are God's co-workers; you are God's field, God's building."

104. The following are examples of Paul's use of figures from Greek athletics, theater, and mystery religions: (1) from Greek athletics: 1 Cor 9:24-26; Gal 2:2; 5:7; Phil 2:16; 3:12, 14, 16; 2 Tim 4:7; (2) from Greek theater: 1 Cor 4:9; Gal 3:27; Rom 13:14; (3) from Greek mysteries: 1 Cor 2:8; 4:1; 13:2; 14:2; 15:51; Col 1:26-27; 2:2; 4:3; Eph 1:9; 3:4; 6:19-20; 1 Tim 3:16, to which might be added Rom 11:33-36.

In regard to these figures, two things are noteworthy:

(1) Greek athletics were always individual contests, for there were no team sports such as our football, baseball, or basketball (to mention only a few). If there had been team athletics, undoubtedly Paul would have used imagery

derived from them to illustrate the necessity of unity and cooperation among Christians, for example, in 1 Cor 12 and Rom 12.

(2) While Paul may use the terminology of mystery religions to refer to the mystery of Christ and Christianity, it is clear that his thinking is worlds apart from those cults based on mythological legends and the cycle of nature.

105. The most recent commentaries to which I refer are *The International Bible Commentary* (1986), *Harper's Bible Commentary* (1988), *The Collegeville Bible Commentary* (1989), and *The New Jerome Biblical Commentary* (1990), all of them listed in my introduction to this volume.

106. 1 and 2 Thessalonians are dubbed "Eschatological Letters" because they both deal with what is called in Greek the *éschaton*, or end time, when Christ will return in triumph.

107. Galatians and Romans are referred to as "*Soteriological Letters*" because they treat the questions of justification and salvation, and the Greek word for "salvation" is *sōtēría* from *sōtḗr*, which means "a savior."

108. In treating the problem of Corinthian disunity first, Paul clearly shows it to be his primary concern. Factionalism arising from personal attachments to individual ministers of the gospel, and usually based, as at Corinth, on the preachers' gifts or abilities, is a perennial danger in the Church. All concerned, preachers and hearers alike, should reflect carefully on Paul's inspired and inspiring response to the problem and heed his formidable warning in 1 Cor 3:16-17, WFD: "Do you not realize that you (the local Church) are a temple of God, and that the Spirit of God dwells in your midst? If anyone destroys the temple of God (by disunity), God will destroy him, for a temple of God is holy, and that is what you are!"

109. It is generally thought among Scripture scholars that the sexual scandal against which Paul inveighs in 1 Cor 5:1-13 is the case of a man cohabiting with his stepmother, something prohibited not only by Jewish but even by pagan law (see *NJBC*, 803). The gravity of the scandal (in the true meaning of leading others into sin) was aggravated by the atmosphere of sexual immorality that pervaded Corinth.

110. Paul's solution, as indicated in 1 Cor 5:2, 9-11, is to excommunicate the offender, that is, to expel him from the Christian community until he reforms. Unfortunately, some preachers and commentators, unaware that "flesh" and "spirit" in Scripture do not mean "body" and "soul," have held that when Paul urges the deliverance of the man to Satan "for the destruction of his flesh so that his spirit may be saved on the day of the Lord" (1 Cor 5:5, NAB), he is literally condemning him to death! (see *NJBC*, 803).

111. What Paul describes in 1 Cor 7:12-16 is the basis of what is known in the Catholic Church as the Pauline Privilege. Richard Kugelman states in the *NCE*, 11:27-28, "*Pauline Privilege*, the term used to express the right to dissolve the marriage bond contracted between two unbaptized persons after the baptism of one of the spouses and the refusal of the other to cohabit peacefully. The term is based on the supposition that St. Paul grants this privilege in 1 Cor 7:12-15, but it is rather a privilege granted by the Church through a broader interpretation of the Pauline text. . . . Since the fourth century the

majority of Catholic commentators have interpreted 1 Cor 7:15 to mean that the marriage bond between two unbaptized persons is dissolvable when the unbaptized spouse refuses peaceful cohabitation with the baptized person, and that it is actually dissolved when the baptized spouse contracts a sacramental marriage.''

See also P. Dulau, ''The Pauline Privilege: Is It Promulgated in the First Epistle to the Corinthians?'' *Catholic Biblical Quarterly* (July 1951) 146–52.

112. For Christians of the first century living in a pagan society, there existed the practical question of whether they could buy and eat meat sold in the common marketplace in view of the possibility that it might have been offered to idols. Paul's solution is quite straightforward: ''Eat freely, knowing that idols or false gods do not exist, but remember two things, namely that you might scandalize another Christian whose faith is not as strong, and that you yourself may possibly revert to idolatry.''

While actual idolatry is no longer the problem it once was, nevertheless the issue and Paul's solution are still relevant today. The issue is relevant because we do live in a neopagan society and must use prudence lest we let ourselves live on a pagan level. Paul's two cautions are also very relevant because, while we may feel immune to the dangers of neopagan temptations, we too must consider the possibility of giving bad example to others as well as that of falling prey to temptations ourselves. Weaker than we think we are, we need a healthy respect for human nature.

113. Paul's account of the institution of the Eucharist is the earliest we have, antedating those in the Gospels. A comparison with the Gospel accounts reveals four things in particular; (1) that no two are exactly the same; (2) that the closest similarity exists between Paul and Luke on the one hand, and between Mark and Matthew on the other; (3) that all accounts use the simple Greek word *estín*, meaning ''is,'' as their connective rather than *homoiázei* or *homoioûtai*, meaning ''is like'' or ''resembles''; (4) that modifying participles are always in the present rather than the future or past tense. Thus, in my own translation:

Paul: ''This is my body (which is) for you. This cup is the new covenant in my blood'' (1 Cor 11:24-25).

Luke: ''This is my body (which is) being given for you. This cup (is) the new covenant in my blood (which is) being poured out for you'' (Luke 22:19-20).

Mark: ''This is my body. This is my blood of the covenant (which is) being poured out for many'' (Mark 14:22-24).

Matt: ''This is my body. For this is my blood of the covenant (which is) being poured out for many for the forgiveness of sins'' (Matt 26:26-28).

It should be noted that Paul declares unequivocalloy in 1 Cor 11:27, REB: ''It follows that anyone who eats the bread or drinks the cup of the Lord unworthily will be guilty of offending against the body and blood of the Lord.'' By doing so, he not only emphasizes that the Eucharist contains the Body and Blood of Christ but also that he is truly present under either the form of bread or the form of wine, though reception of Communion under both forms does carry a greater sign value.

114. A spiritual or charismatic gift (in Greek, *chárisma*) is a special ability or talent given to persons by God, not for their own sanctification (as are the seven gifts of the Holy Spirit, *see* Isa 11:2), still less for their self-glorification, but for the service of others and for the building up of the Church (1 Cor 12:4-11, 27-31; 14:1-40; Rom 12:6-8; Eph 4:7-12). Of these gifts, the one that tends to receive the most attention is the gift of tongues or ecstatic utterances, but evidently Paul did not share in the enthusiasm about this particular gift, as is clear from these facts: (1) Even in his first list of gifts, he places the gift of tongues, together with their interpretation, in the last place (1 Cor 12:10). (2) In the next chapter, he extolls the supremacy of love above all the charismatic gifts, in particular that of tongues (1 Cor 13:1). (3) In 1 Cor 14, he apparently treats the gift of tongues more as a problem than as a great advantage. (4) In his other lists of gifts (Rom 12:6-8; Eph 4:11-13) he never once includes the gift of tongues. I mention the fact not to downplay the charismatic gifts including the gift of tongues, which are noted several times in the Acts of Apostles (Acts 2:4; 10:44-46; 19:6), but to keep them in perspective as Paul does in 1 Cor 12–14. After all, ecstatic utterances (*glossalália*) were known among the Jews (Num 11:24-29; 1 Sam 19:22-24) and even among the pagans (1 Kgs 18:29), but more importantly, Jesus Christ, Son of God and Son of Man is never described as speaking in tongues or ecstatic utterances. (*See* my articles "Charismatic Gifts" and "Gift of Tongues," *NCE*, 3:460 and 6:473).

115. Paul's description of the Church as the (mystical) body of Christ is masterful and has happily promoted a healthy sense of community among Christians. We must, however, bear in mind that the community is composed of persons, and therefore it is essential to keep a balance between the person and the community. Paul's portrait of the Church as the body of Christ will be completed later on in his Letter to the "Ephesians," when he adds the description of Jesus as the head (Eph 1:22-23), and at that time we will have our reflection on Paul and the Church.

116. Paul's lyrical description of the highest gift, that Christian, spiritual, and, indeed, divine love called by the Greek name *agápe*. Of the three well-known Greek words for love, *érōs* (sexual love) is, for whatever reason, never used in the New Testament; *philía*, the Greek word for friendship, can be either purely natural or supernatural; while *agápe* is always supernatural, being a sharing in God's own love through Jesus Christ. It is noteworthy that in Paul's description of Christian love in 1 Cor 13, which forms an excellent examination of conscience, the very first qualities listed are those of patience and kindness.

117. The extremely important questions of the Corinthians about the reality and nature of bodily resurrection, which Paul treats both in 1 Cor 15 and 2 Cor 5, are entirely too important, complex, and fascinating to allow treatment in a note, hence this brief notice here with a promise to include the entire matter in our reflections on the later writings of Paul (ch. 2), particularly in connection with his Letter to the Philippians.

118. In 1 Cor 16:2 Paul directs that the collected funds be gathered on "the first day of the week," thereby indicating for the first time that Sunday had

become "the Lord's Day." It seems that at first the Christians had simply added the Eucharistic celebration at the end of the Jewish observance of the Sabbath. Bearing in mind that the Jewish day began at sundown of the previous day, this was already a celebration on the first day of the week. When the Church spread beyond Israel and became increasingly Gentile, it was inevitable that Sunday, the first day of the week, would become the Christian Sabbath. After all, it was on the first day of the week that creation began (Gen 1:5), that Jesus rose from the dead (Mark 16:2; Matt 28:1; Luke 24:1; John 20:1), and that the Holy Spirit "baptized" the Church on the Jewish feast of (seven) Weeks plus one, or Pentecost (fifty days, see Acts 2:1). Thus, Sunday honors all three persons of the Trinity, though the major (and at first the only) emphasis was on Jesus' resurrection. See Acts 20:7; Rev. 1:10; *see also* my article "The Lord's Day," NCE 8:991.

119. From 2 Cor 2:14 to 6:13, Paul describes the Christian ministry of himself and his co-workers in terms that are among the most sublime in Scripture or Christian literature. We will return to this when we reflect on Paul the missionary and pastor, but perhaps I can summarize his profound teaching on ministry here by quoting 2 Cor 4:6-7, NAB: "For God who said, 'Let light shine out of darkness,' has shone in our hearts to bring to light the knowledge of the glory of God on the face of [Jesus] Christ.

"But we hold this treasure in earthen vessels, that the surpassing power may be of God and not from us." All of us in ministry could well meditate on this for life!

120. The word "covenant" (in Hebrew, *berith*; in Greek, *diathēkē*) is of French origin from the Latin *convenire* meaning "to come together." It describes an agreement establishing a lasting bond of relationship. Whether or not Israel owed much to Hittite suzerainty treaties for its format (see NJBC, 1297–98), it is clear that the covenant relationship between Yahweh and Israel, mainly as established at Mount Sinai (Exod 19:3-8; 24:1-11) and renewed at Shechem (Josh 24:1-28), was central to salvation history in the Old Testament (or covenant), so central that prophets like Hosea, Isaiah, Jeremiah, and Ezekiel, viewing the covenant as a spiritual marriage between Yahweh and Israel, strove desperately to reconcile faithless Israel to her divine spouse (Hos 1–3; Isa 1:21; Jer 3:1-13; Ezek 16:1-63).

In the New Testament (or covenant), we see Jesus not only striving to reconcile Israel and, indeed, all people through himself with the Father (Matt 11:25-30) and emphasizing the relational commandments of love (Deut 6:4-5; Lev 19:18; Mark 12:28-34; Matt 22:34-40; Luke 10:25-28; John 13:34; 15:12, 17) but also instituting a new covenant in his blood at the Last Supper (1 Cor 11:25; Mark 14:24; Matt 26:28; Luke 22:20). As in the old covenant, Yahweh and Israel were the spiritual bridegroom and bride, so in the new covenant, Christ and the Church are the spiritual partners or spouses (Eph 5:22-33), and Christ is referred to, sometimes obliquely, as a bridegroom (Mark 2:18-20; Matt 9:14-15; 22:1-14; Luke 5:33-35; John 3:29). This covenant union, or spiritual marriage, moreover, pertains not only to Christ and the Church as a whole but also to Christ and the local Church (2 Cor 11:2) and even to Christ and the individual

Christian (1 Cor 6:16-17; 2 Cor 6:14; Rom 7:1-4). Into this covenant relationship with the risen Christ we were baptized (Rom 6:1-11), and every Eucharistic
celebration is a personal and communal renewal of our covenant with Christ.
See my treatment on covenant in *To Live the Word, Inspired and Incarnate* (Staten
Island, N.Y.: Alba, 1985) 4–6.

121. "Reconciliation" (in Greek, *katallagē*) is very closely related to the word
"covenant" in the previous note. A covenant connotes relationship, and reconciliation is a resumption of that relationship, especially after the sundering of
the relationship wrought by sin, just as in married life a reconciliation is a
resumption of that life after a separation or even divorce. On sin, repentance,
confession and reconciliation, *see* my book *To Live the Word* 330–34.

122. In 2 Cor 12, Paul, defending his apostolic authority, describes his mystical visions and revelations, then refers to his "thorn in the flesh" (in Greek,
skólops tê sarkí, in 2 Cor 12:7) as a "messenger of Satan" (in Greek *ángelos Satanâ*)
tormenting him. Unfortunately, he does not reveal the exact nature of this
troubling affliction but only its purposes: to humble him after his revelations
(2 Cor 12:7) and to teach him to rely on God's grace (2 Cor 12:9). The principal
theories among scripturists regarding the nature of Paul's "thorn in the flesh"
mention an eye disease, as possibly suggested in Gal 4:15 and 6:11, or malaria,
perhaps contracted in the notorious marshes of Pamphilia on his first missionary
journey (Acts 13:13), which, recurring on the second journey, forced him to
the more northerly and salubrious area of Galatia (Gal 4:13); but it might have
been a skin disease caused by the sun, wind, and dust, which could have made
him feel loathsome (Gal 4:14).

123. For my treatment of the northern Galatian theory, *see* n. 43 above.

124. The celebrated confrontation of Paul against Peter in Gal 2:11-14, sometimes used as an argument against the primacy of Peter in the Church, actually serves to confirm that primacy. It was the very authoritative position
of Peter that gave force to Paul's action. To confront any lesser leader, such
as Barnabas or even James, would not have had the same effect. No, Paul can
argue that he dared to criticize even Peter himself, whose primacy he emphasizes by using his Aramaic name, *Kephas* (Rock), as in 1 Cor 1:12; Matt 16:18;
John 1:42.

And the nature of the confrontation? Surely not a disagreement between
Peter and Paul on the conversion of Gentiles without requiring circumcision
and the Mosaic Law, for Peter himself had been the first to do so (Acts 10).
No, it was rather Peter's failure to live up to his own convictions by associat-
ing only with the Jewish Christians from Jerusalem in a kind of de facto dis-
crimination, perhaps to avoid offending the hypersensitive Judeans or because
he knew a number of them personally or just because he felt more comfortable speaking Aramaic with fellow Jews than Greek with the Gentiles.

125. Paul's landmark statement in Gal 3:28 declares the spiritual unity and
equality of all through baptism into the risen Christ and lays the groundwork
for social unity and equality. Paul, however, like Jesus himself, fully realized
that social changes happen slowly and only with changes in human attitudes.
Hence, like Jesus, he was more immediately concerned with the conversion

and salvation of souls, including the inculcation of justice and charity, than in the overturning of institutional inequities such as slavery, the lower status of women, unjust taxation, unrepresentative government, and the like. However, it is now almost two millennia since Jesus and Paul, surely enough time for not only individual but institutional changes to occur.

126. Paul begins his great Letter to the Romans with an unusually long salutation, which actually comprises a compendium of salvation history. For the sake of my readers, I will attempt to translate it as literally as possible, so that they may have some idea of its complexity. "Paul, a slave of Christ Jesus, called (as) an apostle set apart for the good news of God which was promised through his prophets in (the) holy scriptures, concerning his Son, born of the seed of David according to (the) flesh, delineated (as) Son of God in power according to the spirit of holiness (or Holy Spirit) from resurrection of (the) dead, Jesus Christ our Lord through whom we received grace and apostleship for the obedience of faith, on behalf of his name, among all the Gentiles, among whom are you also, (the) called of Jesus Christ; to all the beloved of God who are in Rome, called (to be) saints, grace (be) to you and peace from God our Father and (our) Lord Jesus Christ" (Rom 1:1-7, WFD).

Note that the Greek word I have chosen to translate as "delineated" is a past passive participle of the verb *horízō*, from *hóros*, meaning "a limit or boundary" and perhaps ultimately from *óros*, meaning "a mountain." To me the word "delineated" captures the meaning better than most translations, especially "made" in the original NAB or even "established" in the revised NAB.

127. In this section, Paul describes the need of redemption on the part of both Gentiles and Jews; the former for failing to acknowledge the Creator from the evidence of his creation, the latter for failing to keep the Mosaic Law. In the first instance, he indicates that because of idolatry pagans have fallen into all kinds of perversity, notably homosexuality. Today, while we may dismiss idolatry as a root cause of homosexuality, that does not negate Paul's description of this activity as contrary to nature (*see* Rom 1:18-32, especially vv. 26–27).

128. Paul's key illustration from Gen 15:6, which has been such a cause of division not only between Jews and Christians but especially between Protestants and Catholics, will receive special treatment in the next section, namely when we reflect upon Paul the theologian.

129. In this section, Paul clearly distinguishes between justification (entry into a state of grace and right relationship with God) and salvation (perseverance in that state to entry into eternal life and glory), as will be treated more fully when we reflect on Paul the theologian.

130. Paul's use of the story of Adam (and Eve) no more establishes the historicity of the account in Gen 2–3 than Jesus' references to Jonah in Matt 12:39-41; and Luke 11:29-32 establish the historicity of that marvelous Old Testament parable. What we commonly refer to as original sin is really the sinfulness of our human race, represented by Adam (which means "mankind" in Hebrew), into which we are born and from which we are raised to a state of grace by baptism into Christ and reception of his life within us. *See* my work *To Live the Word*, 93–95; *see* also Michael Taylor, ed., *The Mystery of Sin and Forgiveness* (Staten Island, N.Y.: Alba, 1971) 215–77.

131. In this section, Paul stresses the crucial role of the sacrament of baptism as the means instituted by Christ for initiation into his death and resurrection for the forgiveness of sin and the beginning of his life in us. Paul had learned well at the time of his conversion that, important as was his surrender in faith to the risen Christ who had appeared to him, it was still necessary for him to be baptized with water and the Holy Spirit by a representative of the Church, namely Ananias of Damascus (Acts 9:10-19).Thus he was incorporated both into the body (that is, the person) of the crucified and risen Christ and into the body (that is, the Church) of all those who were also baptized into Christ. Today, thanks to the ceremonies surrounding the sacrament, it is even more meaningful to meditate on our baptism and more salutary to try to live it to the full. (*See* my treatment of baptism in *To Live the Word*, 316–27.)

132. Here Paul dramatizes the need of redemptive grace even for those who have the Mosaic Law by describing that condition in the first person. The Law, in fact any law, including the Church's canon law, indicates what to do but gives no power to do it, with the result that of ourselves we are more aware of our sinfulness because of the Law but incapable of overcoming that sinfulness and achieving goodness. In the desperation of our errant human nature, Paul cries out: "Wretched creature that I am, who is there to rescue me from this state of death? Who but God? Thanks be to him through Jesus Christ our Lord!" (Rom 7:24-25, REB, a somewhat freer translation but more intelligible).

133. In ch. 8, we come to the very heart of Paul's Letter to the Romans: his magnificent description of life in Christ, lived according to the Holy Spirit rather than according to the flesh, that is, our natural inclinations. Too rich for a note, it will be largely included in our reflection on Paul the mystic and missionary-pastor.

134. Many people who have become acquainted with the writings of Pierre Teilhard de Chardin, the great Jesuit anthropologist, philosopher-theologian, and mystic, are surprised to find the basis of his vision in Paul's description of all creation awaiting ultimate redemption with us (Rom 8:19-25).

135. Just as Paul's Old Testament illustration in Rom 4:3 (and Gal 3:6) was the occasion of Luther's theology about justification, so his Old Testament illustrations in Rom 9-11 were the occasion of Calvin's theology of predestination and prereprobation. Both of these questions we will consider in depth when we reflect on Paul the theologian.

136. Having completed his doctrinal presentation, Paul now introduces his moral exhortation with a magnificent plea for the complete gift of oneself to God and transformation into Christ, which alone render the fulfillment of all his Christian directives not only possible but even easy. We will return to this in our reflections on Paul.

137. Paul's insistence on unquestioning obedience to the authority of Rome was obviously written before the outbreak of Nero's cruel persecution of Christians in A.D. 64., following the Great Fire at Rome, which began on July 19.

138. Paul's references, here and in Gal 3:27, to "putting on Christ" will be treated in our reflection on Paul the mystic and in n. 144 below.

139. After reminding the Roman Christians of his apostolic mission to ful-

fill the priestly duty of preaching the good news to the Gentiles (which we will reflect on under Paul the missionary) and after reporting on his fulfillment of that mission to date, Paul then reveals his plan to go to Jerusalem with the collection for the poor there and then to visit Rome and even Spain (Rom 15:14-29). In our next chapter, on Paul's later letters, we will see whether and in what way Paul's plans would be fulfilled.

140. In the New Testament's only mention of a deaconess, Paul writes in Rom 16:1-2, WFD: "I recommend to you Phoebe our sister, who is a deaconess [in Greek, *diákonos*, masculine in form but either masculine or feminine in meaning, like *theós*, god or goddess] of the Church in Kenchreai [or Cenchreae, the eastern port of Corinth], in order that you may receive her in the Lord in a manner worthy of the saints and assist her in whatever matter she may need your aid, for she has been a helpful friend of many, including myself." Whether Phoebe was a deaconess in the full sense of the ordained diaconate or whether she simply helped the women receiving baptism by immersion is not altogether clear, but the fact that she is called a deaconess deserves very special consideration. *See* the comprehensive work of Aime Georges Martimort, *Deaconesses: An Historical Study*, trans. K. D. Whitehead (San Francisco: Ignatius, 1986).

141. It is the general opinion of Scripture scholars that Paul never knew Jesus of Nazareth during his earthly life but encountered him for the first time in his risen state on the Damascus Road. (2 Cor 5:16 simply indicates that he no longer thinks of Jesus in a merely human way.) This may account for the fact that almost his entire interest is not in Jesus' earthly life and ministry, as seen later in the Gospels, but rather in the risen Christ living in the Church and in Christians. This is also the focus of Luke's Acts of Apostles and the Johannine writings, even John's Gospel with its typical realized eschatology, that is, the portrait of the risen Christ read back into his life.

142. Recall that lyrical description in Isa 40:29-31, NEB: "He gives vigor to the weary, / new strength to the exhausted. / Young men may grow weary and faint, / even the fittest may stumble and fall; / But those who look to the Lord / will win new strength, / They will soar as on eagles' wings; / they will run and not feel faint, / march on and not grow weary."
And, along the same lines, The *Imitation of Christ*, trans. Abbot Justin McCann (Westminster, Md., 1955) 3:5, "The noble love of Jesus impels a man to do great things, and ever excites him to desire that which is more perfect. . . . The lover flies, runs, and rejoices; he is free and is not bound. . . . Love feels no burden, thinks lightly of labors, aims beyond its strength, complains not of impossibility, for it conceives that all things are possible to it, and all things free." Paul's famous declaration in 2 Cor 5:14, usually rendered "the love of Christ impels us" would seem to fit here, but since the Greek text translates somewhat differently from this familiar version from the Latin Vulgate, I will reserve it until later.

143. In almost all the English translations, there seems to be a contradiction between the experience of Paul's companions in Luke's report of his encounter with Christ (Acts 9:7) and in Paul's own description (Acts 22:9), but for-

tunately the NIV, recognizing that the Greek verb for hearing, *akoúō*, takes a partial genitive in the former text but an accusative in the latter, translates properly: Acts 9:7, "The men traveling with Saul stood there speechless; they heard the sound but did not see anyone." Acts 22:9, "My companions saw the light, but they did not understand the voice of him who was speaking to me."

144. The Greek verb, *endúomai*, meaning "I put on or play the role of someone," is so used, for example, by Dionysius of Halicarnassus in reference to the role of Tarquin. (See Colin Brown, ed., *New Testament Theology* (Grand Rapids: Brown, Zondervan, 1971) 1:314. Some feel the reference is rather to the practice in mystery religions of "putting on or clothing oneself with" a certain god, goddess, or mythical figure, or perhaps the old Testament concept of adopting another's moral dispositions or outlook (Job 29:14; 2 Chr 6–41), but the former seems less likely and the latter does not seem justified by the Old Testament references (see *NJBC*, 787). More importantly, in baptism the clothing with the white garment should remind us of our "putting on Christ" in Gal 3:27 and Rom 13:14 and our call to live his life throughout our own.

145. In Gen 2:7 and throughout the Bible generally, we are flesh (in Hebrew, *bashar*; in Green, *sárx*), referring to our whole being in all its human weakness; person (Hebrew, *nephesh*; Greek, *sôma*; "body-person" or *psychě*, "soul-person"); and spirit (Hebrew, *rhuah*; Greek, *pneûma*, both meaning "breath," "wind," or "spirit"), the latter describing our entire being aspiring to union with God. Note above all that Paul, in describing the lifelong struggle within us between flesh and spirit (Gal 5:16-26; Rom 8:1-17), is not talking about a struggle between our body and our soul, as it had been misunderstood by so many out of our Greco-Roman background.

146. See St. Augustine, *The Confessions of St. Augustine*, trans. F. J. Sheed (New York: Sheed & Ward, 1943) 1:1, 3.

147. Paul seems to be quoting Isa 40:13-14 and perhaps alluding to Wis 9:13.

148. James' recommendations obviously concern practices that were forbidden to Jews but not to Gentile Christians, namely eating food that may have been offered to idols, marrying within forbidden degrees of kinship (the probable idea here of the Greek word *porneía*, meaning "an uncleanness"), and eating the meat of strangled animals or with the blood otherwise still in them, for the life of any human or animal was thought (not unreasonably) to reside in the blood (Gen 9:4-6; Lev 17:10-16).

149. The word "dogma" is simply a transliteration of the Greek word *dógma* meaning "a decision," from the impersonal verb *dikeî* meaning "it seems good" (Acts 15:28).

150. The Great Western Schism (1378-1415), which had so divided and demoralized Christianity by the scandal of three rival claimants to the papal throne, had finally ended with the election of Pope Martin V in 1417 at the Council of Constance (1414-18). Between the end of the Great Schism in October 1417 and the beginning of the Protestant Reformation in October 1517, exactly one hundred years passed in which the Church tried in vain to reform

the abuses that had multiplied for some time and become acute during the schism.

The "reforming" Fifth Lateran Council (1512–17) was to be the great attempt at Church reform, but it ended in March of 1517 with the condemnation of Wyclif and Hus and a few decrees about ecclesiastical taxation, episcopal selection, and religious education. Within six months, on October 31, 1517, Martin Luther nailed his ninety-five theses to the door of the Castle Church in Wittenberg, launching the Protestant Reformation. *See* Hans Margull, ed., *The Councils of the Church: History and Analysis* (Philadelphia: Fortress, 1966) 245–46.

151. Out of the vast literature on Martin Luther, some of it biased for or against him, some of it more objective, let me mention just two books, one on Luther's younger years, the other on his later years: Martin Brecht, *Martin Luther: His Road to Reformation, 1483–1521*, trans. James L. Schaaf (Philadelphia: Fortress, 1985); H. G. Haile, *Luther: An Experiment in Biography* (Princeton, N.J.: Princeton University Press, 1983).

152. The official definition of an indulgence, according to the new *Code of Canon Law* (Washington: Canon Law Society of America, 1983) 365, can. 992, follows: "An indulgence is a remission before God of the temporal punishment for sin, the guilt of which is already forgiven, which a properly disposed member of the Christian faithful obtains under certain and definite conditions with the help of the Church, which as the minister of redemption dispenses and applies authoritatively the treasure of the satisfactions of Christ and the saints." In brief, the practice of indulgences is based on the reality of temporal punishment due to sin even after its forgiveness (2 Sam 12:1-20; 24:1-15), the possibility of vicarious satisfaction (Col 1:24), and the Church's power of binding and loosing (Matt 16:19; 18:18). For a fuller study of indulgences, including their history and abuses, see *NCE*, 7:482–86. Whatever the value of indulgences, it should be borne in mind that the best indulgence is an act of pure *agápe* love, "for love covers a multitude of sins" (1 Pet 4:8, NRSV).

153. It is informative to observe from his own words how Martin Luther changed his interpretation of Gen 15:6 and his theology of justification between his *Commentary on Romans* in 1515–1516 (before his break with Rome) and his *Commentary on Galatians* in 1535, twenty years later. In his *Lectures on Romans*, ed. Hilton C. Oswald, in *Luther's Works* (St. Louis, Mo: Concordia, 1972) 25:254–84, he inveighs against hypocrites who consider themselves righteous because of their works rather than humbly seeking their justification from God, which of course is nothing more than an echo of Jesus' beautiful parable of the Pharisee and the publican in Luke 18:9-14. However in his *Lectures on Galatians, 1535, Chapters 1–4*, ed. Jaroslav Pelikan, in *Luther's Works* (St. Louis, Mo.: Concordia, 1963) 26:226-36, Luther declares: "Therefore this is a marvelous definition of Christian righteousness: it is a divine imputation or reckoning as righteousness or to righteousness, for the sake of our faith in Christ . . . [233]. So far as the words are concerned, this fact is easy, namely, that righteousness is not in us in a formal sense, . . . but is outside us, solely in the grace of God and in his imputation. . . . Here we are in a divine theol-

ogy, where we hear the Gospel that Christ died for us and that when we believe this we are reckoned as righteous, even though sins, and great ones at that, still remain in us [234]."

154. As a result of Lutheran-Catholic dialogues on justification since 1978, there was drawn up a joint declaration of consensus in five points, contained in George Anderson, Austin Murphy, and Joseph Burgess, eds., *Justification by Faith: Lutherans and Catholics in Dialogue VII* (Minneapolis: Augsburg, 1985) 73–74. Of the five points, I will quote only the first, which is by far the longest and most important: "We believe that God's creative graciousness is offered to us and to everyone for healing and reconciliation so that through the Word made flesh, Jesus Christ, 'who was put to death for our transgressions and raised for our justification' (Rom 4:25), we are all called to pass from the alienation and oppression of sin to freedom and fellowship with God in the Holy Spirit. It is not through our own initiative that we respond to this call, but only through an undeserved gift which is granted and made known in faith, and which comes to fruition in our love of God and neighbor, as we are led by the Spirit in faith to bear witness to the divine gift in all aspects of our lives. This faith gives us hope for ourselves and for all humanity and gives us confidence that salvation in Christ will always be proclaimed as the gospel, the good news for which the world is searching."

155. Regarding the Septuagint, *see* n. 101 above.

156. *he'emin* is the hiphil or causative form of the Hebrew verb *aman* which basically means "stand" and is so familiar to us in the form *amen*, that is, "let it stand; let it be; I agree." In its hiphil form, *he'emin*, when it is used of a human response to God in the Old Testament, almost always means "believe" rather than "obey," as some of our Jewish brothers contend. In Isa 7:9, WFD, Yahweh challenges King Ahaz through Isaiah in this typical play on words in Hebrew, "If you do not believe (*ta'aminu*), you will not stand (*te'amenu*)," both expressions being from the same verb, *aman*, even the same form, *he'emin*. *See* G. Johannes Botterweck and Helmer Ringgren, eds., and John T. Willis, trans., *The Theological Dictionary of the Old Testament* (Grand Rapids: Eerdmans, 1974) 1:298–309, especially 308.

157. The perceptive Catholic theologian F. X. Durrwell sums up nicely the meaning of biblical faith as viewed today both by Catholics and Protestants: "By faith, man gives up making himself the center of his own life, the basis of his own salvation, and places that center and basis outside himself, in God who gives life to Christ. Whereas the Jew relies upon the privileges of his race and upon his works and remains bounded by the sufficiency of his own justice (Phil 3:9; Rom 9:32; 10:3) the believer considers everything that seemed gain according to the flesh as valueless and even harmful (Phil 3:8), he comes out of himself to seek a justice he has not merited by any works (Rom 3:28; 4:5; Gal 2:16; Eph 2:8-9; Phil 3:9). He believes in the justice of God which is communicated in Christ, and he is in turn glorified, but not for his works, for his glory is in God alone (2 Cor 10:17; Phil 3:9). He has crazily cast his anchor of certainty beyond all the assurances of the flesh to fix it in the death and resurrection of Jesus Christ." See F. X. Durrwell, "The Church's Assimi-

lation of the Easter Mystery,'' in Michael Taylor, ed., *A Companion to Paul*, (New York: Alba, 1975) 69.

158. Regarding ''grace'' in Paul's theology, one of the outstanding American Catholic Scripture scholars, Joseph A. Fitzmyer comments in *NJBC*, 1397: ''Related to the foregoing question (on *pneûma*, ''spirit'') is the use of *cháris*, ''grace.'' For Paul, it most frequently designates God's ''favor,'' the gratuitous aspect of the Father's initiative in salvation (Gal 2:21; 2 Cor 1:12) or of Christ's own collaboration (2 Cor 8:9). Thus it characterizes the divine prevenience in the promise to Abraham (Rom 4:16), in the apostolic call (Gal 1:6, 15; 1 Cor 15:10; Rom 1:5), in election (Rom 11: 5), in the justification of human beings (Rom 3:24; 5:15, 17, 20-21). Moreover, it characterizes the dispensation that supersedes the law (Rom 6:14-15; 11:6). But at times Paul speaks of *cháris* as something that is given or manifested (Gal 2:9; 1 Cor 1:4; 3:10; 2 Cor 6:1; 8:1; 9:14; Rom 12:3, 6; 15:15). It accompanies Paul or is in him (Phil 1:7; 1 Cor 15:10). One may debate whether this is to be conceived of as something produced or not. In any case this last group of texts led in time to the medieval idea of ''sanctifying grace.'' Even though to read this notion into such Pauline passages would be anachronistic, one must remember that the Pauline teaching about the Spirit as an energizing force is likewise the basis of that later teaching.''

To this I would only add that today, both among scholars and Christians generally, the emphasis is not so much on ''sanctifying grace'' as it is on ''uncreated grace,'' that is, the life of Christ in us, which is regularly mentioned by Paul, for example, in 2 Cor 4:10; 6:15; 13:3, 5; Gal 2:20; 4:19; Rom 8:10; Phil 1:21; 3:12; Col 1:27. Add to this those places where Paul refers to the Spirit in us (e.g., 1 Cor 6:19; Gal 4:6; Rom 5:5; 8:9-17) and even of God in us (2 Cor 5:20) and we begin to see the picture of the indwelling Trinity later developed in the Johannine writings, particularly the final discourse of Jesus in John 13–17.

159. It is interesting that the Greek word *misthós* is used both for a worker's pay or salary and for spiritual rewards, a clear indication of the fact that once justified, once Christ lives and acts in us, then we can earn in justice the rewards he has promised. In 1 Tim 5:18; Matt 20:8; and Luke 10:7, for example, the word *misthós* means ''a wage or salary,'' while it refers to spiritual rewards in 1 Cor 3:8, 14; 9:17-18; Mark 9:41; Matt 5:12, 46; 6:1-2, 5, 16; 10:41-42; Luke 6:23, 35; and John 4:36.

160. Possibly because Luther was twenty-six years older than Calvin, more flamboyant throughout his life, and more influential in the Protestant Reformation, there is a far greater number of biographies about the former than the latter. Of the few modern biographies about Calvin, let me mention just one, T. H. L. Parker, *John Calvin: A Biography* (Philadelphia: Westminster, 1975).

161. With regard to God's attitude to Esau and Jacob, three things should be borne in mind: (1) As indicated in the reflection, the reference is not to individual persons but to peoples, namely the Edomites and Israelites, as is clear from the complete text of Gen 25:23, WFD: ''Two nations are in your womb, and / two peoples will be divided from birth. / One shall be stronger than the other / the elder shall serve the younger.'' (2) In the quotation from Mal 1:2-3,

"Jacob I have loved, but Esau I have hated," one should remember that the Greek verb *miséō* used here can also mean "I love less," as we see in Jesus' own words, for example in Luke 14:26 compared with Matt 10:37. (3) The quotation is from Malachi, the last of the prophets, hence written after the treachery of Edom against Israel during the Babylonian invasion (Ps 137:7), which climaxed centuries of enmity (Num 20:18-20; 1 Sam 14:47; 2 Chr 20:1-30) and led to its condemnation through the prophets (Isa 34:5-17; 63:1-6; Jer 49:7-22; Ezek 25:12-14; 35:1-15, etc.).

162. That the pharaohs of Egypt considered themselves as the embodiment of the country and people is manifested in many ways, for example, their statues depicting them with the staff and scourge, their elaborate monuments (pyramids, obelisks, temples, etc.), and even their name ("pharaoh" comes from the Egyptian word *per*, meaning "house," probably signifying not only their palace but the whole people, in the same way as Peter speaks of the "whole house of Israel" in Acts 2:36.

163. Among the ten plagues, it is mentioned only after the sixth, eighth, and ninth that God hardened Pharaoh's heart, whereas normally it is simply recorded that Pharaoh became obstinate or hardened his own heart.

164. That predestination as such is an orthodox teaching is evident from Rom, 8:29, NAB: "For those he foreknew he also predestined to be conformed to the image of his Son," as well as from Eph 1:3-6.

165. Lest I be accused of misrepresenting Calvin's teaching on prereprobation, let me quote directly from his *Commentary on Romans*, ed. David and Thomas Torrance, trans. Ross Mackenzie (Grand Rapids: Eerdmans, 1961): "Paul's first proposition, therefore is as follows: 'As the blessing of the covenant separates the people of Israel from all other nations, so also the election of God makes a distinction between men in that nation, while He predestinates some to salvation, and others to eternal condemnation' [199–200]. . . . Paul does not inform us that the ruin of the ungodly is foreseen by the Lord, but that it is ordained by His counsel and will [207]. . . . Although Paul is more explicit in this second clause in stating that it is God who prepares the elect for glory, when before he had simply said that the reprobate were vessels prepared for destruction, there is no doubt that the preparation of both is dependent on the secret counsel of God [212]." Calvin's *Commentary on Romans* was first published in 1540, but a perusal of his work *De aeterna predestinatione Dei*, published in 1552, clearly indicates that his doctrinal position on prereprobation remained unchanged.

166. "God is love" (1 John 4:8, 16, NIV), "who wants all men to be saved" (1 Tim 2:4, NIV), "not wanting anyone to perish, but everyone to come to repentance" (2 Pet 3:9, NIV).

167. Mark 1:17; Matt 4:19; Luke 5:10. See W. Wuellner, *The Meaning of Fishers of Men* (Philadelphia: Westminster, 1967).

168. The concept of shepherding has enjoyed a long and much loved tradition in both Testaments from Abel (Gen 4:2) to Abram (Gen 12:16), Isaac (Gen 26:14), and Jacob (Gen 30:29-43); to Moses (Exod 3:1) and David (1 Sam 16:11); in both the Prophetic and Wisdom literature (Isa 40:11; Jer 33:12-13; Ezek

34:11-16, 23-31; Pss 23; 80:1-7; 95:7); to the Gospels (Matt 18:12-14; 25:31-40; 26:30-31; Luke 15:3-7; John 10:11-18, 25-30; 21:15-17); to Paul in Acts (20:28-29); to Peter (1 Pet 5:1-4).

169. *See* Isa 61:1; Luke 4:18.

170. *See* John 10:11, 14; 1 Pet 5:4.

171. Paul's quotation is from Isa 52:7.

172. Time and space prohibit extensive references here, but the primary duty of priests to preach is clear, for example, from the Vatican II Decree on the Ministry and Life of Priests, Dec. 7, 1965. *See* Austin Flannery, ed., *Vatican Council II: The Conciliar and Post Conciliar Documents* (Northport, N.Y.: Costello, 1975) 863–902, especially 868–70, from which I quote part of the second sentence: "It is the first task of priests as co-workers of the bishops to preach the Gospel of God to all men."

173. In *The Roman Pontifical*, published in 1978 by the International Commission on English in the Liturgy, pp. 208 and 368, the bishop's instruction to those called to the priesthood begins thus: "My sons you are now to be advanced to the order of the presbyterate. You must apply your energies to the duty of teaching in the name of Christ, the Teacher. Share with all mankind the word of God you have received with joy. Meditate on the law of God, believe what you read, teach what you believe, and put into practice what you teach."

174. The tools are now available not only for seminarians and priests but also for religious and laypeople, not only to learn New Testament Greek but to continue its use indefinitely. The tools I have in mind are the following: (1) my concise introduction, *Greek Without Grief: An Outline Guide to New Testament Greek* (Chicago: Loyola University Press, 1989); (2) Kurt Aland and others, eds., *The Greek New Testament*, 3rd ed., with dictionary (New York: United Bible Societies, 1975); (3) Max Zerwick and Mary Grosvenor, *A Grammatical Analysis of the Greek New Testament* (Rome: Biblical Institute Press, 1981; distributed in U.S. by Loyola University Press, Chicago). The great advantage of this last-named tool is that, unlike a dictionary or lexicon, it takes up and explains everything as it comes along in the New Testament, beginning with the first verse of Matthew and ending with the last verse of the Apocalypse or Book of Revelation.

175. I have been unable to find the source, if any, of this saying which I have heard and repeated so often. In its place, however, I can offer two similar and noteworthy aphorisms: (1) George Borrow, "Translation is at best an echo" and (2) a pithy but powerful Italian proverb, *Traduttore, traditore* (Translator, traitor), both quoted in H. L. Mencken ed., *A New Dictionary of Quotations* (New York: Alfred Knopf, 1942) 1212.

176. Paul's farewell to his presbyters of the province of Asia (western Asia Minor) on the Island of Miletus, recorded (and perhaps revised) by Luke in Acts 20:18-35, is a masterpiece and deserves a place of honor alongside that of Moses (supposedly) in Deuteronomy, Jesus in John 13–17, and Paul himself in 2 Timothy.

177. The Greek word *epískopos*, literally "overseer," is the origin of our Latin

word *epíscopus* and our English word "bishop." However, in the time of Paul, no distinction was yet made between an *epískopos* (overseer) and a *presbýteros* (elder, whence the word "priest"), as we can see in Acts 20:17, 28 where Paul's hearers are called in v. 17 *presbýteroi* and in v. 28 *epískopoi*. Only in the *Letters* of St. Ignatius of Antioch, around A.D. 110 is the distinction clearly made which continues until now.

178. With all due respect for the efforts of psychiatrists, psychologists, and counselors to prevent "burnout" among people in ministry, I personally believe that the problem is primarily spiritual, stemming largely from a failure to let Christ continue his life and ministry in us rather than trying to do everything ourselves with our limited natural resources.

179. How can anything be lacking to the sufferings of the God-man, Jesus Christ, whose slightest suffering was of infinite value? Only in the mystical sense that through union with his Church ("I am Jesus, whom you are persecuting" Acts 9:5, REB) he can continue to suffer in and through us, his followers, especially those who surrender themselves entirely to him, like Paul and other saints. *See* Alfred Wikenhauser, *Pauline Mysticism: Christ in the Mystical Teaching of St. Paul* (New York: Herder and Herder, 1960) 154–62; *see also* my own treatment in *To Live the Word*, 252–55, 266–73, 335–36.

180. One of the many commercials that exemplify the antisuffering attitude so pervasive in our soft society is this recent one: "We haven't got time for the pain!"

181. Belief in life after death, with rewards and punishments therein, did not develop in Israel until the final centuries before Christ (Dan 12:2-3; 2 Macc 12:39-45; Wis 3), and even then not among all the Jews, for example, the Sadducees (Mark 12:18-27; Matt 22:23-33; Luke 20:27-40; Acts 23:6-8). Consequently, rewards and punishments were regarded as taking place in this life. This theology of temporal rewards and punishments came to be called Deuteronomic mainly for two reasons: (1) The Book of Deuteronomy, more than other books of the Torah, or Law, offers temporal motives for obeying the Lord's commands, for example, Deut 5:16; (2) The Deuteronomic history (Joshua–Judges; 1 and 2 Samuel; 1 and 2 Kings) exemplifies the teaching of Deuteronomy, namely the cause-effect connection between personal and communal conduct on the one hand and temporal rewards and punishments on the other, for example, 2 Sam 12. *See* H. Cunliffe-Jones, *Deuteronomy: Introduction and Commentary* (London: SCM Press, 1971) 21–23; *see also* Calum M. Carmichael, *The Laws of Deuteronomy* (Ithaca, N.Y.: Cornell University Press, 1974) 37–40.

182. This thought-provoking statement is part of the appeal for contributions to the United Negro College Fund.

183. *See* Matt 13:44.

184. The theological virtues are faith, hope, and charity or love; the principal moral virtues are prudence, justice, fortitude, and temperance. In my book on biblical spirituality, *To Live the Word*, I prefer to divide them into the "Virtues of Letting Go" (humility, purity, and detachment) and the "Virtues of Holding On" (faith, trust, and love).

185. These missionary and pastoral virtues, availability, adaptability, and affability, whose practitioners I like to refer to as members of the spiritual AAA Club, are referred to in my book, *To Live the Word*, 264–65, but borrowed originally from James E. Walsh, *Maryknoll Spiritual Directory* (New York: Field Afar Press, 1947) 55–70.

186. *See also* the only parable unique to Mark's Gospel, that of the seed growing of itself (Mark 4:26-29).

187. *See* n. 102 above on *Carmen Christi*, the "Hymn of Christ."

188. *See* nn. 33 and 73 above. The problem of the Judaizers lies behind both 2 Corinthians and Galatians, not to mention Philippians, which will be examined later.

189. *See* Charles Hugo Doyle, *Pride: Thief of the Holocaust* (Milwaukee: Bruce, 1959).

190. *See* Gen 3:1-5; 2 Cor 11:3.

191. *See* n. 114, on charismatic gifts.

192. *See* Rev 2:4.

193. *See* 1 Thess 2:11.

194. *See* 1 Thess 2:7.

195. The original meaning of the Greek word *paidagōgós*, usually translated "tutor or instructor," referred to a slave who accompanied a child to school. This is clear from the component parts *paîs* (child) and *agō* (I lead), but whether in that original sense or in the later one of a pedagogue or instructor, Paul's claim still retains its force, namely that he is their (spiritual) father because he has "begotten" them through his preaching of the gospel.

196. It was characteristic of Paul that many of his converts also became his close friends, for example, Timothy, Titus and Luke, Aquila and Priscilla, Lydia and Phoebe.

197. The meaning of the Greek verb *synéchō* is "I hold together, I control," from *sýn* (with, together) and *échō* (I have, I hold). The common and much loved translation, "The love of Christ impels us" is from Jerome's Vulgate Latin version *Caritas Christi urget nos*. In any case, the important consideration is that the "love of Christ" is not just Paul's love for Christ but Christ's love in Paul, controlling him and, yes, impelling him to "spend himself and be spent" (2 Cor 12:15) for God and for others.

RECOMMENDED READING LIST

Drane, John. *Paul: An Illustrated Documentary on the Life and Writings of a Key Figure in the Beginnings of Christianity.* New York: Harper & Row, 1976.

Fitzmyer, Joseph. *Paul and His Theology.* Englewood Cliffs, N.J.: Prentice-Hall, 1988.

Flanagan, Neal. *Friend Paul.* Wilmington, Del.: Michael Glazier, 1986.

Morrow, Stanley. *Paul: His Letters and His Theology.* New York: Paulist, 1986.

Taylor, Michael, ed. *A Companion to Paul: Readings in Pauline Theology.* Staten Island, N.Y.: Alba, 1975.

QUESTIONS FOR REFLECTION AND DISCUSSION

1. What is your personal picture of St. Paul, and what is his importance to Christianity?

2. What were the circumstances that moved Paul to write his Eschatological Letters?

3. How many letters did Paul write to the Corinthians, and what is the general makeup of the two that we have?

4. How are Paul's letters to the Galatians and Romans similar and how are they different? Please explain in full.

5. What are the main ideas that you have derived from our reflections on St. Paul as mystic, theologian, and missionary-pastor? What ideas would you like to add?

ROME IN 67–68 A.D.

N

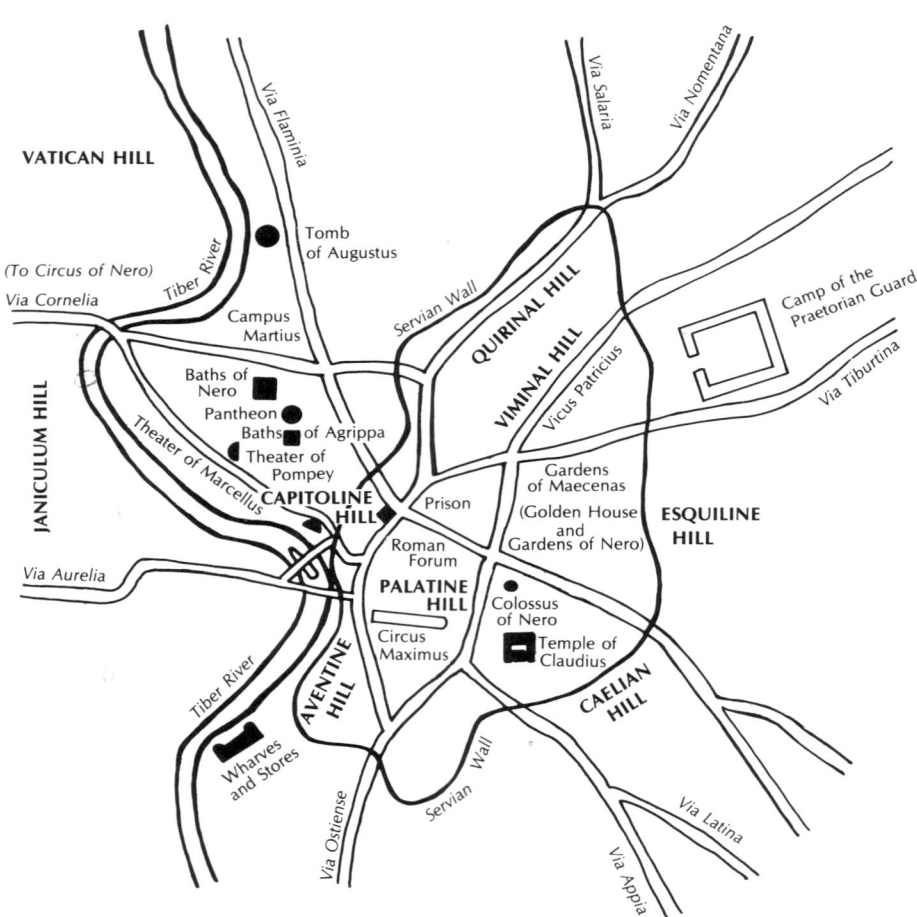

VATICAN HILL

(To Circus of Nero)
Via Cornelia

Via Flaminia

Via Salaria

Via Nomentana

Tiber River

Tomb
of Augustus

Campus
Martius

Servian Wall

QUIRINAL HILL

VIMINAL HILL

Camp of the
Praetorian Guard

Via Tiburtina

JANICULUM HILL

Baths of
Nero

Pantheon
Baths of Agrippa

Theater of
Pompey

Theater of Marcellus

CAPITOLINE
HILL

Prison

Roman
Forum

Vicus Patricius

Gardens
of Maecenas

(Golden House
and
Gardens of Nero)

ESQUILINE
HILL

Via Aurelia

PALATINE
HILL

Circus
Maximus

Colossus
of Nero

Temple of
Claudius

Tiber River

AVENTINE
HILL

Wharves
and Stores

Via Ostiense

Servian Wall

CAELIAN
HILL

Via Latina

Via Appia

2

Prolific Paul[1] and the Later Letters[2]

THE LATER STORY OF PAUL

Life Is Christ and Death Is Gain![3] (Phil 1:21)

The darkness was depressing enough but the dampness and piercing cold were far worse, and the combination of all three seemed to invade and possess his very soul. As Paul languished day after day in the ancient and infamous *carcer*[4] of Rome, his thoughts drifted with just a touch of envy to Simon Peter. He smiled ruefully as he thought of Peter's crown of curly white locks, which had gone with him to the cross some four years earlier.[5] Though confined in this same prison, he must not have experienced to the same extent this aching cold from the top of his head to the toes of his sandaled feet. Even more crucially, Peter, as a "Jewish Christian" in Rome, had been summarily condemned and promptly crucified, while here he was, Paul the Roman citizen, finding little solace in his prized citizenship with its privilege of a just and thorough trial free of any threat of crucifixion.

"Just and thorough trial indeed!" huffed Paul. "What a farce! It's perfectly obvious that I've already been tried, condemned, and sentenced to death by this hypocritical court, yet I still have to endure this bone-chilling imprisonment between hearings just to satisfy the appearance of Roman justice." The more he brooded about it, the deeper became his depression, until he felt utterly alone and abandoned—by Roman authorities, by his friends, even by God himself!

"Wait a minute!" groaned Paul. "What's happening to me? I've been in prisons before![6] Why am I letting this final incarceration get to me? Is it the injustice of it all? My disappointment in Roman ad-

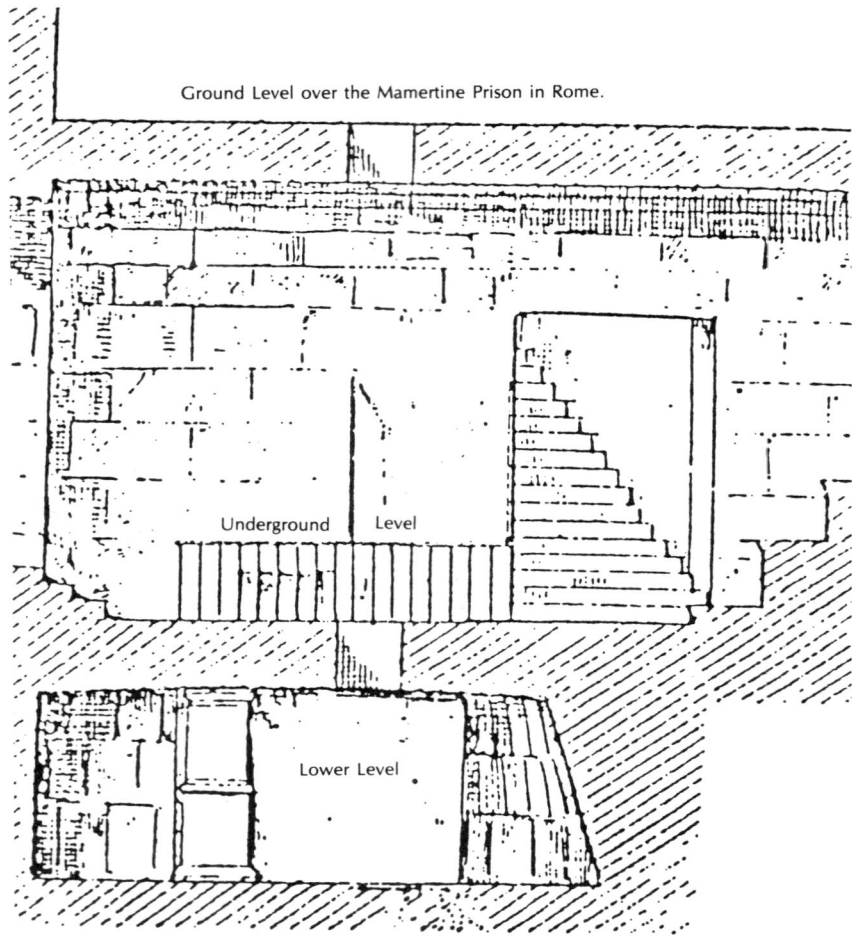

Ground Level over the Mamertine Prison in Rome.

Underground Level

Lower Level

Plan of the Carcer Tullianum, later called the Mamertine Prison, situated in Rome between the Capitoline Hill and the Forum.

ministration? My anguish at the defection or forced absence of my friends?[7] Or am I having second thoughts about the wisdom of my returning to Rome during Nero's persecution? After all I've been through since my conversion, why am I so depressed over my present situation? There must be a reason!"

The answer did not come easily. "Perhaps I'm simply exhausted in body, mind, even spirit. Or maybe I'm just getting old and cranky. No, it has to be something more than that!" Little by little, it began to dawn on him that he was experiencing something of what Jesus had felt during his passion and crucifixion: the hypocrisy and injustice of officialdom, both Jewish and Roman; the deep personal pain of betrayal, denial, and desertion on the part of his chosen apostles, even the profound sense of abandonment by God the Father himself![8]

"Yes, that's it!" cried Paul as he broke into tears of love and gratitude. "Thank you, precious Lord, for this special grace to plumb the depths of internal suffering that you must have endured beyond all the physical pain you had to bear. And, as if that were not enough, you choose to continue your suffering in those of us, your followers, who allow you to do so! Now I understand more than ever all that's involved in my claim to the Colossians that, by my tribulations, 'I am bringing to completion in my own weak human nature whatever Christ still desires to suffer for his body, the Church.'[9] Oh, may I always be ready and even happy to let you continue suffering in me!"

An interesting possibility suddenly occurred to Paul. "Lord, is it because, as a Roman citizen, I can't undergo the excruciating pains and humiliations of crucifixion as you and Peter and so many others have done that you've let me feel your interior sufferings so deeply?" No answer was forthcoming, but Paul was content. "After all, I really don't need to know. It's enough for me to be here where I belong, imprisoned in Rome, one with my persecuted fellow Christians and, above all, one with you, my gracious Lord, who confronted me years ago with those unforgettable words, 'I am Jesus whom you are persecuting!' "[10]

With that sense of oneness peace came to Paul, a peace that no hardships, internal or external, would be able to disturb. And with that peace there arose, almost without his even adverting to it, the urge to think back over the Lord's loving providence, especially in that segment of his life, labors, and sufferings since his letter to Rome.[11]

Ah, his letter to Rome! It seemed like just yesterday that he was writing about the mystery of God's saving call to the Gentiles: "Oh, the depth of the riches and wisdom and knowledge of God! How inscrutable are his judgments and how unsearchable his ways!"[12] Little had he known that those very words would also apply to his ardent wish to visit Rome.[13] For God had certainly chosen his own way of fulfilling that desire!

Not long after completing that most painstaking of all his letter-writing efforts, Paul and his faithful friend Titus gathered the collection for the poor of Palestine and left Corinth for Jerusalem to deliver it. Normally, the easiest and safest method of travel would have been by ship out of Kenchreai to Ephesus and then to the coast of Syria or Israel.[14] That was their original intention, but learning of a Jewish plot against Paul's life on that route, they had decided to go overland through Macedonia in northern Greece.[15] Paul quickly recognized this turn of events as a blessing in disguise because, with the Holy Spirit informing him of imprisonment at Jerusalem,[16] he would have the opportunity to bid farewell to his Churches and friends in Greece as well as western Asia Minor in a final swing around the Aegean Sea, which would turn out to be both a triumphal tour and a funeral procession.

Thus they had set out for Philippi, wasting no time at proud Athens and making only brief, surreptitious visits with the Christians of Beroea and Thessalonica. From the former city they were joined by Sopater, the son of Pyrrhus; from the latter, by Aristarchus and Secundus. At Philippi the little band was enlarged by the addition of Luke, leader of the Church there as well as Gaius of Derbe and Timothy of Lystra, both in southern Asia Minor. Aware that this was Paul's farewell journey, many of his converts and friends were anxious to escort and protect him as far as they were allowed. Among them were Tychicus and Trophimus of Ephesus,[17] but instead of accompanying Paul and his band from Philippi, they were persuaded by Luke to go on ahead of them to Troas in order to announce their coming and make the appropriate preparations for Paul's farewell sermon there at the next celebration of the Eucharist on the Lord's Day.[18]

"Troas! How can I ever forget it?" Paul wondered to himself. The entire experience was extremely moving, not only because of the large turnout of faithful Christians but, in addition because of the conscious parallel with the Lord's own farewell discourse in the upper room at Jerusalem, when he instituted the Eucharist and inaugurated the new covenant. However, the evening was unforgettable for another reason as well, one that was at the same time deadly serious and yet somewhat humorous.

Paul could not help smiling as he recalled the incident.[19] "The upper room in Troas was so full of Christians of all ages that one youngster named Eutychus, who perhaps should have been home in bed, had to content himself with sitting in an open window. That in itself was not a major problem. No, the problem arose when I became so overwhelmed with the realization that I would never see these, my friends, again, and so determined to leave them with all the advice I could give them for the difficult years ahead, that I'm afraid I preached far too long. Little by little, poor Eutychus' eyes began to close and his head to nod. All of a sudden, he was no longer in the window but sprawled out in the stone courtyard, the life breath gone from his broken body. Well, what else could I do but raise him to life again, since it was actually my fault that he had died! Thanks, Lord, for your graciousness and power in bringing him back to life at my hands. And thanks also for reminding me of that priceless incident in the midst of this depressing prison.''

One might have thought that Paul's long sermon and his raising of Eutychus would have been enough for one evening, but no, after completing the celebration of the Eucharist, he and his converts had carried on a lively conversation until daybreak.[20] Then, leaving Troas behind, Paul and his entourage sailed by way of the Aegean islands of Assos, Mitylene, Chios, and Samos to Miletus,[21] off the coast of Ephesus, for his farewell meeting there with the presbyters of the Roman province of Asia, arguably at that time the area with the most Christians in the Gentile world.

Paul's eyes misted as he remembered that touching scene at Miletus.[22] After reminding them of his tireless labors of evangelization among them for three years and of the trials he had undergone in their midst, he candidly confided that he was now en route to Jerusalem and imprisonment. He would not be seeing them again, so he wanted to leave with them as a last will and testament the grave responsibility to guard the flock of God from the wolves who were certain to ravage it, even from among their own number. Then, with an exhortation to work selflessly for the Church just as he had and a reminder that ''it is more blessed to give than to receive,''[23] he entrusted them to Divine Providence with these inspired and inspiring words: ''I commend you to God and to that gracious word of his that can build you up and give you the inheritance among all who are consecrated.''[24]

Then, after heartfelt prayers with unrestrained tears and embraces, they reluctantly bade him Godspeed and escorted him to the waiting ship.[25] ''What a wrenching and draining experience that was,'' mused Paul, ''but at the same time, what a consolation it is now in this wretched prison to be able to recall the loving solicitude of my friends!''

As Paul continued his reminiscences, he could almost sense the growing warmth as their ship sailed southward on the daylong legs

One of two aqueducts at Caesarea Maritima.

of their voyage to the Aegean Isles of Cos and Rhodes, then to the port of Patara on the lower coast of Asia Minor.[26] There Paul and his party had transferred to a Phoenicia-bound ship, which swung below Cyprus and arrived in good time at Tyre,[27] where they spent a week visiting with local Christians. There and at Caesarea-by-the-Sea,[28] which they reached after a stop at Ptolemais, the disciples (including Paul's own traveling companions) tried in every way possible to dissuade him from continuing his fateful journey to Jerusalem.

"By this time," Paul vividly recalled, "I was losing patience with all the well-meaning but misguided entreaties. It was at Caesarea, I remember, that I finally confronted my friends in much the same way as Peter once told me that Jesus had challenged him and the other apostles:[29] 'What are you doing, weeping and breaking my heart? I am prepared not only to be bound but even to die in Jerusalem for the name of the Lord Jesus!'[30]

"Surprisingly, though, things seemed to flow smoothly in Jerusalem, and I was beginning to feel a warmth from the Church there that I'd hardly ever experienced before. It may have had something to do with the large collection I was bringing them from the Churches in Greece, but I like to think not. No, I really believe that it was out of a combination of Christian charity and a misguided hope to attract more Jews to belief in Jesus by using me as an example of Jewish Christian devotion to the Mosaic Law and the Temple of God at Jerusalem. For that reason, they begged me to accompany some Jewish Christians in the prescribed ceremonies for the fulfillment of their vows. In this way, they argued, the Jews themselves would be able to see that, contrary to reports, I am fully devoted to the Law and the Temple.[31]

"Well, I ought to have realized that the whole idea was a mistake. Why should I pretend to be devoted to the Law and the Temple when, as I'd just written so vigorously to the Galatians and Romans,[32] our justification comes from our faith and baptism in the crucified and risen Christ? Sure enough, the whole scheme backfired! Some of the Jews from Ephesus who'd seen my Gentile Ephesian convert, Trophimus, with me in Jerusalem, rashly assumed that he'd also gone with me into the Temple,[33] and thereupon they promptly and publicly accused me of sacrilege. What a riot ensued! I'd certainly have been beaten to death if I hadn't been rescued by a Roman commander[34] who, when he discovered that I wasn't the Egyptian troublemaker he thought I was, even let me tell my story to my fellow Jews of Jerusalem. It almost worked, too! The crowd quieted down and listened respectfully as I addressed them in Aramaic,[35] but as soon as I mentioned my mission to the Gentiles, the riot started all over again, and the commander was forced once more to take me into protective custody, especially when he learned that I was a Roman citizen.[36]

"Poor man, he still couldn't understand why the Jews had such a hatred for me! After all, how could he? I felt sorry for him because, as a Roman, he knew nothing about the Law, the Temple, or the Messiah, and yet here he was caught up in the midst of a riot about them! I have to give him credit, though, for when he realized he couldn't get at the truth by scourging me, a Roman citizen, he did the only thing he could to settle the matter by submitting my case to the Sanhedrin.[37]

"It seemed so strange to come before that august body as a suspected criminal or at least a troublemaker, when not many years before I myself had been their champion in persecuting the very movement I was now representing and defending!" Then Paul chuckled as he recalled the ploy he had used to split and immobilize the assembly. "Aware that the Sanhedrin was composed of Pharisees who believe in resurrection and Sadducees who don't, it was a clever but simple maneuver on my part to declare openly that it was my belief in resurrection from the dead that was the basis of any charges against me. Ha! Ha! Immediately, the Pharisees as a body leapt to my defense. I had managed to divide and conquer![38] So back into custody I went, but as soon as my nephew was able to get word to me about a Jewish plot to assassinate me, the commander sent me off under guard to Caesarea.[39] Well, so far so good! At least I hadn't been dispatched by the Jerusalem Jews before I even had a chance to get to Rome! That was the positive part.

"The negative part was that even though Felix, the Roman governor, couldn't find anything substantive in the charges by the Jewish representatives from Jerusalem, he still kept me imprisoned at Caesarea, obviously hoping I'd offer to buy my freedom with a generous bribe.[40] Little did he know that I neither could nor would stoop to that expedient! So I stayed in that stinking prison for two long years, until finally Felix's term of office expired and he was replaced by Festus.[41] During that time, Lord, I clearly remember how consoled I was, first of all by your strengthening presence, and then also by the visits of my friends,[42] particularly my faithful companion and physician, Luke. If only they could still visit me here in this *carcer*, what a consolation that would be!"

Festus proved to be a more honest and humane governor than Felix. No sooner had he taken command than he tried to resolve Paul's situation. But when, at the request of the Jews in Jerusalem, he proposed that Paul return there for a new trial, the apostle felt he had no alternative but to exercise his right as a Roman citizen and demand a trial before the Roman emperor.[43] Ironically, when King Herod Agrippa II and his wife, Bernice, who was also his sister, paid Festus a courtesy call and, at the latter's request, had an informal hearing of Paul's case, Agrippa's final statement to Festus was, "This man could have been set free if he had not appealed to Caesar."[44]

As Paul remembered his journey to Rome in chains, the terrifying northeaster that attacked the ship in the open sea, and, particularly, the disastrous shipwreck at Malta, he could not keep from shivering. It had been a nightmare experience indeed, and he would just as soon pass over it quickly. Much more to his liking was the recollection of the Lord's providence in saving all hands[45] and, later on, the gracious welcome of the Christians in Puteoli and in Rome itself,[46] which filled

The Roman Forum from near the Mamertine Prison.

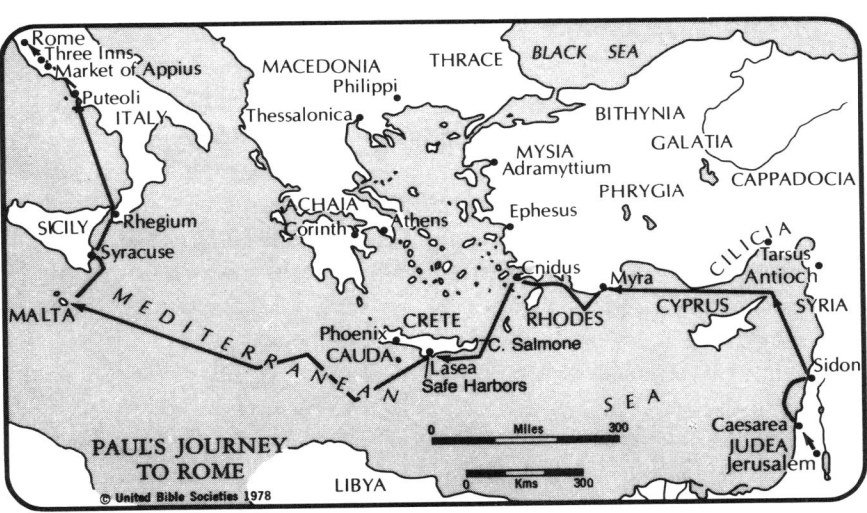

PAUL'S JOURNEY TO ROME

his heart with such gratitude to God and to his friends that, even in his dark, damp, and freezing confinement, he managed to feel suddenly warm and comfortable.

Of course, Paul remained in custody for two full years[47] while the imperial court waited for his accusers to show up from Jerusalem with their charges against him. In the meantime, though still in chains, he was able to live in rented quarters with only a soldier to guard him and with complete freedom not only to receive his friends but also to preach the good news of Jesus Christ freely to all who would listen, including leaders of the Jews in Rome.[48] "The important thing," Paul remembered with a smile of satisfaction, "was that, regardless of the chains and custody, I was finally in Rome, thanks and praise to my gracious God and his loving Son, Jesus Christ. My dream of coming to Rome had been marvelously, miraculously fulfilled!"

Two years! A lot can happen during that time, and a lot did! Not so much in Paul's situation, for his Jewish accusers never appeared, so there was no trial, and after the two years he was released. No, what happened was that Paul, insisting on being informed of the conditions of his Churches in Asia Minor and Greece and unwilling to remain idle during his confinement, wrote four of his thirteen letters during this period, namely those to the Philippians and Philemon as well as to the Colossians and Ephesians. These are all known as his Captivity Letters.[49]

As Paul reflected on those four letters, written from his first Roman captivity, his mind dwelt on the diverse situations that had occasioned them: (1) his overwhelming joy and gratitude toward the Philippians; (2) his desire to settle in a Christian manner the case of Philemon and his runaway slave, Onesimus; and (3) the dangerous growth of false teaching and conduct in the Churches of Colossae and Laodicea.[50]

Paul's heart warmed with affection and gratitude as he thought of his beloved Philippian community, which under the inspiring guidance of his dear friend Luke, had from the beginning been so solicitous for his welfare, sending him assistance of all kinds at every opportunity.[51] While he always boasted that he was self-supporting and not at all dependent on his Churches,[52] he could not help making an exception in the case of Philippi. How could he do otherwise when it obviously gave them such joy to see to his needs and him such joy to accept their ministrations? He could truly call them "my joy and my crown!"[53]

And by the same token, it was with his beloved Philippians that he could open up his heart and bare his soul. Especially in the face

The Famous Egnatian Way at Philippi.

of the threatened incursion from his old nemesis, the Judaizers, he could with great confidence share the autobiographical account[54] of his own conversion, which had involved nothing less than a total rejection of his past life as a Pharisee and, without a backward glance, his complete dedication to the goal of possessing Jesus Christ, who had already taken possession of him. Even now, he could already claim in truth and love, "Life to me is Christ and death is gain!"[55]

Then there was the strange but touching arrival of the runaway slave Onesimus, whom he had come to know, admire, and befriend in the household of his convert and friend, Philemon, during his three years at Ephesus. Onesimus, Paul had come to realize, was one of those extraordinary human beings who combined a handsome appearance, active intelligence, broad education, and deep sensitivity. He was a slave not out of any inferiority but simply from the misfortune of defeat in war. The very presence of Onesimus had lightened Paul's confinement, and when the erstwhile slave expressed his desire to become a Christian, Paul was overjoyed.

"I would have been delighted to keep him with me, not as a slave but as a cherished friend. However, I knew that such a decision would have been not only against Roman law but also against my friendship with Philemon. So I had to send him back, but with the urgent request of Philemon that he would now regard Onesimus as a brother in Christ and seriously consider before God the possibility of setting him free."[56] And Paul smiled warmly as he recalled his gentle pressure tactic with Philemon, but quickly added, "Knowing that the plight of Onesimus was and is prevalent throughout the Roman world, I made sure to address my letter not only to Philemon himself but to all the members of the Church that met at his house.[57] I can't singlehandedly overthrow the practice of slavery, but perhaps I can change enough minds and hearts so that in the not too distant future slavery will be a thing of the past!" Little did he realize how long it would take!

"Finally, there were my twin letters to the neighboring Churches of Colossae and Laodicea, both in the province of Asia, whose capital is Ephesus. During those three years that I'd spent at Ephesus and in spite of all I'd borne there (or perhaps because of it), we'd managed to spread the good news throughout the whole province. I shouldn't even say 'we,' for evangelization beyond the capital was largely done by others. Epaphras[58] in particular carried the word with wonderful success to such cities as Colossae, Hierapolis, and Laodicea. But while the good seeds of God's word were growing toward the harvest, we became painfully aware that very dangerous weeds were growing among them.[59]

"It was Epaphras himself who hurried to Rome to bring me sad tidings about the dangers threatening our young Churches of the Asian province, dangers especially from syncretism,[60] to which the entire area is singularly vulnerable because of its location at the crossroads between east and west. Our poor Christians! They're literally besieged with the crosscurrents of Greek philosophy and mystery religions,[61] Hellenistic Judaism,[62] various kinds of Eastern religions,[63] and most insidious of all, something that's beginning to be called gnosticism.[64]

"Dear Jesus, all those movements have one thing in common: in their 'superior wisdom' they deny that you are the Son of God and Savior of the world. Instead, they regard you as only one of a whole host of heavenly beings (called the fullness of God) who are thought to rule the world.

"In my twin letters, then, I tried to make it perfectly clear that you, Jesus, are the true fullness of God and Lord of the universe,[65] through whom alone we have access to God our Creator and Father, and that your fullness is your body the Church, whose head and bridegroom you are.[66] Those letters were a real joy to write, for they gave me the opportunity to express my love and praise for you, my blessed Lord, and for your Church in no uncertain terms.

"But they were not to be my final letters. As soon as I was released from my two years of confinement, I hurried back to our Churches in Greece and Asia Minor.[67] My former wish to visit Spain,[68] I realized, was not to be, so I put it behind me. I knew that my time was short, that my work of evangelization was largely completed, and that my task now was primarily to ensure the preservation[69] of what you, my Lord, had enabled me and my co-workers to establish. For that reason, I sent my dear son Timothy to Ephesus to be my representative in that troubled area and to oversee the preservation of the faith there. Titus, my stalwart companion, I dispatched to Crete to organize the Church there and also to be close enough to return to Corinth if his presence should again be needed there. And to both of them I wrote letters of instruction [70] on how I felt they should conduct themselves in the roles entrusted to them.

"Finally, with the outbreak and continuation of the terrible persecution of our Roman Christians, and particularly with the news of Peter's martyrdom, I knew just as surely as I breathed, dear Lord, that it was here in Rome that I was to fill up in my own being the sufferings that you still wanted to suffer for your body the Church.[71] So here I am, Lord, ready to follow you when you call me to yourself. Truly, you are my very life, and death my gain![72]

"There's just one more letter that I want to write, a farewell to my spiritual son, Timothy. We've been so close for so long, like father and son,[73] that I feel I owe it to him to tell him good-bye. Besides, there may even be time for him to join me[74] before my date with the sword. And if he can come in time, perhaps he can bring my Cilician cloak from Troas to help me bear this cold, and my scrolls and parchments to help me pass the time.[75] Oh! And if he can also bring Mark,[76] with whom I was gladly reconciled during my first Roman imprisonment through the good offices of my dear friend Luke, then I would be content indeed. Just as you, my Lord, were accompanied in the Garden of Gethsemane by your three closest apostles[77] and surrounded at the cross by your dear mother and her sister, along with John and Mary Magdalene,[78] so I would have my special three, Luke and Mark and Timothy. Yes, Lord, I am indeed ready! I have fought the good fight, I have finished the race, I have kept the faith!"[79]

Whether Timothy and Mark were able to reach Paul before his martyrdom, we do not know. What we do know is that after a second trial Paul was condemned to death, taken out to the Ostian Way, and summarily beheaded, probably sometime between December of 67 and July of 68.[80] And I like to think that, just before lowering his head for the sword, Paul's mind and heart traveled back over some thirty years to that day outside the walls of Jerusalem when he had witnessed the stoning of the young Stephen, whose prayers had later haunted him and now returned to him as the perfect expression of his own heart, "Lord Jesus, receive my spirit!" and "Lord, do not hold this sin against them!"[81]

Today, outside of Rome on the Ostian Way stands the beautiful Basilica of St. Paul, within which, around the confessional containing his body, can be found the words[82] *Mihi vivere Christus et mori lucrum!*[83] (To me to live is Christ and to die is gain!).

ANALYSIS OF PAUL'S LATER LETTERS

Having already provided an overview of Paul's letters in general, there is no need to retrace our steps in that regard. Instead, let us take a brief overview of Paul's later letters only, leaving to the specific analysis of each one questions concerning that particular letter.

I. Overview: The Later Letters of Paul in General
  A. Division and Chronology
     1. The later letters are divided into two groups, generally identified as the Captivity Letters (Philippians, Philemon, Colossians, "Ephesians") and the Pastoral Letters (1 Timothy, Titus, 2 Timothy). The order of their listing here is obviously not that found in the New Testament, where all the letters to churches come before those to individuals and where the listing is according to length rather than chronology. Instead, I have chosen to put them in what I consider to be their probable chronological order.
  B. Authenticity or authorship
     1. Of these later letters, the only ones about which there is no question regarding Pauline authorship are the first two, Philippians and Philemon. The others, together with 2 Thessalonians, are often referred to these days as Deutero-Pauline

(literally, "Second-Pauline"), meaning that they are of doubtful Pauline authorship. Various reasons are offered for this distinction, such as differences in style, vocabulary, and theology between these letters and those universally accepted as genuinely Pauline.

2. As I have indicated previously, I choose to follow the more traditional position, accepting all of the letters attributed to Paul as of Pauline authorship except Hebrews which is universally regarded by scholars today as nonPauline and is listed in the New Testament after all of Paul's letters. I prefer this position, not because it is more traditional but for the following reasons:

   a) To me, the arguments against Pauline authorship are not proven beyond a reasonable doubt, and therefore the Pauline authenticity should continue to be held.

   b) There are other factors accounting for differences in these letters, which to me are not being given due consideration, such as the use of different secretaries, divergent situations requiring the use of different words, and, above all, Paul's own spiritual and theological development as well as his changing situation from an earlier, dynamic evangelization to a later period of actual or impending imprisonment. This, along with advancing age and infirmities, quite naturally tended to emphasize preservation of what had already been established against growing dangers of many kinds.

   c) Assuming, as most scholars do, that Paul was freed from his house arrest in Rome around A.D. 62 and not martyred until A.D. 67 or 68, it would be nothing short of incredible to think that he suddenly quit writing letters or that Christians ceased to preserve them. Even more unbelievable is the idea of some, who consider Philippians and Philemon as written during an earlier but unnamed captivity at Ephesus (2 Cor 1:8-11), that Paul wrote nothing at all after his great Letter to the Romans, penned around A.D. 56-57. Such a position would contend that Paul ceased his very important apostolate of letter writing for the final ten years of his life!

    d) Attributing all the "Pauline Letters" to Paul does not preclude the possibility of contributions by others in the form of additions or revisions, even posthumously,[84] any more than attributing the Fourth Gospel to John rules out additions and revisions by one or more of his disciples.

    e) Particular attention should be given to the names of Paul's friends, many of which appear in more than one of the Deutero-Pauline Letters,[85] for example, Timothy, Mark, Luke, Tychicus, and Onesimus.

C. Letting these remarks suffice for our overview of Paul's later letters as a whole, let us move forward to an analysis of the individual letters. As we do so, it will be convenient and helpful to consider more than one at a time. Thus, let us begin with Philippians and Philemon, then proceed to Colossians and "Ephesians," and close with 1 Timothy, Titus, and 2 Timothy.

II. Analysis and Outlines of Paul's Later Letters

A. Captivity Letters I: Philippians and Philemon

    1. General impression

        a) Philippians: Paul's most joyous and loving letter (1:7-8) and, with 2 Corinthians, his most self-revealing, although somewhat disjointed either from a combination of his letters or from an abrupt change of mood due to an interruption in dictation or to the receipt of disturbing news about the Judaizers

        b) Philemon: Paul's most tactful letter, balancing concern for a runaway slave with regard for his master's legal rights and feelings

    2. Circumstances

        a) Philippians

            (1) If one letter: written from Paul's first Roman captivity[86] out of joy and gratitude for the Philippians' concern and help along with Paul's response to the danger of the evil influence of the Judaizers

            (2) If two letters: chapters 1, 2, and 4 written from Paul's first Roman captivity out of joy and gratitude for the Philippians' concern and help; chapter 3 taken from

an earlier letter, perhaps from Ephesian captivity, against Judaizing influence

b) Philemon: from Paul's first Roman captivity[87] to his friend Philemon and those who meet at his house, probably in Ephesus, regarding Philemon's runaway slave, Onesimus, baptized by Paul and now being returned with the request and hope that Philemon will receive him as a brother rather than a slave

3. Purposes

a) Philippians: to express Paul's joy and gratitude, to warn against Judaizers, and to exhort to greater pursuit of Christ and his virtues

b) Philemon: to explain to Paul's friend, to the local Church, and perhaps to the whole Church that a Christian slave is a brother in Christ

4. Characteristics

a) Philippians: joyous and loving at beginning and end; firm in the middle. Important references to life in Christ and acceptance of life or death (1:21-26), unity in humility in imitation of Christ (2:1-11), salvation worked out with fear and trembling (2:12), autobiographical race for Christ (3:7-16), resurrection with Christ (3:21), joy and the practice of all virtues (4:4-9)

b) Philemon: very brief (one chapter long) but rich in expressions of Paul's affection and respect for both Philemon and Onesimus, with clear indications of his desire to see his landmark statement on equality in Gal 3:28 brought to realization (v. 16)

5. Authorship: no questions about the authenticity of both Philippians and Philemon, though another may have joined two or three of Paul's letters to the Philippians into one

6. Outlines

a) Philemon: too brief to need an outline

b) Philippians: also brief but this may help—

(1) Greetings from Paul and Timothy, slaves of Christ, to the holy ones of Philippi, with their overseers and deacons[88] (1:1-2)

(2) Thanksgiving and prayer (1:3-11)
  (a) Joyous, loving thanks for the Philippians as faithful fellow workers from the beginning[89] (1:3-8)
  (b) Paul's prayer for their continued growth in love, knowledge, discernment, purity, and holiness in Christ (1:9-11)
(3) Body of the letter (1:12–4:20)
  (a) Paul's report on how his imprisonment and possible death[90] work for the spread of the good news (1:12-26)
  (b) Paul's exhortation to faithfulness in conduct and suffering (1:27-30); unity and humility in Christ[91] (2:1-11); obedience, witness, and service (2:12-18); joyous welcome of Timothy and Epaphroditus (2:19-30)
  (c) Paul's warning against the Judaizers and appeal to his own example of the rejection of (Pharisaic) Judaism for the sake of Christ[92] (3:2-21)
  (d) Paul's further exhortation to harmony, joy, peace, and holiness through the practice of every virtue (4:1-9)
  (e) Paul's gratitude for the Philippians' faithful care of his needs (4:10-20)
(4) Exchange of greetings, especially from Paul's friends and co-workers, and his final blessing (4:21-23)

B. Captivity Letters II: Colossians and "Ephesians"
  1. General impression
    a) Both letters together: so similar in structure, style, vocabulary, and content that they deserve to be considered and treated as twin letters, which we will do in this study
    b) Colossians: an almost lyrical letter featuring the risen Christ as the fullness of God and Lord of the cosmos but also as living in each of his followers
    c) "Ephesians": almost as lyrical as Colossians, with major emphasis on the Church as the very fullness of Christ and rightly called his body, bride, temple, people, city, etc.

2. Circumstances

   a) Both letters seem to be written about the same time during Paul's first Roman captivity,[93] sent to the same area in the Roman province of Asia, and delivered by the same courier, Tychicus.

   b) The address to the Christians of Colossae, a town in the Lycus Valley east of Ephesus no longer preserved even in ruins, which had not been evangelized by Paul but by Epaphras,[94] is certain enough from the manuscript evidence.

   c) The address to the Ephesians, however, is at least doubtful, being missing from some of the most important manuscripts.[95] Since Colossians mentions the letter to Laodicea in the same area (Col 4:16), that may well have been the original address, which was later changed to the Ephesians for certain reasons.[96]

3. Purposes of both letters: to combat the growing danger of religious syncretism in general and Gnosticism in particular[97] and to inculcate good Christian conduct, mainly in the family

4. Characteristics

   a) The letters are so similar to each other that they really constitute twin works.

   b) Colossians is primarily Christological, featuring the "Hymn of the Cosmic Christ."[98]

   c) Ephesians is primarily Ecclesial, featuring a "Blessing Hymn of Christian Destiny."[99]

5. Authorship: Pauline authorship of Colossians and "Ephesians" is widely questioned, but see my remarks above on the authorship of these Deutero-Pauline Letters in general.

6. Outlines of these twin letters are best given in parallel columns, to show their similarity.

   a) Colossians
      (1) Address and greeting (1:1-2)
      (2) Thanksgiving and prayer (1:3-14)

   b) "Ephesians"
      (1) Address and greeting (1:1-2)
      (2) Blessing Hymn of Christian Destiny (1:3-14)

(3) Hymn of Christ in the cosmos and us (1:15–2:3)	(3) The Church's unity in Christ (1:15–2:22)
(4) Beware teachings against Christ (2:4-23)	(4) The Church's world mission in Christ (3:1–4:24)
(5) Christian life in home and world (3:1–4:6)	(5) Christian Life in home[100] and world (4:25–6:20)
(6) Greetings, conclusion, blessing (4:7-18)	(6) Conclusion and blessing (6:21-24)

C. Pastoral Letters: 1 Timothy, Titus, 2 Timothy
   1. General Impression
      a) Great similarity among all three, especially between 1 Timothy and Titus. 2 Timothy contains the added element of Paul's farewell to his beloved spiritual son before his death.
      b) Even greater conservatism in the Pastorals than the Captivity Letters, but this should be quite understandable considering Paul's premonition of his impending end and therefore his concern to preserve what he has gained and built up for Christ.
   2. Circumstances
      a) 1 Timothy and Titus written from somewhere in Greece, possibly Philippi,[101] to Paul's main co-workers in Ephesus and Crete respectively
      b) 2 Timothy written from Paul's final Roman imprisonment[102] to his spiritual son in Ephesus
   3. Purposes
      a) 1 Timothy and Titus written to instruct Paul's "delegate bishops" on how to fulfill their pastoral duties in Ephesus and Crete
      b) 2 Timothy likewise written to instruct Paul's son in Christ on his duties but also to bid farewell to his most constant companion

4. Characteristics of all three

    a) Marked by conservatism in the insistence on exemplary conduct, avoidance of and preaching against false doctrine, portrait of the Church as "pillar and foundation of truth,"[103] living "in faith" and keeping "the faith,"[104]and careful choice of good ministers who will teach, serve, and guard the faithful

    b) Containing short hymns or "creeds"[105] about our salvation through Christ (1 Tim 2:5-6; 3:16; Titus 2:11-14; 3:4-7; 2 Tim 2:11-13), somewhat reminiscent of Phil 2:5-11; Col 1:15-20; Eph 1:3-14

    c) Featuring careful instructions about the qualifications required of *epískopoi-presbýteroi* (bishops-priests, not yet distinguished,[106] for example in 1 Tim 5:17 and Titus 1:5-7) as well as *diákonoi* (deacons, 1 Tim 3:8-10, 12-13), *gynaîkes* (women, deaconesses?[107] 1 Tim 3:11), and *chêrai* (widows, 1 Tim 5:3-16)

    d) Dotted with typical Pauline terminology, for example, tender expressions toward Timothy and Titus (1 Tim 1:2, 18; Titus 1:4; 2 Tim 1:2-5), athletic imagery (1 Tim 1:18; 4:8; 2 Tim 2:5; 4:7), and favorite teachings familiar from letters universally accepted as genuine, for example, God's will of salvation for all (1 Tim 2:4), Paul's vocation to teach the Gentiles (1 Tim 2:7), handing someone over to Satan[108] (1 Tim 1:20), and many more.

5. Authorship

    a) Whatever may be said of letters like Colossians, "Ephesians," and 2 Thessalonians, it is almost taken for granted today in Scripture circles that the Pastorals were not written until a generation or two after Paul. This is based largely on the argument that Paul's life, thinking, and times could not have shown the conservatism, the advanced state of ministry, the vocabulary, and so forth found in the Pastorals.

    b) I suggest that a careful reading of the characteristics of the Pastorals listed above will show that they have very much in common with the so-called genuine Pauline letters.

  c) Can we imagine anyone else except Paul, the spiritual fa-
     ther of Timothy, saying something like "Stop drinking
     only water, but have a little wine for the sake of your
     stomach and your frequent illnesses"?[109] And the same
     is true of other expressions,[110] especially of Paul toward
     his beloved sons, Timothy and Titus.

  d) While it is true that attributing some of Paul's letters to
     anonymous authors does not affect their inspiration and
     canonicity, it does seem to affect their use and importance
     in our lives, as a moment of reflection will confirm.[111]

6. Outlines: It would be helpful to examine all three of the
   Pastorals in parallel columns, but since that is impractical,
   let us view 1 Timothy and Titus together, and then outline
   2 Timothy alone.

a) 1 Timothy	b) Titus
(1) Address and greeting (1:1-2)	(1) Address and greeting (1:1-4)
(2) Apostolic charge	(2) Apostolic charge
(a) Beware false teaching (1:3-11)	(a) Appoint good presbyters (1:5-16)
(b) God's mercy on Paul (1:12-17)	(b) Teach Christian conduct (2:1-10)
(c) Prayer and role of women (2:1-15)	(c) Teach change of life (2:11–3:8)
(d) Appoint good leaders (3:1–5:25)	(d) Avoid false teaching (3:8-11)
(e) Advice and exhortation (6:1-21)	(e) Advice and directives (3:12-14)
(3) Final blessing (6:21b)	(3) Greetings and final blessing (3:12)

  c) 2 Timothy
     (1) Address and greeting (1:1-2)
     (2) Thanksgiving (1:3-5)
     (3) Exhortations to sound teaching (1:6–2:13)

(4) Warnings on false teachers and the last days[112]
(2:14–4:8)
(5) Requests and final greetings (4:9-21)
(6) Blessing (4:22)

REFLECTIONS ON PAUL'S LATER LETTERS AND OUR LIFE

In this final segment of our treatment of Paul, namely our reflections on his later letters, I would like to concentrate especially on three subjects concerning which I have promised the reader a fuller consideration at this time. Those three subjects are (1) Paul's vision of the "cosmic Christ,"[113] particularly in Colossians; (2) Paul's vision of the Church as the "fullness of Christ,"[114] mainly in "Ephesians"; and (3) Paul's vision of our bodily resurrection,[115] especially in Philippians, with a flashback to his Corinthian letters. Then, to avoid leaving these prime considerations in the abstract, I intend to apply each one, at least briefly, to our own life and ministry.

Paul's Vision of the Cosmic Christ
It is interesting to observe how Paul, the consummate Jew as well as the consummate Christian, tended to mirror the development of Jewish thought in his own life. For centuries the Israelites evidently regarded Yahweh as their national God, in special relationship with them as his people, but with little or no realization, at least in practice, of his uniqueness as the only God and Lord of the universe. However, with the Babylonian Captivity six centuries before Christ,[116] there occurred a fundamental change in Jewish thinking and practice. Beginning with Ezekiel's fantastic vision of Yahweh present, mobile, and active apart from the Temple in Jerusalem,[117] where Jewish thought had largely confined him,[118] and culminating in the eye-opening and mind-expanding universalism of Deutero-Isaiah,[119] God's revelation and inspiration succeeded in developing a far greater and more accurate understanding of himself as the Creator, Lord, and Savior of all beings.[120]

Not that this portrait of Yahweh was entirely new. The very name "Yahweh"[121] (I am who am), revealed to Moses back in Exod 3:14, probably means "I am the only God who truly exists!" And even the beautiful invitation to a covenant relationship in Exod 19:3-6 contains the clear reminder that "all the earth is mine!"[122] However, in addition to Israel's apparent failure to grasp such a universal idea so early in her history, there is evidence that the wording of the invitation itself may have been embellished under later Deuteronomic[123] and possibly Priestly[124] influence.

At any rate, just as Israel evidently did not fully appreciate Yahweh's uniqueness and greatness until the Babylonian Captivity, so it seems that Paul may not have completely understood Jesus' uniqueness and greatness as the "cosmic Christ" until his own "Babylonian Captivity" in Rome.[125] Before that time, his emphasis had been mainly on Jesus as Messiah[126] and Son of God[127] and as one with his followers in the Church,[128] especially with Paul himself.[129] Now however, apparently faced with the baleful influence of incipient Gnosticism[130] in western Asia Minor and possibly helped by contemplation of personified wisdom in the Hebrew Scriptures,[131] Paul's own vision of Christ underwent a dramatic expansion, or should I say explosion?

He now saw Christ not only as the mirror image[132] of the Father himself but also as personally involved in past and present creation,[133] as Redeemer and Lord of the cosmos,[134] and as Ultimate Purpose of the universe.[135] This is all contained in Paul's "Hymn of the Cosmic Christ" (Col 1:15-20, WFD), which seems to lend itself to the following divisions:

I. *The uniqueness of Christ:*[136]
> He is the image of the invisible God,
>> the firstborn of all creation.

In creation:[137]
> For in him were created all things
>> in heaven and on earth,
>> the visible and the invisible,
>> whether thrones or dominations
>> or principalities or powers;
> all things have been created
>> through him and for him.

II. *The primacy of Christ:*[138]
> He is before all things,
>> and in him all have held together.

In redemption:[139]
> He is the head of his body, the Church.
> He is the beginning,
>> the firstborn from the dead,

that in all things he himself
might hold the primacy.
For in him all the fullness
was pleased to dwell,
and through him to reconcile
all things into himself,
having united them in peace
by the blood of his cross,
whether the things on earth
or those in the heavens.

However, it would be a mistake to view this magnificent hymn in isolation. The portrait of Christ as the image of the invisible God probably has antecedents in both Rom 8:29 and 2 Cor 3:18 with a possible reference to Gen 1:27[140] and an even clearer allusion to Wis 7:25-26,[141] while his personal role in creation seems to be clearly foreshadowed in the personification of the wisdom of God in Prov 8:22-31.[142] In addition, Christ's role as redeemer of creation is fully in keeping with Rom 8:19-23,[143] and his headship of his body, the Church, is a development of 1 Cor 12 and Rom 12.[144]

In fact, the entire "Hymn of the Cosmic Christ" ought to be read in conjunction with the famous "Hymn of Christ," already noted[145] in Phil 2:5-12 (portraying Jesus' glorious preexistence, self-emptying incarnation, humiliating but redemptive death-resurrection, and consequent supreme glorification), as well as with the "Blessing Hymn"[146] of Eph 1:3-12 and the "Creedal Hymns"[147] of 1 Tim 2:5-6; 3:16.

To those who are familiar with the remarkable vision of Pierre Teilhard de Chardin,[148] it should be clear that he has drawn his fascinating doctrine of cosmic thought and spirituality largely from Paul[149] and, to some extent, from John.[150] All well and good, I seem to hear you say, but what has all this cosmic stuff to do with our life, especially our spiritual life? A great deal indeed!

First of all, it reminds us of the unique greatness of Jesus Christ. As heirs of two millennia of belief in and relationship with Jesus as our brother and Savior, it is not always easy for us to remember the infinite leap of love and humility involved in the incarnation, the mystery of God-become-human. We can only imagine the amount of faith required for a Jew in Jesus' time, with a heritage of six centuries' emphasis on God's transcendence, to accept a lowly carpenter of Nazareth in Galilee not only as his Messiah but as the very Son of God, equal to Yahweh himself![151] We cannot recapture that same situation, but we can, by developing a realistic sense of the universe and of Christ's creative-incarnate-redemptive primacy over it, come to know him in all his greatness and all his self-emptying love for us.

It is also not easy for us, in our self-centeredness, to keep in mind our own responsibility for the ongoing creation, preservation, and redemption of the world about us. In the memorable words of John Donne, "No man is an island, entire of itself; every man is a piece of the continent, a part of the main."[152] By the way in which we live, we affect the world in which we live. Our holiness, or rather Christ's holiness in us, contributes greatly to the hominization and Christification[153] of the world, just as surely as our sinfulness not only impedes it but even reverses it toward the level of the beasts. There simply is no such thing as a victimless crime,[154] for we are all the victims of every crime, every sin, as we are all the beneficiaries of every saintly life. Ours is a global, a cosmic, responsibility.

It is so tempting for us to flee the world as dangerous to our spiritual life, and indeed, that may be our need and our vocation,[155] but in most cases our vocation is to live in the world and allow Christ to continue in and through us his creative and redemptive role in the world and in the universe. We need to heed his invitation to "launch out into the deep,"[156] not just the deep waters of the Sea of Galilee, but the awe-inspiring depths of space. We are not living in the ancient world or even in the Middle Ages but in the "age of space." Each of us is a "child of the universe,"[157] one with him who is "the Alpha and the Omega,"[158] the beginning and the end of all things.

Paul's Vision of the Church as the Fullness of Christ

Incipient Gnosticism taught that emanating from the transcendent Deity are innumerable demigods or demiurges, which together form the *plērōma*, or "fullness," of the universe.[159] To Jewish Gnostics this fullness comprises the many kinds of angels;[160] to Christian Gnostics, Christ himself would be included as part of the *plērōma*.[161] Hence, Paul in Col 1:19 stresses that Jesus Christ is not just contained in the fullness of God. He *is* the fullness of God![162] Indeed, he is the fullness of the entire universe. At the same time, in Col 1:18, Paul develops his analogy of the Church as the body of Christ from 1 Cor 12:12-31 and Rom 12:4-8 by pointing out that Christ, as the "firstborn of all creation" (Col 1:15) and the "firstborn from the dead" (Col 1:18) is, of course, the "head of his body, the Church." It should not be surprising, then, that in Eph 1:22-23, NAB, Paul refers to the Church not only as the body but also as the fullness of Christ: "And he [God] put all things beneath his [Christ's] feet and gave him as head over all things to the church, which is his body, the fullness of the one who fills all things in every way."

For our part, just as we attempted to probe the depth of meaning in Paul's "Hymn of the Cosmic Christ" in his Letter to the Colossians, so it will enrich us to pursue some of the fullness of meaning in Paul's "Ephesian" portrait of the Church.

First of all, the Greek word *ekklēsía*[163] (Church), which in Paul's writings antedates its usage in "Matthew," serves to remind us of our Jewish roots, for it is the Septuagint translation of the Hebrew *qahal*[164] (assembly), used of the Israelite community in the desert and afterward. The word *ekklēsía* literally means "called out"[165] and aptly identifies the Church as called out of all the nations to be God's own people, a major emphasis in "Ephesians."[166]

And let us not forget the importance of that expression "the people of God," which is in Greek *ho laòs toû theoû*, for the Greek word translated "people" is *laós*, whence we have the term "laity." At one time the Church was largely identified with the hierarchy, and the laity expected and were expected to "pray, pay, and obey,"[167] but ever since the Second Vatican Council,[168] it is generally recognized that the laity primarily comprise the "people of God" and are to represent the Church in the world and the world to the Church. Of course, the role of the clergy continues to be one of leadership, but a leadership of service, of genuine shepherding after the example of Christ himself.[169]

At the end of chapter 2 of "Ephesians," Paul expands his portrait of the Church. Speaking especially of the Gentile Christians (which includes the vast majority of Church members), Paul tries to inculcate in them a sense of belonging, assuring them in Eph 2:19-21, WFD, that now you "are no longer strangers and outsiders but rather fellow citizens with the saints and members of God's own household, built on the foundation of the apostles and prophets, the keystone being Christ Jesus himself, in whom the entire closely fitted building is growing into a sacred temple in the Lord; in whom indeed you are also being built up into a dwelling place of God in the Spirit."

What an outpouring of descriptions of the Church, each suggesting the next in a beautiful chain of figures that together provide us with a magnificent portrait of what it means to be Christians! We are no longer strangers exiled far away from God, but rather full-fledged *citizens* of God's realm, enjoying all the rights and privileges of his holy people. In fact, as Christians we are even members of God's own household, his intimate *family*! We form his very *home*, built on the firm foundation of the apostles and prophets and held solidly together by the capstone of Jesus Christ himself, a closely fitted structure that is actually alive and constantly growing into a holy *temple*, where God himself, Father, Son, and Holy Spirit, is pleased to dwell! Is this not what it means to be the fullness of Christ, as he is the fullness of the Father?

But wait! There is still more, much more! In Eph 5:21-33[170] Paul does not hesitate to compare the union of the Church with Christ to the union of a wife and her husband. Evoking the Gen 2:21-24 account of the formation of Eve from Adam and their reunion in marriage,[171] he unfolds the mystery of the Church as both the bride and the body of her divine-human spouse. This is, of course, in the tradition of the covenant relationship of Yahweh and Israel, pictured as a marital union in Hosea, Isaiah, Jeremiah, and Ezekiel,[172] and yet it transcends that relationship with the emphasis on the Church as not only the bride but the body of Christ, her head.[173]

No wonder, then, that in view of all these privileges, Paul breaks out in his impressive "Blessing Hymn"[174] of Eph 1:3-12, WFD, which I have rearranged in poetic form, with principal segments indicated by Roman numerals and key expressions highlighted by italics:

> I. Blessed be the God and Father
>   of our Lord Jesus Christ,
> who has *blessed* us in Christ
>   with every spiritual blessing
>   in the heavens,
> in that God *chose* us in him
>   before the world's creation
> to be holy and blameless
>   in his presence in love,
> having predestined us
>   for *adoption* into him
>   through Jesus Christ,
> according to the favor of his will
>   for the *praise of the glory*
>   of his favor

with which he has graced us
  in his beloved.

II. In him we have *deliverance*
     through his blood,
    the forgiveness of our sins
     according to the riches
      of his favor,
   which he has showered on us
     in all wisdom and insight,
   revealing to us the *mystery*
     of his will, that
   according to his choice,
   established beforehand in him,
     as a settled plan,
   he would *recapitulate* everything
     in the fullness of time
      in Christ,
      those in the heavens
      and those on the earth.

III. In him we have been chosen,
     predestined acccording to his plan
       which *accomplishes* all things
       according to the decision
        of his will,
     that we who have hoped in Christ
       should be to the *praise*
         of his glory.[175]

No wonder also that Paul has sprinkled this remarkable letter with pleas for Christlike love[176] as well as for unity in the Church[177] and harmony in the home.[178] The entire letter provides us with a strongly challenging portrait of what we are called to be as Christians, nothing less than the fullness of Christ, who is the fullness of the Father.

Paul's Vision of Our Bodily Resurrection
In Phil 3:20-21, WFD, Paul tells his dear friends, ''For our citizenship is in heaven, whence we are also awaiting a savior, the Lord Jesus Christ, who will transform these lowly bodies of ours, conforming them to his glorified body according to the power which enables him to subject all things to himself.''

This statement clearly expresses Paul's belief in and expectation of bodily resurrection. It even describes to some extent what our risen body will be like, namely, like the glorified body of Jesus after his resurrection. However, it does not clearly declare just when this bodily resurrection will occur, whether at the end of time or at our individual deaths. For information in that regard, we need to return to Paul's Letters to the Corinthians. But, before we do that, it would be well for us to review in brief what the so-called traditional teaching is regarding bodily resurrection, and what problems may lie therein.

It is my observation that most Christians, at least most Catholics, grow up, as I did, with an understanding of our human nature and therefore of our resurrection, which is derived from Greek philosophy. We see ourselves as human beings composed of body and soul, united in life and separated at death, after which the soul continues a separate and purely spiritual existence until the end of time, when God will reunite our body with our soul in the general resurrection of the dead. Such is our generally accepted conception of bodily resurrection, but it seems to contain certain problems that warrant consideration.

First of all, it seems to involve a dichotomy, regarding the body and soul as two distinct entities united in life but separated at death, perhaps for centuries. Secondly, a separated soul does not enjoy a personal existence for, even by Greek definition, a person is a composite of body and soul, Thirdly, it requires of God an innumerable series of miracles in reuniting our souls with our bodies, considering that human bodies virtually disintegrate into nothingness after some time and that many are cremated or blown to smithereens here on earth or in space. And what about the whole problem of transplants? To whom will they belong in the general resurrection? But fourthly, and to me most importantly, our familiar body-soul picture says absolutely nothing about any relationship with God. For these negative reasons and for as many positive ones, I prefer the biblical description of our human nature in Gen 2:7 as both more complete and more accurate.

In this simple depiction of our formation, we are seen as one being in three dimensions, which throughout the Bible are referred to generally as flesh, person, and spirit. Flesh[179] here is not the body but rather our whole being in all our human weakness, subject to sickness, accident, death, temptation, sin. Spirit[180] here is not the soul but rather our whole being naturally oriented to union with God. And person[181] is our whole being, body and soul, with intelligence and free will and involved in a lifelong struggle[182] between living the life of the spirit and living that of the flesh.

Now in considering bodily resurrection in the light of this three-dimensional anthropology, it is natural and logical to view our individual resurrection as occurring at the time of our death. When we die, this body can be buried, cremated, donated to medicine or science. No matter! At the moment of death, we receive a new, glorified body with all the special attributes we see in that of Jesus after his resurrection but with one difference. We are not Jesus, or Mary either. Jesus rose with the selfsame body with which he had lived, suffered, and died. And Mary was assumed into heaven, according to our Catholic belief, with her lifetime body. We do not enjoy that privilege, but we receive the next best: a new and glorified body at the time of our death.

This, of course, is my own speculation, but it rests on the biblical anthropology that I have explained as well as on Paul's descriptions of bodily resurrection in his two Letters to the Corinthians.[183] It is supported by the Church's current rite of funerals[184] with its major emphasis on the resurrection, and it finds support also in the works of some important current theologians.[185] Nor, to my mind, is it contradicted by the tradition of the Church[186] over the centuries. The truth of the matter is that very little has been revealed about life after death, but that should not surprise us when we realize that Israel had no clear revelation that there is an afterlife until late in her history.[187]

For the purpose of our reflections on Paul's later letters, it is significant that evidently with the passage of time Paul became less concerned with physical resurrection at or after death and more concerned with spiritual or mystical death and resurrection with Christ during this life. Not that this was an entirely new development in his thinking, for in Rom 6:1-11 he clearly dwells on this, notably in connection with baptism. But, especially in his later letter to the Colossians, it becomes a prime consideration, as we see in Col 3:1-4, NAB: "If then you were raised with Christ, seek what is above, where Christ is seated at the right hand of God. Think of what is above, not of what is on earth. For you have died, and your life is hidden with Christ in God. When Christ your life appears, then you too will appear with him in glory."

For us also this is a salutary consideration. Just when and how our bodily resurrection will take place is not nearly as important for us in this life as is our commitment to die to ourselves and our selfishness with Christ and to live his risen life as totally as possible. This does not mean, of course, that we should live in splendid isolation but rather that we detach ourselves from earthly things so that we may be free and open channels of Christ's life and ministry to others.

Paul is such a fascinating person, such a towering figure in the history of the Church, that it is not easy to leave him, but leave him we must. And our parting is rendered less painful by the realization that the next and final human author of the New Testament whom we will study is none other than the beloved disciple,[188] who not only reclined closest to Jesus at the Last Supper[189] but was the only apostle at the foot of Jesus' cross and was given the care of his own mother;[190] the traditional author of the Fourth Gospel, three epistles, and the mysterious Apocalypse;[191] the "eagle"[192] among the evangelists, St. John!

NOTES

1. I have chosen the description "Prolific Paul" for the second part of our Pauline study because this chapter comprises seven letters, one more than the first chapter, and these letters are not characterized by the same amount of passion that we have seen in the previous chapter, largely because Paul is older and his ministry is now less that of a "fisher of men" (see ch. 1, n. 167) than that of a "shepherd of souls" (see ch. 1, n. 168), less of a missionary and evangelizer and more of a preserver.

2. Under the heading of "later letters," I am including the Captivity Letters (Philippians, Philemon, Colossians, and "Ephesians") and the Pastoral Letters (1 Timothy, Titus, and 2 Timothy). Their authorship and chronology, which are disputed, will be examined shortly.

3. The complete sentence in Phil 1:21, NAB, REB, is this: "For to me life is Christ, and death is gain." An even more exact translation of the infinitives used in Greek is that of the NIV, "For to me, to live is Christ and to die is gain." At any rate, this pithy statement seems to sum up beautifully the life and death of Paul after his monumental Letter to the Romans.

4. The word *carcer* simply means "prison" in Latin and provides the origin for the English word "incarcerate." At the foot of the Capitoline Hill adjacent to the Roman forum and near the Curia, or senate house, the ancient *carcer* of Rome still remains today under a variety of names: (1) the Tullianum, from the small lower, vaulted section containing springs (*tullii*) where state prisoners like Jugurtha, Catiline, and Vercingetorix perished of cold and hunger; (2) the Mamertine, a medieval name derived from a nearby statue of Mars (Mamers); and (3) San Pietro in Carcere, from the tradition that both Peter and Paul were confined in this prison, though not necessarily at the same time or in the lower cramped part.

We do not know for sure exactly where Peter and Paul were imprisoned in Rome, but the *carcer* is the most famous of the three prisons existing in Rome at the time of their martyrdom, one being nameless and the other being known as the Lautumiae (stone quarries), possibly after stone quarries at Syracuse in Sicily that were used as prisons. It is important to remember that, unlike the world of today, the ancient world, including Greece and Rome, had no system of penal imprisonment. Punishment took the form of fines, exile, or execution. Prisons existed solely as holding places before a trial or execution and sometimes as places of execution. If Paul spent some time in the *carcer*, he was indeed exposed to relentless cold, dampness, and loneliness. And, as important leaders of Christianity, which Nero had condemned to extermination as inimical to Rome and the human race, both Peter and Paul may well have qualified as state prisoners, at least for temporary confinement, most probably in the upper and larger part of the *carcer*. *See* Harry Thurston Pech, ed., *Harper's Dictionary of Classical Literature and Antiquities* (New York: Cooper Square Publishers, 1962) 277–79.

5. If Peter was crucified in the Circus of Nero at Vatican Hill not long after the beginning of Nero's persecution in A.D. 64 and Paul was beheaded on the Ostian Way not long before its end in A.D. 68, the interval was about four years. The liturgical celebration of their martyrdom on the same day, June 29, the feast of Sts. Peter and Paul, is simply a convenient way of honoring the "Princes of the Apostles" and "Founders of the Church at Rome."

6. Paul had been imprisoned at Philippi (Acts 16:16-40), possibly at Ephesus (2 Cor 1:8-10; 11:23), at Jerusalem (Acts 22:24; 23:10), as well as two years each at Caesarea (Acts 23:33–26:32) and Rome (Acts 28:16, 30-31).

7. In 2 Tim 4:9-16, Paul describes his sense of abandonment by his friends, especially at his first trial, and in any case they obviously did not have access to him in his final Roman imprisonment as they had in his first.

8. The reference here is to Jesus' sense of abandonment on the cross when he cried out, "My God, my God, why have you forsaken me?" (Mark 15:34; Matt 27:46, NAB, etc.), whereby he identified himself with the suffering Messiah in Ps 22 and also expressed, through his union with sinful humanity, an actual sense of abandonment by God. "God made him who had no sin to be sin for us, so that in him we might become the righteousness of God" (2 Cor 5:21, NIV).

9. This is a rather free translation of Col 1:24, WFD, in an attempt to bring out its meaning.

10. This clear identification of the risen Christ with his suffering followers, which became the cornerstone of Paul's thinking, preaching, and writing, is located in Acts 9:5; 22:8; 26:15.

11. Assuming with most historians and Scripture scholars that Paul wrote his great Letter to the Romans sometime around A.D. 56 or 57, this last segment of his life embraced a span of about ten years.

12. Rom 11:33, NAB.

13. *See* Rom 1:15; 15:22-24, 28-29.

14. This was the route taken by Paul at the end of his second missionary

journey (Acts 18:18-22). Normally, in those days seamen preferred to remain within sight of the coastline, but, fortunately, between Kenkreai and Ephesus, there lay a very convenient string of Greek islands, which made navigation from Greece to Asia Minor relatively safe and swift.

15. *See* Acts 20:3.

16. *See* Acts 20:22-23.

17. For these additions to Paul's group, *see* Acts 20:4-5.

18. Luke uses the expression "breaking bread" as a description of the Eucharist, reflecting the words of institution in 1 Cor 11:24; Mark 14:22; Matt 26:26; Luke 22:19. *See* Acts 2:42; 20:7, 11; and possibly Luke 24:30. It is clear that the Eucharist came to be celebrated on "the first day of the week," (Sunday) as we see here in Acts 20:7 and in 1 Cor 16:2, when the collection is to be taken up. Later, this came to be called the Lord's Day (Rev 1:10). *See* my article "The Lord's Day," NCE 8:990-91.

19. *See* Acts 20:7-12.

20. *See* Acts 20:11.

21. *See* Acts 20:13-17.

22. *See* Acts 20:18-35. Whether Luke somehow recorded Paul's farewell address at Miletus or, as many scholars believe, placed the words in Paul's mouth, rhetorically speaking, it reflects thoughts and concerns found in Paul's letters, those universally accepted as his and the others as well.

23. Acts 20:35. This saying of Jesus is not found in any of the Gospels and indicates the existence of an oral or written collection of Jesus' sayings, represented perhaps by the lost collection commonly called *Q* (for the German word *Quelle*, "source"), which seems to underlie the sayings in common between the Gospels of "Matthew" and Luke but not found in that of Mark.

24. Acts 20:32, NAB.

25. *See* Acts 20:36-38.

26. *See* Acts 21:1. Both Cos and Rhodes were famous islands in the ancient world, the former as the birthplace of the prestigious Greek physician Hippocrates and the location of his great school of medicine, where Luke himself may well have studied and trained; the latter, for its Colossus of Rhodes, a statue of Helios, the sun god, 100 feet high, which straddled the main harbor. Built from 292 to 280 B.C., it was destroyed by an earthquake in 225 B.C., but was still listed among the seven wonders of the ancient world. At another part of the island called Lindus, there is a small inlet that bears the name "Bay of St. Paul." *See* the *New Encyclopedia Brittanica* 10:24-25.

27. *See* Acts 21:2-6. Of ancient Tyre, famous in history and Scripture (e.g., 1 Kgs 5:15-32; Isa 23:1-18; Ezek 26:1-28:19, etc.), there is virtually nothing visible remaining.

28. *See* Acts 21:7-12. In contrast with Tyre, many of the Herodian, Roman, Byzantine, and Crusader ruins of Caesarea Maritima have been excavated and provide an exotic backdrop to the modern seaside resort. Built by Herod the Great in 10 or 9 B.C. to honor Caesar Augustus, his patron, it was a marvel of engineering and architecture, perhaps the finest port on the Mediterranean. With the deposition of Herod's son Archelaus in A.D. 6, Caesarea became the

seat of Roman government in the province of Judea, and there still remains an inscription commemorating the dedication of a building to Tiberius by Pontius Pilate. *See* F. F. Bruce, *Jesus and Paul: Places They Knew* (Nashville: Nelson, 1983) 111–15.

29. *See* Mark 8:31-38; Matt 16:21-28; Luke 9:22-26.

30. Acts 21:13, NAB.

31. *See* Acts 21:17-24.

32. *See* Gal 2:15–3:29; Rom 3:21–4:25.

33. *See* Acts 21:26-29.

34. *See* Acts 21:30-40.

35. *See* Acts 21:40–22:21. Paul is said to have addressed his fellow Jews in Hebrew, but since Hebrew had largely become a dead language in favor of its cousin, Aramaic, he probably spoke in the latter medium. The Qumran (Dead Sea) Scrolls, however, indicate that Hebrew may have been more alive than commonly thought, and, of course, it has again become the official and common language of Israel.

36. *See* Acts 22:22-29.

37. *See* Acts 22:30. On the Sanhedrin, see ch. 1, n. 26.

38. *See* Acts 23:6-9.

39. *See* Acts 23:12-35.

40. *See* Acts 24:1-26.

41. *See* Acts 24:27.

42. *See* Acts 24:23.

43. *See* Acts 25:1-12.

44. Acts 25:13–26:32, NAB.

45. For Luke's thrilling description of the voyage and shipwreck, see Acts 27:1–28:1.

46. *See* Acts 28:11-16.

47. *See* Acts 28:30.

48. *See* Acts 28:16-28.

49. On the authorship of the Captivity Letters, see the next section, "Analysis of Paul's Later Letters." Even if all are Pauline, however, the question remains, From which captivity did Paul write the Captivity Letters? From an assumed captivity in Ephesus (2 Cor 1:8-11)? From his two-year captivity in Caesarea (Acts 23:33–26:32)? Or from his two-year captivity (or house arrest) in Rome (Acts 28:16, 30-31)? An increasing number of Scripture scholars favor the supposed Ephesian captivity, mainly on the grounds of the distances involved. In response to this, I would like to point out that the famous Appian Way ran directly from Rome to Brundisium (Brindisi), whence an easy Adriatic voyage took one to Dyrrhachium in Greece, from which the Egnatian Way ran due east through Philippi to the Aegean port of Neapolis (Kavalla) whence ships traveled regularly to the great city of Ephesus and its environs. Actually in the unlikely event that Paul wrote all the Captivity Letters at about the same time in his Roman "house arrest," he could have had them all delivered by the same messengers, presumably Tychicus and Onesimus (Col 4:7-9; Eph 6:21; Phlm 12), who would have stopped at Philippi anyway.

50. My substitution here of the name Laodicea for that of Ephesus will be explained in the "Analysis," which follows.

51. *See* Phil 4:15-20.

52. *See* Acts 20:33-35; 1 Cor 9:1-18; Phil 4:10-13.

53. Phil 4:1, WFD.

54. *See* Phil 3:4-16.

55. Phil 1:21, WFD.

56. *See* Phlm 10--20.

57. *See* Phlm 1-3.

58. On the work of others, especially Epaphras in Asia outside of Ephesus, *see* Col 1:4, 7-8; 2:1-3; Eph 1:15-17.

59. *See* the parable of the weeds in Matt 13:24-30.

60. The word "syncretism," which seems originally to have meant "a federation of Cretan cities," came to designate "the combination of different forms of belief or practice." See *Webster's Ninth New Collegiate Dictionary*.

61. The Greek emphasis on knowledge (*gnôsis*) and wisdom (*sophía*) had a profound influence on Hellenistic Judaism, incipient Gnosticism, and even Christianity itself (1 Cor 1:17-2:16). This emphasis is symbolized by the inscription on the Athenian treasury at Delphi, GNOTHI SAUTON (know thyself). For the mystery religions, for example, those of Eleusis, Dionysus, and Orpheus, *see* Edwin Yamauchi, *Harper's World of the New Testament* (New York: Harper & Row, 1981) 34--37.

62. Hellenistic Judaism, exemplified by Philo of Alexandria, attempted a union between Jewish wisdom as found in the Bible and Greek philosophy, developing a system of allegorical interpretation of the Scriptures that may have provided part of the origins of Jewish Gnosticism. *See* Edwin Yamauchi, *Pre-Christian Gnosticism* (Grand Rapids: Eerdmans, 1973) 143-62. *See also* other works on Gnosticism in n. 64 below.

63. Among Eastern religions, the most influential seem to have been those of Cybele and Artemis of Asia Minor, Isis and Serapis of Egypt, Adonis and Atargatis of Phoenicia and Syria, Mazdaism, Mithraism, and Manicheism of Persia. *See* Yamauchi, *Harper's World of the New Testament*, 55-63.

64. Gnosticism, as represented in the Nag Hammadi (Chenoboskion) writings, discovered in Egypt in 1945, two years before the Dead Sea Scrolls, was not a truly organized movement until the second century A.D. However, it is commonly believed today that the roots of Gnosticism predate Christianity, and it was probably against inroads of this incipient Gnosticism as well as other forms of syncretism that Paul wrote Colossians and "Ephesians."

Some of the Gnostic tendencies that may have invaded and confused the Christians of the province of Asia are these: (1) the enticement of (secret) knowledge (*gnôsis*) rather than faith as the basic condition of salvation; (2) the dualistic antagonism between spirit and matter leading some to hyperasceticism and others to unbridled license; (3) the cosmic view of an infinite series of emanations from God, called collectively the "fullness of God" (*plêrōma toû theoû*), consisting of demigods or demiurges or angels or even all of us if we have the knowledge (*gnôsis*), like Christ and other elite persons, to truly "know ourselves."

Besides the work on Gnosticism already mentioned, see also *The Nag Hammadi Library in English,* trans. James M. Robinson, (New York: Harper & Row, 1977); Kurt Rudolf, *Gnosis: The Nature & History of Gnosticism,* trans. Robert Wilson (New York: Harper & Row, 1987); George W. McRae, *Studies in the New Testament and Gnosticism* (Wilmington, Del.: Michael Glazier, 1987).

65. For Paul's teaching on Christ as the fullness of God and Lord of the universe, *see* Col 1:15-20; 2:9-10.

66. For Paul's teaching on the Church as the fullness of Christ as well as his body of which he is the head, *see* Col 1:18; 2:10; Eph 1:22-23; 5:22-33.

67. *See* 1 Tim 1:3; Titus 3:12.

68. *See* Rom 15:24, 28.

69. Paul's concern with preservation of what had been accomplished explains why his Captivity and Pastoral Letters have a more conservative flavor than his earlier letters.

70. *See* 1 Timothy and Titus.

71. *See* Col 1:24.

72. *See* Phil 1:21.

73. *See* Phil 2:19-22; 2 Tim 1:2, 5.

74. *See* 2 Tim 4:9, 13, 21.

75. *See* 2 Tim 4:13. Paul's cloak (*phailónēs*) was most probably one of those sturdy mantles of Cilician goathair (the same as used in tents) which were highly prized for being virtually impervious to cold and dampness. It is not farfetched, in fact, to imagine that he had personally woven the cloth and perhaps even fashioned the cloak.

The scrolls (*biblía*) and especially the parchments (*membránai*) refer to written works, possibly biblical, and writing materials. Parchment, made from stretched and smoothed animal skins, was invented at Pergamum in the second century B.C., when papyrus was no longer exported to that city by Egypt, allegedly to prevent the library at Pergamum from surpassing that of Alexandria. The word itself comes from *pergaménē* through French, *parchemin.*

76. *See* 2 Tim 4:11.

77. Peter, James, and John. *See* Mark 14:33; Matt 26:37.

78. *See* John 19:25-27.

79. *See* 2 Tim 4:7.

80. This indication of the year of Paul's martyrdom is provided both by Eusebius and Jerome, quoted in Giuseppe Ricciotti, *Paul the Apostle,* trans. Alba Zizzamia (Milwaukee, Bruce, 1953) 501.

81. Acts 7:59-60, NAB.

82. *See* Ricciotti, *Paul the Apostle,* 504.

83. This is the Vulgate translation of Phil 1:21.

84. It is quite possible that Philippians, like 2 Corinthians, is a conflation of two or three Pauline letters, put together after his death.

85. The study of the personal names of Paul's friends in his later letters and in his entourage in Acts 20:4-6 is quite interesting and instructive. Numerically, for example, there are twenty-two names in 2 Timothy, eleven in Colossians, ten in Philemon, eight in Acts 20:4-6, five in Titus, three in Philip-

pians and 1 Timothy, and only one in "Ephesians." This in itself does not argue for or against Pauline authorship, but it does cast doubt on the identification of the addressees in "Ephesians," for Paul had spent three years there (Acts 20:31) and surely would have had greetings for a number of friends.

Taking the largest collections of names in probable chronological order (Acts 20:4-6; Philemon; Colossians; and 2 Timothy), we find Timothy and Luke in all four (one of Luke's "we sections" begins at 20:5); Aristarchus in the first three; Mark and Demas in the last three; Tychicus in the first, third, and fourth; Trophimus in the first and last; and finally Archippus, Epaphras, and Onesimus in the second and third. To me, the large number of the identical names showing up in Acts, Philemon (accepted by all as authentically Pauline), Colossians (doubtfully Pauline in the minds of many), and 2 Timothy (rejected as Pauline by many if not most) clearly indicates more in common among these letters than admitted by many. And notice that I have not even touched on names that appear in these lists but are well known elsewhere, for example Aquila and Priscilla, who appear in Acts 18:2, 18, 26 as well as 1 Cor 16:19; Rom 16:3; 2 Tim 4:19.

Add to the above the incidence of the names of Clement in Phil 4:3 and Linus in 2 Tim 4:21, both of whom lived in Rome and (along with Cletus) succeeded Peter as bishops of Rome and visible heads of the Church, and the argument for a Roman provenance of these letters grows stronger.

86. *See* nn. 49 and 85 above about the distances and names involved respectively in these letters.

87. *See* n. 86 above.

88. Phil 1:1. Paul's salutation to the "overseers and deacons" (*epískopoi kaì diákonoi*) reflects the fact that there was not yet a distinction between overseers (bishops) and priests (*presbýteroi*, literally, "elders"), and that lack of distinction remained until the *Letters* of Ignatius of Antioch early in the following century. We will return to this point when discussing the Pastoral Letters.

89. *See* especially Phil 1:7-8, NAB: "It is right that I should think this way about all of you, because I hold you in my heart, you who are all partners with me in grace, both in my imprisonment and in the defense and confirmation of the gospel. For God is my witness, how I long for all of you with the affection of Christ Jesus." Note also that, in this letter, which all recognize as genuinely Pauline and many locate early in Paul's life, he is already thinking and speaking in fairly conservative terms, for example, "the defense and confirmation of the gospel."

90. It is in this section in Phil 1:21 that we encounter that revealing statement of Paul's that provides our basic biblical key to this study of Paul's later letters.

91. In Phil 2:5-11 we find the famous *Carmen Christi*, the "Hymn of Christ," which, whether original with Paul or borrowed, admirably summarizes the incarnation, sufferings, death, and exaltation of Jesus Christ. *See* my own translation of this remarkable hymn in ch. 1 in my reflection about humility as the first quality of Paul's ministry.

92. In Phil 3:10-14, REB, within Paul's defense against the Judaizers, which

may be all or part of an earlier letter, we encounter that thrilling self-revelation of Paul. The REB translation that I am using here is admittedly more free than I normally like, but it is thoroughly alive. Having described his former Pharisaic righteousness and then having expressed his rejection of it in favor of the holiness of Christ achieved by faith, he goes on as follows: ''My one desire is to know Christ and the power of his resurrection, and to share his sufferings in growing conformity with his death, in the hope of somehow attaining the resurrection from the dead.

''It is not that I have already achieved this. I have not yet reached perfection, but I press on, hoping to take hold of that for which Christ once took hold of me. My friends, I do not claim to have hold of it yet. What I do say is this: forgetting what is behind and straining towards what lies ahead, I press towards the finishing line, to win the heavenly prize to which God has called me in Christ Jesus.''

93. Accepting the Pauline authorship of Colossians and ''Ephesians,'' both for positive and negative reasons already presented, the very content of the letters, responding to an apparent syncretistic and especially Gnostic threat to these Churches, suggests their having been written later in Paul's life, as would be the case in his first Roman confinement.

94. *See* Col 1:4, 7-8; 2:1-3; Eph 1:15-17; Phlm 23.

95. The expression ''in Ephesus'' (*en Ephésō*), is placed in brackets in the United Bible Society's excellent edition of *The Greek New Testament*, indicating that it is at best doubtfully original for the simple reason that it is missing from some of the most important early manuscripts, including the *Chester Beatty papyrus P46*, dating to A.D. 200 and the original, uncorrected *Codex Vaticanus* and *Codex Sinaiticus*, both from the fourth century and considered the two most reliable uncial (capital letter) manuscripts in existence.

96. The most probable reasons why a letter addressed to the Laodiceans might be changed to one addressed to the Ephesians are: (1) a negative one, that Laodicea was considered disgraced by what was later written in the letter sent to that Church in Rev 3:14-19; and (2) a positive one, namely that Ephesus, the capital of the Roman province of Asia and one of the four great cities of the ancient world, was also a great Christian center from Paul's three years of evangelization there and hence deserving, especially in the minds of Ephesians, of a special letter from Paul. As mentioned earlier, however, the utter lack of any greetings to friends there in itself casts suspicion on the alleged address of the letter.

97. For an explanation of syncretism and Gnosticism, *see* nn. 60–64 above.

98. For the ''Hymn of the Cosmic Christ,'' *see* Col 1:15-20. We will examine this hymn more closely in the reflections.

99. For the ''Blessing Hymn of Christian Destiny'' (my own title), *see* Eph 1:3-14. It is interesting to compare this hymn with *berakoth*, or blessing hymns in Jewish rituals, as well as with the blessing hymn in 1 Pet 1:3-12. This blessing hymn of Paul's we will also consider when we come to the reflections.

100. It is in this section, specifically in Eph 5:22-33, that Paul gives us that magnificent parallel between the union of a husband and his wife and that

of Christ and his Church. However, one does not appreciate the full force of the comparison without advertence to the story of Adam and Eve in Gen 2:18-24, where Eve is not only the wife but the very body of Adam. So the Church is at once the bride and the body of Christ.

The same can be said of the husband and wife in Christian marriage. However, Paul's directive to wives to be subordinate or submissive to their husbands should not be interpreted in any slavish fashion. One should bear in mind not only the different cultural situation of his time but also the meaning of the verb used here, namely *hypotássomai*, which means "I defer to another for the sake of good order" (*táxis*, "order," from *tásso*, "I order, arrange"). This is confirmed by the preceding verse, Eph 5:21, in which Paul urges everyone to "defer to one another out of fear of (or reverence for) Christ."

101. The centrality of Philippi, its convenience because of the Egnatian Way, its comparative calm and freedom from harrassment, as well as its general proximity to Nicopolis on the Adriatic coast, where Paul plans to spend the winter (Titus 3:12), all seem to point to that Roman colony as the place where Paul wrote 1 Timothy and Titus, but this is only an educated guess, for nothing is clearly stated.

102. The entire tenor of 2 Timothy, especially of Paul's report of his first trial, of his loneliness, of his urgent request for Timothy to join him, and, above all, of his conviction that his "race" is over, his "fight" won in 2 Tim 4:6-8, indicates his final Roman imprisonment as the time when Paul wrote his final letter.

103. 1 Tim 3:15. As mentioned before, a conservative view of the Church such as this is quite understandable in Paul's final years, when evangelization was yielding to preservation of what had been accomplished.

104. One of the main arguments for discounting the Pauline authorship of the Pastorals is that the idea of faith in these letters seems to have departed from *pístis* (faith) as the condition of justification to *hē pístis* (the faith) as a deposit of truths and beliefs. Admittedly, the author certainly does employ the second usage, for example, in his famous declaration, "I have kept the faith!" (2 Tim 4:7), but a careful study of the Pastorals easily reveals the use of both important concepts, which would be compatible with the time of life in which Paul was writing (see 2 Tim 3:15).

105. Another contention is that the Pastoral Letters contain "creeds," such as in 1 Tim 2:5-6; 3:16; Titus 3:4-7; and possibly 2 Tim 2:11-13, but this argument seems to fall of its own weight when we consider the "Hymn of Christ" in Phil 2:5-11, which is clearly more creedal than the rest.

106. Another very common argument against Pauline authorship of the Pastorals is that a distinction is already made between *epískopoi* (overseers, bishops) and *presbýteroi* (elders, priests), as seen in a comparison of 1 Tim 3:1-7 and 1 Tim 5:17-22. However, in Titus 1:5-7, the two terms are obviously used interchangeably. To me, the explanation is that in 1 Timothy, they are also used interchangeably, and that, in the second instance, Paul is emphasizing the support that *epískopoi-presbýteroi* should receive and the care Timothy should take in appointing them. Frankly, it has always sounded less ambitious to me

and more in keeping with Paul's thought to translate 1 Tim 3:1, "Whoever desires the office of priest desires a noble task."

107. It is conjectured by some that the word *gynaîkes* (women), used here in 1 Tim 3:11 in the midst of instructions about deacons (diákonoi), must refer either to deaconesses or the wives of deacons. Either possibility is valid, but the former is more likely. And as discussed before regarding Rom 16:1, it is not clear just what the status and role of a deaconess was in the early Church.

108. Paul's statement about "handing over to Satan" in 1 Tim 1:20 is certainly reminiscent of his similar declaration regarding the incestuous man in 1 Cor 5:5-6. In both instances the reference is to excommunication from the community rather than physical death, as some maintain.

109. 1 Tim 5:23, NAB.

110. Another such expression, by way of example is that in 2 Tim 1:4-5, NAB: "I yearn to see you again, recalling your tears, so that I may be filled with joy, as I recall your sincere faith that first lived in your grandmother Lois and in your mother Eunice and that I am confident lives also in you." *See also* Paul's reference in 2 Tim 3:10-11 to his persecutions at Antioch (in Pisidia), Iconium, and Lystra, with which we are also familiar from Acts 13:13-14:20.

111. For example, it is my observation that in seminaries the Pastorals are often not included in the course on the writings of Paul, and for that reason they are sometimes not taught at all, thereby neglecting a very important source of instruction about ministry, which is exactly what the seminarians are supposed to be preparing for.

112. In this section, precisely in 2 Tim 3:14-4:5, NAB, Paul presents unforgettable directives to Timothy about the importance of the Sacred Scriptures and the duty of preaching the word of God: "But you, remain faithful to what you have learned and believed, because you know from whom you have learned it, and that from infancy you have known [the] sacred scriptures, which are capable of giving you wisdom for salvation through faith in Christ Jesus. All scripture is inspired by God and is useful for teaching, for refutation, for correction, and for training in righteousness, so that one who belongs to God may be competent, equipped for every good work.

"I charge you in the presence of God and of Christ Jesus, who will judge the living and the dead, and by his appearing and his kingly power: proclaim the word; be persistent whether it is convenient or inconvenient; convince, reprimand, encourage through all patience and teaching. For the time will come when people will not tolerate sound doctrine, . . . but you, be self-possessed in all circumstances; put up with hardship; perform the work of an evangelist; fulfill your ministry."

113. *See* n. 98 above.

114. *See* n. 99 above.

115. *See* ch. 1, n. 117.

116. 597–538 B.C. See *NJBC*, art. 75, pp. 1236–37.

117. *See* Ezekiel's vision of Yahweh on the cherubim in Ezek 1, 10, 43.

118. In spite of Solomon's declaration in 1 Kgs 8:27, NAB, "If the heavens and the highest heavens cannot contain you, how much less this temple which I have built!"

119. Deutero-Isaiah is the name usually given the anonymous prophet who prophesied in the spirit of Isaiah, but over a hundred years after him. His prophecy begins with Isa 40, which provides a good example of his universalism.

120. Unfortunately, Israel's new reverence for Yahweh went to the extreme of regarding him at such a distance that his sacred name, Yahweh, was no longer pronounced, the word for Lord, *adonah*, being substituted instead. Sadly, some Christian translators combined the two words into the nonword "Jehovah.") Another development was that of a complex and pervasive angelology, which (at least among some Jews) may have evolved into Jewish Gnosticism.

121. This is the so-called Hebrew tetragrammaton (four letters), namely *yod, heth, waw, heth*, written, of course, from right to left, as in Oriental languages generally.

122. Exod 19:5.

123. Compare the reference to eagle wings in Exod 19:4 with Deut 32:11, NAB: ''As an eagle incites its nestlings forth by hovering over its brood, so he spread his wings to receive them and bore them up on his pinions.''

124. Compare Exod 19:5, ''though all the earth is mine,'' with the Priestly creation account in Gen 1.

125. *See* the use of ''Babylon'' for Rome in 1 Pet 5:13.

126. *See*, for example, Acts 13:16-41; 22:1-21; 26:2-23; Rom 9-11.

127. *See*, for example, 1 Thess 1:10; 1 Cor 1:9; 2 Cor 1:19; Gal 1:16; 2:20; 3:26; 4:4, 6; Rom 1:3, 9; 5:10; 8:3, 29, 32.

128. *See*, for example, Acts 9:5; 22:8; 26:15; 1 Cor 6:15; 12:12-31; Rom 12:3-8; plus the many instances of Paul's expression ''in Christ'' some 164 times, according to A. Wikenhauser, *Pauline Mysticism: Christ in the Mystical Teaching of St. Paul* (New York: Herder & Herder, 1960) 21–22; regarding Christ in Christians, *see* for example, in 2 Cor 13:5; Gal 4:19, Col 1:27.

129. *See* for example, 2 Cor 13:3; Gal 2:19-20; Phil 1:20; 3:7-14.

130. *See* n. 64 above.

131. *See* especially Prov 8:22-36; Wis 7:24-8:1; Sir 24:1-31.

132. The noun *eikōn*, from which is derived ''icon,'' denotes here not just a similarity or representation but an exact likeness, a ''carbon copy,'' of the Father. This is confirmed by Col 2:9, WFD, ''For in him dwells all the fullness of the deity bodily.''

133. The reference here is to creation, not just as something accomplished in the past, an event over and done with, but as something still continuing until the end of time. This is clearly indicated by the use of the perfect tense in Col 1:16, *éktistai* (have been created), as well as in Col 1:17, *synéstēken* (have held together). Note that in Greek the perfect tense designates an action or a state that began in the past but continues in the present.

134. That Christ, by his death and resurrection, is the Redeemer and Lord of the cosmos is clear from Col 1:18: ''. . . the firstborn *prōtótokos* from the dead, that in all things he himself might hold the primacy [be preeminent].'' Bear in mind all the ancient privileges of the firstborn son, who held a natural

place of honor and succession to authority in the family, who had the right to a double inheritance, and who was specially consecrated to Yahweh because of being spared during the tenth plague in Egypt. *See*, for example, Gen 25:13; Exod 13:1-16; Deut 21:15-17; Luke 2:6, 22-24; 1 Cor 15:20; Rom 8:29; Rev. 1:5.

135. That Jesus was and is the purpose of creation seems clear from a proper translation of Col 1:16, "All things have been created through him and *eis autòn* (into, unto, or for him)."

136. Cf. the prologue of John's Gospel.

137. Cf. John's prologue, but note the additional idea of Christ's superiority over all forms of spiritual beings, such as angels or demigods.

138. The expression *prò pántōn* (before all things) is temporal. Christ pre-existed all things. Compare with John the Baptist's statement in John 1:30, WFD: "This is he of whom I said, 'After me comes a man who has taken his place ahead of me because he existed before me.' "

139. Many scholars feel that the statement about Christ's headship of his body the Church in Col 1:18a is out of place here and probably interpolated, but this theory is not supported by the manuscript evidence, and indeed the expression is not incongruous with what follows.

Note in Col 1:19 that far from Jesus' being part of the *plērōma*, or fullness, all the fullness dwells in him! Also, regarding reconciliation in Col 1:20, compare this with Paul's description of his ministry of reconciliation in 2 Cor 5:11-21, and with recapitulation in Eph 1:10.

140. The reference here is to the creation of the first humans "in the divine image." If this is true of humans generally, how much more so of Christ, the God-man, uncreated in his divine person and nature, created perfect in his human nature.

141. To underline the remarkable comparison between the personified portrait of divine wisdom in Wis 7:25-26, NAB, and the description of incarnate wisdom in our "Hymn of the Cosmic Christ," I am taking the liberty of changing the feminine gender of "*sophía* (wisdom) to the masculine of Jesus Christ, as follows: "For he is an aura of the might of God / and a pure effusion of the glory of the Almighty; / therefore nought that is sullied enters into him. / For he is the refulgence of eternal light, the spotless mirror of the power of God, / the image of his goodness."

142. Here again, this description of personified wisdom in Prov 8:22-31 is in the feminine gender because the Hebrew word for wisdom, *hochmah*, like the Greek word *sophía*, is feminine. For this reason, this passage, like the previous one from Wisdom, is sometimes used of Mary, the mother of Jesus, but there is no scriptural basis for this. It should be noted that I have not made any reference to the description of personified wisdom in Sir 24 for the simple reason that there divine wisdom is portrayed far more exclusively, being largely confined to Israelite wisdom and especially the Torah, or Law.

143. This mysterious passage in the midst of Paul's portrayal of life in the Spirit is clearly a favorite of Pierre Teilhard de Chardin in his vision of all creation in evolution and seeking ultimate redemption in Christ, the "Omega

Point'' of all creation. For a readable resumé of Teilhard's often abstruse theories, I recommend the following books: Christopher Mooney, *Teilhard de Chardin and the Mystery of Christ* (Garden City, N.Y.: Doubleday, 1968); George Maloney, *The Cosmic Christ: From Paul to Teilhard* (New York: Sheed & Ward, 1968); Robert Hale, *Christ and the Universe: Teilhard de Chardin and the Cosmos* (Chicago; Franciscan Herald, 1972).

144. In these passages, particularly 1 Cor 12, Paul uses the analogy of the body, including the head, to inculcate humility, love, and unity in the use of charismatic gifts, but from there it was a natural progression to regarding Christ as head of his body the Church in terms of primacy.

145. *See* ch. 1, Reflections, part 3.

146. *See* ch. 2, Reflections, part 2.

147. I refer to those as ''Creedal Hymns'' because they seem to be written in the form of early creeds or professions of faith about Jesus Christ and may well not have been written by Paul. To these may be added the hymns of Titus 3:4-8 and 2 Tim 2:11-13, both of which are designated as ''trustworthy sayings.''

148. Pierre Teilhard de Chardin (1881–1955), mentioned here and in n. 143 above, is the famous Jesuit priest, anthropologist, philosopher, theologian, spiritual writer, mystic, poet, and man of vision whose theories and books have caused such a stir in Catholic circles and beyond. In addition to the works about him listed above in n. 143, some of his own more notable works, published posthumously like all his writings, are *The Phenomenon of Man, The Future of Man, The Divine Milieu,* and *The Hymn of the Universe,* all published in New York by Harper & Row in 1959, 1960, 1964, and 1965, respectively.

149. The principal sources of Teilhard's thought in Paul are Rom 8:19-23, Col 1:15-20, and Eph 1:3-12.

150. The principal sources of Teilhard's thought in John are the prologue to his Gospel and his Apocalypse.

151. In Luke 4:16-30, we see the Jews' reaction to Jesus' messianic claim, and in Jesus' ''trial'' before the Sanhedrin (Mark 14:60-64; Matt 26:63-66; Luke 22:66-71) we see the reaction of their religious leaders to Jesus' claims as Messiah and Son of God. I have not included the many reactions in John's Gospel because, as we will see, John's Gospel is written in a very different way.

152. See John Donne, *Devotions* (Ann Arbor, Mich.: University of Michigan Press, 1960) 108.

153. ''Hominization'' and ''Christification'' are favorite terms of Teilhard de Chardin, indicating two stages in upward evolution, first the humanizing of the world and then its transformation into Christ, its ''Omega Point,'' or final end and purpose. Unfortunately, with our free will, we humans seem to be opting for returning to a more primitive and bestial level, as evidenced by the little regard for life, the substitution of lust for love, and other aberrations.

154. ''Victimless crime'' is a common expression today, indicating a transgression of the law or of morality in which ''no one is hurt,'' as in the common case of ''two consenting adults'' engaged in premarital or extramarital sexual acts.

155. Some are called to ''flee the world'' for their own salvation and for the

good of others, but the vast majority are called to live, work, and achieve salvation and sanctification in the world, at the same time working for the salvation and sanctification of the world.

156. Luke 5:4.

157. *See* Max Ehrman, *Desiderata: Found in Old St. Paul's Church, Baltimore, dated 1692* (Boston: Crescendo Publishing Company, 1954).

158. *See* Rev. 1:8. Since alpha and omega are the first and last letters of the Greek alphabet, this is an apt way of describing Jesus as the beginning and end of all.

159. *See* the summary of incipient Gnosticism in n. 64 above.

160. This is reflected in the "Hymn of the Cosmic Christ" by the listing in Col 1:16 of "thrones and denominations, principalities and powers."

161. Obviously, considering Christ as only part of the *plērōma*, or fullness, of the universe was nothing less than a denial of his essential uniqueness and greatness, as emphasized in the "Hymn of the Cosmic Christ."

162. Besides the "Hymn of the Cosmic Christ," this truth is also crystal clear in Col 2:9, NAB: "For in him dwells the whole fullness of the deity bodily!"

163. The Greek word *ekklesía* is a composite of the little preposition, *ek* (out, out of), and the verb *kaléō* (I call), hence it refers to the Israelites called out of Egypt to be God's own people at Mount Sinai.

164. Qahal is the Hebrew word for the assembly of God's people in the desert. When the Hebrew Bible was translated into Greek in what is known as the Septuagint (LXX) version about two centuries before Christ, the word *ekklēsía* was chosen over all others to translate *qahal*.

165. Whether Jesus himself ever used either *qahal* or *ekklēsía* in Matt 16:18 or 18:17 is debatable. It is quite possible that he employed the Hebrew and Aramaic term *malkuth* (kingdom), of which the Greek equivalent would be *basileía*. But at any rate, the early Church providentially chose to continue the Septuagint tradition by employing *ekklēsía* (called out) as the most appropriate description of Christ's followers, called out of every nation to be God's new chosen people according to the new covenant inaugurated at the Last Supper.

166. Paul's Letter to the "Ephesians" is commonly referred to as his ecclesial letter just as the Gospel according to "Matthew" is commonly designated the ecclesial gospel.

Of Paul's other later letters, the ones that would best qualify as "ecclesial" would be his Pastoral Letters, especially 1 Timothy, which in 3:15, WFD, refers to "the Church of the living God" not only as the "house of God" very much as in Eph 2:19, but also as "the pillar and foundation of the truth." To some, this static picture of the Church seems very un-Pauline, but in these final years of his life, it is understandable that he would be conservative, seeking to preserve all that he had built.

167. See Warren Dicharry, *To Live the Word, Inspired and Incarnate* (Staten Island, N.Y.: Alba, 1985) 388.

168. The documents of the Second Vatican Council that in particular redefine the role of the laity in the Church are the Decree on the Apostolate of

Lay People and the Pastoral Constitution on the Church in the Modern World. *See* Austin Flannery, ed. *Vatican Council II: The Conciliar and Post Conciliar Documents* (Northport, N.Y.: Costello, 1975) 766–98 and 903–1014.

169. *See* John 10:1-18; 21:15-19; Acts 20:28; 1 Pet 5:1-4.

170. It is true that this analogy is found in the moral section of "Ephesians," where Paul is promoting domestic harmony, but it obviously ends with special emphasis on the union of Christ and the Church, as we see in Eph 5:32.

171. *See* Gen 2:18-25.

172. *See* Hos 1-3; Isa 54:4-8; 62:4-5; Jer 2:2; 3:20; Ezek 16 and 23.

173. Before leaving Paul's marriage analogy of the union of Christ and his Church in Eph 5:21-33, I would like to make two observations: (1) Paul is in no way demanding servile submission of a wife to her husband; the verb used is *hypotássomai* (from *tássō*, I order or arrange), meaning "I defer for the sake of good order." Note that in Eph 5:21, all are urged to "defer to one another for the sake of good order," the same verb, *hypotássomai* being used. (2) How can the portrait of the Church here as one "without spot or wrinkle or any such thing" (Eph 5:27) be reconciled with the picture of the Church in Matt 13:24-30 and Matt 18:6-9, both of which predict a Church of sinners as well as saints? To me, the answer is that in "Ephesians" Paul is portraying what Christ desires the Church to be, as indicated by the use of the conjunction *hína* (so that, in order that) in Eph 5:26-27.

174. Compare Paul's "Blessing Hymn" here with the *berakoth* (blessing hymns) of Jewish worship. Note, for example, how we Christians ask God to bless us or others, but Jews tend to bless God. *See Jewish Encyclopedia* (New York: Funk & Wagnalls, 1916) 3:47–50.

175. This expression, "the praise of his glory," which occurs twice in Paul's "Blessing Hymn" is obviously one of special significance as a kind of epitome of the entire hymn. It was adopted by St. Elizabeth of the Trinity as her spiritual self-identification. *See*, for example, Jean Lafrance, *Elizabeth of the Trinity: The Charism of Her Prayer* (Bangalore, India: Asian Trading Co., 1987) 68.

176. *See*, for example, Eph 3:14-21; 5:1-2, 25-29.

177. *See*, for example, Eph 1:15-2:22; 3:14-4:24.

178. *See*, for example, Eph 4:25-6:9.

179. "Flesh" is expressed by the Hebrew *bashar* and the Greek *sárx*.

180. "Spirit" is expressed by the Hebrew *rhuah* and the Greek *pneûma*. The same words also mean "breath" and "wind."

181. "Person" is expressed by the Hebrew *nephesh*, but since the Greek terms for "person" are entirely too abstract, the Hebrew word is normally represented in Greek either by *sôma* (body) or by *psychē* (soul), depending on the context and emphasis. Hence, the words "body" and "soul" in English translations may refer to the whole person.

182. *See* Paul's description of this struggle between the spirit and the flesh in Gal 5:16-26 and Rom 8:1-13.

183. Paul's teaching on bodily resurrection is found primarily in 1 Cor:15 and 2 Cor 5:1-10. In regard to resurrection at the time of death, it is significant that Paul in 1 Cor 15:25-58 uses analogies, such as that of a seed, which apply

more aptly to immediate than to endtime resurrection. So with Paul's analogy of the old and new tents in 2 Cor 5:1-10, representing old and new bodies, with the implication that the latter will replace the former at death with no lapse of time.

184. Happily, the Church has changed from a gloom-filled, black-robed, *Dies irae* (day of wrath) funeral service to a joyous celebration of resurrection, Christ's and our own, as symbolized by the paschal candle, white vestments and pall, resurrection music, etc.

185. One of the outstanding champions of resurrection at death is Ladislaus Boros, whom I quote extensively in my book *To Live the Word*, app. A, 404–5. *See* Ladislaus Boros, *Living in Hope: Future Perspectives in Christian Thought*, trans. W. J. O'Hara (Garden City, N.Y.: Doubleday, 1973) 37–39. Another writer cited is Eduard Schweizer, *Psyché* in Kittel, ed. *Theological Dictionary of the New Testament*, 9:656. To these, I would like to add the additional testimony of F. F. Bruce, one of the most respected moderate Scripture scholars, in his article "The Idea of Immortality in Paul," included in Michael Taylor, ed., *A Companion to Paul: Readings in Pauline Theology* (Staten Island, N.Y.: Alba, 1975) 130–34.

186. *See* my treatment of this question in *To Live the Word*, app. A, 407.

187. Interestingly, references to an afterlife appear only in Israel's late writings, but they do appear in all three kinds of literature, (1) historical: 2 Macc 7 and 12:38-46; (2) prophetic: Dan 12:1-4 (actually an apocalyptic book); and (3) wisdom: Wis 3–4.

188. Identification of the Beloved Disciple with John the apostle and evangelist is not accepted by all scholars, but the truth remains that this beautiful description does not fit anyone else quite as well as it does John.

189. *See* John 13:23.

190. *See* John 19:25-27.

191. Because of the tradition of Johannine authorship, whose pros and cons we will examine in our next and final study, The Apocalypse, or Book of Revelation, will constitute the final study of this work.

192. The eagle is one of the "four living creatures" of Rev 4:6-10, which in turn recall the "four living creatures," each with four faces, in Ezek 1:5-28. In both of those references, the "four living creatures" apparently represent all of living creation: humans, wild animals, domesticated animals, and birds. However, the Fathers of the Church, following Irenaeus in the second century, saw in these mysterious figures appropriate symbols of the four evangelists: the lion for Mark, who begins his Gospel with the voice of the Baptist roaring (*boôntos*) in the desert; the human for Matthew, who commences his Gospel with Jesus' human genealogy; the ox for Luke, whose Gospel opens at the Temple, where oxen and other animals were sacrificed; and the eagle for John, who, in his highly mystical Gospel and Letters and his mysterious Apocalypse, seems to soar higher and farther than the other evangelists. *See* Irenaeus, *Against Heresies*, bk. 3, ch. 11, par. 8, in *The Ante-Nicene Fathers*, ed. Alexander Roberts and Joseph Donaldson (New York: Charles Scribner's Sons, 1926) 1:428–29.

RECOMMENDED READING LIST

Cerfaux, Lucien. *The Spiritual Journey of Saint Paul*. New York: Sheed & Ward, 1968.

Grant, Michael. *Saint Paul*. Charles Scribner's Sons, 1976.

Hagner, Donald, and Murray Harris, eds. *Pauline Studies: Essays Honoring F. F. Bruce*. Grand Rapids: Eerdmans, 1980.

Schillebeeckx, Edward. *Paul the Apostle*. New York: Crossroad, 1983.

Wikenhauser, Alfred. *Pauline Mysticism: Christ in the Mystical Teaching of St. Paul*. New York: Herder and Herder, 1960. (Older than usually recommended, but a classic.)

QUESTIONS FOR REFLECTION AND DISCUSSION

1. Which are the seven later letters (excluding Hebrews) traditionally attributed to Paul, and what seem to have been the circumstances of their writing?

2. What are your own personal preferences among Paul's later letters, and why?

3. In which letter and in what terms does Paul describe the ''cosmic Christ,'' and how has this description influenced later thought?

4. In which letter and in what terms does Paul describe the Church as the ''fullness of Christ,'' and how has this description influenced later thought?

5. Does Paul give us any indication, in earlier or later letters, of his beliefs regarding the nature and time of our bodily resurrection?

EPHESUS IN THE FIRST CENTURY A.D.

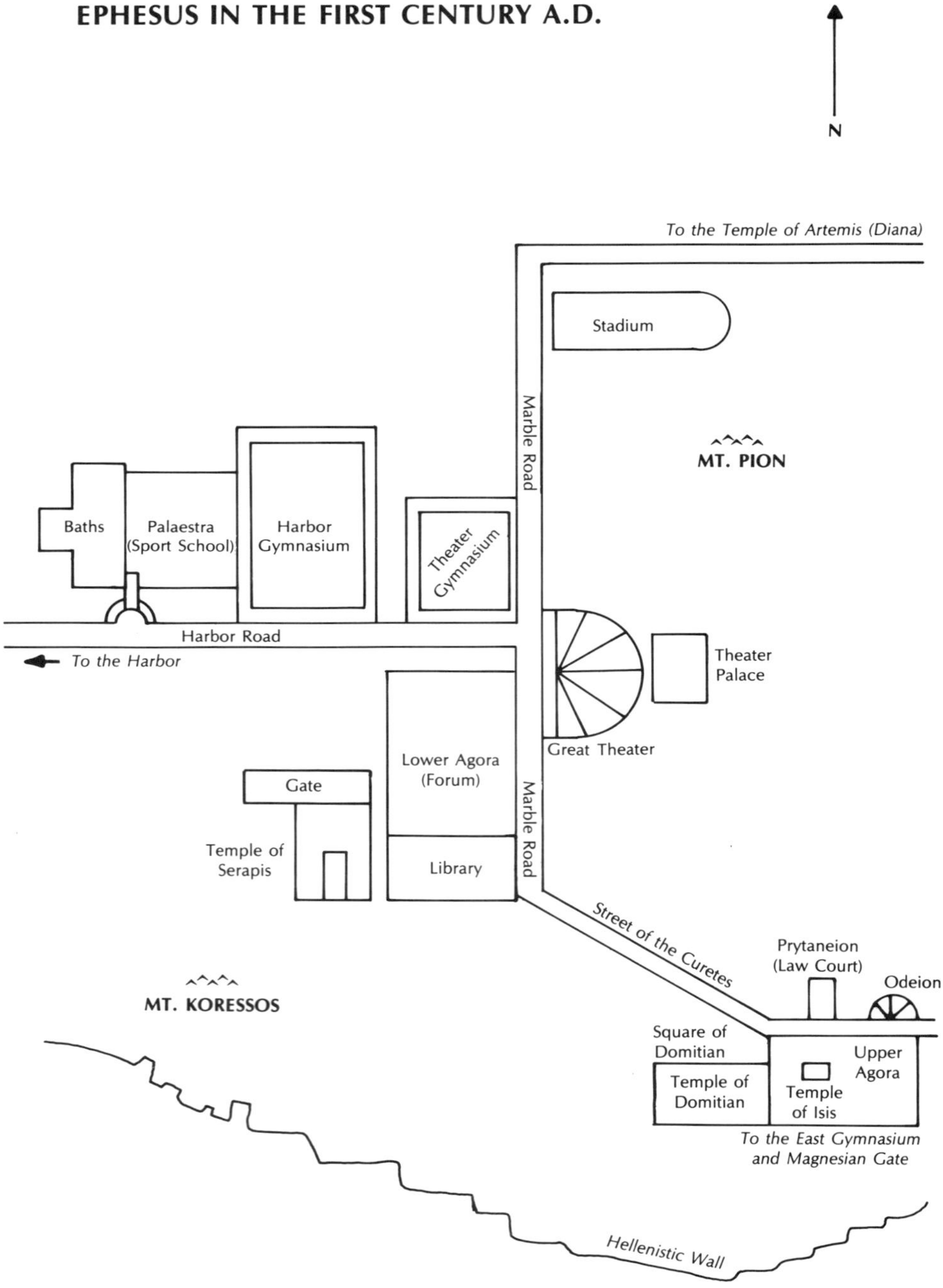

N

To the Temple of Artemis (Diana)

Stadium

Marble Road

MT. PION

Baths

Palaestra
(Sport School)

Harbor
Gymnasium

Theater
Gymnasium

Theater
Palace

Harbor Road

To the Harbor

Great Theater

Lower Agora
(Forum)

Gate

Marble Road

Temple of
Serapis

Library

Street of the Curetes

Prytaneion
(Law Court)

Odeion

MT. KORESSOS

Square of
Domitian

Upper
Agora

Temple of
Domitian

Temple
of Isis

To the East Gymnasium
and Magnesian Gate

Hellenistic Wall

3

Ingenuous John and the Sublime Gospel[1]

THE STORY OF JOHN'S GOSPEL AND FIRST EPISTLE

The way and the truth and the life[2] (John 14:6)

To John and his companions, the great city of Ephesus[3] had never looked more beautiful or more dangerous. As they took their early morning stroll from the area of the upper agora near the Magnesian gate[4] and, after traversing the famous Way of the Curetes,[5] ambled down the magnificent Marble Road[6] to the great theater,[7] and finally wended their way past the lower agora and along the monumental Harbor Road[8] to the bustling port,[9] they could not help contrasting the splendor of the city with the obvious signs of her notoriety as the crossroads of pagan cults.[10] After all, they were unable to take a leisurely walk through the heart of Ephesus without seeing not only splendid agoras, gymnasia, baths, odeon[11] and theater, library[12] and stadium, but also such impressive yet infamous temples as those of Diana, Serapis, and Domitian.

The temple of Diana, or Artemis,[13] one of the fabled seven wonders of the world, featured the many-breasted figure of that goddess, not the chaste huntress and sister of Apollo of Greek mythology but the Asian fertility goddess sometimes identified with the earth-mother, Cybele.[14] Ephesus did not take a backseat to Corinth[15] when it came to sexual immorality under the guise of religion. In fact, romantic and sexual stories were commonly called Ephesian Tales.[16]

The massive Serapeion, or temple of Serapis,[17] honored Osiris and Apis of Egypt, united into one by Ptolemy I and sculpted either as a

The Great Theater of Ephesus from the Harbor Road.

powerful man or as a bull. Perhaps more importantly, it exemplified the popularity of uniting different deities in so-called religious syncretism,[18] for which Ephesus was the world center. To Christians and Jews alike, there was always the temptation to unite the worship of the one true God with that of popular pagan deities.

Of more recent construction, yet possibly more dangerous to Christianity, was the smaller but just as conspicuous temple of Domitian,[19] the current Roman dictator. Emperor worship had actually begun in Asia Minor,[20] but not until Domitian had it been taken seriously by the emperor himself. Domitian not only enjoyed divine worship, he even insisted on it. The first emperor to demand that he be addressed as "Lord and God,"[21] his usurpation of divine honors could not but cause a dilemma for Christians and Jews, whose loyalty to Rome had to stop short of giving the emperor the worship that was due to God alone.

And finally, the very name of Curetes[22] attached to one of the principal streets of Ephesus traversed by John and his companions evoked the idea of demigods, which, besides their involvement in religious

142

syncretism, played such an important part in the thinking of the Gnostics,[23] whether pagan, Jewish, or Christian. Or could they truly be considered Christian if they regarded Christ as only one of a multitude of demigods filling the atmosphere between God and humans?

It was these very concerns that gradually invaded the conversation of John and his companions, Prochorus[24] and Polycarp.[25] What could, what should, they do in the growing crisis facing the Christians of the city of Ephesus as well as the Roman province of Asia generally and, indeed, of the entire Roman Empire? The atmosphere of paganism surrounding Christians was dangerous enough, but the temptation to unite Christian worship with that of pagan deities in religious syncretism and with that of Domitian in emperor worship might prove too powerful to a large number of the laity. In fact, the time might not be far away when Christians, and Jews as well, could be faced with the very difficult choice of worshiping the emperor or sacrificing their lives. Add to that the insidious attraction of incipient Gnosticism, and the faith of Christians was in real danger.

What to do, then? This was the question that occupied the minds of the white-bearded John,[26] the gray-haired Prochorus,[27] and the dark-haired, beardless Polycarp.[28] What to do? Redouble their efforts in preaching and teaching? Of course! But, as John was quick to point out, Bishop Timothy was already doing a heroic job of fulfilling blessed Paul's solemn injunction, which had been graciously shared by Timothy with them all from Paul's touching farewell letter to his beloved child in Christ (2 Tim 4:1-2, NIV): "In the presence of God and of Christ Jesus, who will judge the living and the dead, and in view of his appearing and his kingdom, I give you this charge: 'Preach the Word, be prepared in season and out of season; correct, rebuke and encourage with great patience and careful instruction.' "

"Yes, I certainly agree," added Prochorus, "Timothy is an admirable overseer, especially in his office of preaching and teaching." Then, after a pause, he continued as if thinking aloud, "But I wonder if that office of preaching and teaching doesn't need the support of something more concrete and permanent, something in the form of writing."

"Hmm! That may be an inspired idea," chimed in young Polycarp, "but do you have something specific in mind?"

"Not exactly," replied Prochorus, "but as we talk I'm beginning to glimpse the outlines of what may be called for by the times, and indeed by the Holy Spirit. To put it into simple words, I guess we may need another gospel! Moreover, I can't help thinking that our beloved John here is the very man best suited to write that gospel!''

Up to this point, John had happily let his two closest friends grapple with the current needs of the Church, but at this turn in the conversation he could remain silent no longer. ''Wait just a minute, my dear Prochorus,'' he blurted out. ''Aren't you forgetting something? I'm over eighty years old, and while I still like to keep my hand in, especially by teaching the youngsters about Jesus, I can hardly claim the kind of mental and physical strength needed to write a gospel. Besides, we already have three wonderful gospels, carefully written and with broad appeal. Why do we even want another gospel? And why do you think of me at my age as the possible author?''

''Ah! I was hoping you'd ask that!'' countered Prochorus with a smile, ''for I'm confident I can give you an answer that'll not only make sense to Polycarp here but even to you, my dear John. In fact, the more I think about it, the more I wonder why I haven't made this suggestion before. You're the last living apostle,[29] the beloved disciple[30] of the Master, one of the special three apostles[31] whom Jesus wanted with him at his most sacred times, and, last but far from least, the chosen protector of his holy mother[32] for the rest of her life. What a wealth of personal experience you have of Jesus Christ, the Son of God! Wealth that we all need, especially in these difficult times! I beg you, my dearest friend, don't let all of that go with you to the grave! Polycarp and I will be happy to help you in any way we can, but it's you who hold the treasure of intimate, loving knowledge of Jesus such as no one else has ever known. All we ask is that you share it with the rest of us in a permanent way. Didn't Jesus himself say, 'Freely you have received; freely give?' ''[33]

They walked on a few more paces in absolute silence, while John pondered the eloquent appeal of Prochorus. Was this the sign he had been waiting for? Was the Lord letting him know through his faithful friend Prochorus just what he wanted of him? Why else would the somewhat timid and reticent Prochorus be suddenly able to make such an impassioned appeal? Was this not the Holy Spirit speaking through him? ''Dear Jesus, are you asking me to share with all our Christians what I've learned about you from my personal experience of you and your holy mother as well as from my years of contemplation? If only this will enable others to know and love you as I do, then old as I am,

I will do my best, with your never-failing help and that of my friends, to obey your holy will in this matter.''

Before John could reply, however, Polycarp decided to administer the coup de grâce in the argument for a new gospel, a Johannine gospel. ''If it's your age[34] that worries you, revered master, believe me, as perhaps your youngest close friend, just barely in my twenties, that you in your eighties and for that matter Prochorus here in his seventies do not seem old at all. Your step is lively, your eyes are sharp, your mind and especially your heart seem forever young and vigorous. In all honesty I must say that I've never known anyone to exemplify as you do the truth of that remarkable statement of Isaiah (Isa 40:30-31, NAB):

> Though young men faint and grow weary,
>   and youths stagger and fall,
> They that hope in the Lord
>   will renew their strength.
> They will soar as with eagles' wings;
>   They will run and not grow weary,
>   walk and not grow faint.

John was about to respond at last when Prochorus chose to add one more statement calculated to win the day. ''If, my dear friend, your humility has persuaded you that writing is not one of your gifts, let me reassure you to the contrary. The one pastoral letter[35] that you wrote at the urging of Timothy is among the most powerful and moving pieces that I've ever seen. In fact, I've practically memorized it. Such authority combined with such sensitivity! No one, not even Paul, has given us your lucid portrayal of God as light and love and life![36] If somehow you can provide us with a similar portrayal of Jesus as the very embodiment[37] of that light and love and life, as human, of course, but above all as our true Lord and God, far above and beyond emperors and angels, let alone demigods and false deities, what a service you will render to the Church not only here at Ephesus but everywhere and for all time!''

At last, Prochorus and Polycarp had apparently ''rested their case,''[38] so John finally seized the opportunity to respond. ''All right, all right, you two! You've convinced me at least that we could use another gospel and that I should have something to do with it. But there's more to the picture than you've been willing to mention. That so-called pastoral letter of mine was not mine alone but ours! I could never have produced it without your substantial assistance, not to mention, of course, the inspiration of the Holy Spirit. It was you two who cast it in its final form. It was you who gave it that lyrical flavor that is so attractive. And if, as you propose, I am to write a gospel, it will have to be with your substantial help again. Just considering the language alone, I'm not ignorant of Greek, of course. I even grew up with a rudimentary knowledge of it, being from Galilee of the Gentiles.[39] But my native language is Aramaic, and even though I've now lived most of my life here at Ephesus, speaking Greek almost exclusively, especially since Mary's departure,[40] I still don't feel that I've mastered its many nuances. So I need your invaluable help in polishing the vocabulary, grammar, and style of whatever I may write.

"In addition to the language, I also feel a real need to sample your opinions about such things as the content and the structure involved. For example, should a fourth gospel be very similar to the other three? If so, why write it? If not, how should it differ from them? I would indeed want to emphasize certain basic themes such as those you've already mentioned, Prochorus: light, life, and love. But how can I weave these through a gospel? I also am very devoted to the use of symbols, particularly from God's loving creation all about us as well as from his gracious intervention in our history, as we read in the Holy Scriptures.

"Oh, and while I think of it, let's not forget two other concerns we ought to address in addition to the religious syncretism, emperor worship, and incipient Gnosticism already mentioned. I refer to the need of clarification in regard to the followers of John the Baptist[41] as well as the need of ongoing defense against aggressive Pharisaic Judaism.[42] Yes, I know that's why Mattathias wrote his Gospel[43] and why Apollos wrote his long epistle,[44] but the problem remains, so why not incorporate some help in meeting these needs in our gospel if that can be done without being too obvious and too awkward? And finally, let me just mention something that has probably already occurred to you, namely that we need to present this entire proposal to Bishop Timothy for his approval. Not that I anticipate any difficulty on his part, for we have the most cordial relationship imaginable, but we owe it to him, to ourselves, to the Christian community, and above all to our blessed Lord Jesus himself to do everything in keeping with his holy will, and that means according to the authority that he himself has established in his Church. Yes, I know, I'm an apostle, but for the sake of good order,[45] I defer to Timothy, the local bishop, just as I defer to Peter's successor in Rome.[46]

"Now, are we agreed that we'll all consider what we've been talking about this morning so that the next time we meet we'll perhaps be able to visualize more clearly what this proposed gospel will look like? Till then, my dear friends, farewell! And let's all pray assiduously for the special guidance of the Holy Spirit in this important endeavor. As you've made so clear, the need is great, so the answer to the need should also be as great as we can make it, with the never-failing help of God's grace. May he bless and keep you both in his gracious love!"

On returning to his modest home, John's mind and heart began to race with speculation about the content of the proposed gospel. He felt fully confident that his two friends would be able, with God's grace, to arrange and develop the material into a work that would not only enlighten his fellow Christians but move them to be more completely attached to the Lord Jesus than ever before. For the material itself, however, he felt personally responsible. After all, he was the apostle, one of the favored three, the beloved disciple who had enjoyed the great privilege of accompanying Jesus during those three unforgettable years of his public ministry,[47] who had even rested his head on the Master's bosom at the Last Supper, who alone among the apostles had been with Jesus as he was dying on the cross and had heard those blessed words placing Mary in his charge,[49] and, finally, who had pondered the meaning of the Lord's life, death, and resurrection for all those years with Mary and after Mary until now. If anyone were to supply the content of this gospel, it would have to be he. So, given the urgent needs of the Church, especially in the area of Ephesus, he needed to decide as quickly as possible what this fourth gospel should contain. Without further ado, therefore, he began to attune his mind and heart to those of the Lord and his Holy Spirit in order to discern as clearly and completely as possible this new gospel's content.

First of all, he felt very strongly that it ought to be a deeply spiritual gospel,[50] one that would not be content to present the words and deeds of Jesus but somehow would enable the reader to penetrate the deepest meaning of what his life and saving events were all about. Secondly, it was clear to him that in order to counter emperor worship, religious syncretism, and incipient Gnosticism, it would be essential to emphasize not only the humanity but, above all, the divinity of Christ as Son of God and King of Kings, even if this meant anticipating in the life and discourses of Jesus what became evident only after the resurrection.[51]

Thinking of the resurrection reminded John that the proposed work would not even qualify as a gospel without a passion, death, and resurrection account and, at least in some way, the rest of the kerygma,[52] namely the baptism and witness of John the Baptist, the Galilean ministry, and the journey to Jerusalem. He could see immediately, however, that in all of this his own material would differ quite sharply from that of the other three Gospels. They had all followed the same general order, confining Jesus' ministry largely to Galilee until the very end of his public life, when he journeyed to Jerusalem for the saving events there. Apparently that arrangement, which seemed to be original with Mark and then followed by Mattathias and Luke, was necessitated by the need of compressing the story in the interest of time. He, however, need not feel obliged to follow suit, especially since he had accompanied Jesus to Jerusalem for most if not all of the major Jewish feasts[53] during his three years of public life. In fact, it was above all on those occasions that the Lord, by his miracles and discourses, had made it increasingly evident to his fellow Jews just who and what he was.[54] And, besides all this, John knew that he could add details[55] from Jesus' life that, for whatever reason, had been omitted in the other three Gospels.

In thinking about Jesus' public ministry and to some extent also about his saving events in Jerusalem, John recognized the fact that if he were to provide fresh new material that would assist the reader in penetrating the meaning of the Master, then he would have to omit a good amount of what was already known from the other Gospels[56] for two reasons: first, because otherwise the work would end up entirely too long and cumbersome, and secondly, because there simply was no need of repeating what was now so well known from the previous three accounts. Some of that material, however, he might not omit altogether but include in a different and perhaps more concise fashion.[57]

So far so good! Now, what were some of the principal themes, ideas, sayings, and events that he should suggest to Prochorus and Polycarp for inclusion in their common gospel? Well, first of all, there was the excellent suggestion of Prochorus himself to include the major themes from his pastoral letter identifying Jesus Christ as the light and the love and the life of all people.[58] Then, there would be the question of

View from the Sheep Pool to the Church of St. Ann.

The Synagogue at Capernaum.

miracles and discourses, which so filled the other three Gospels. For this gospel, would it not be wise to limit the number of miracles to a few, say to the perfect biblical number of seven and, in fact, not even to treat them so much as miracles but as signs[59] or symbols, of deep truths, which could be brought out especially in Jesus' discourses?[60]

And, while on the subject of numbers and symbols, would it not be helpful to identify the perfect biblical number of seven in various ways with Christ and Christianity[61] and the imperfect biblical number of six with Pharisaic Judaism[62] in order to demonstrate that the former were intended by God as the fulfillment and conclusion of the latter? Not only that, but the judicious choice of symbols from nature[63] and especially from the Jewish Testament[64] itself could go a long way in affirming the same conclusion.

Finally, since it was so important not only to be understood but also not to be misunderstood, would it not be wise to make it crystal clear that a spiritual gospel was not to be interpreted as a denial of the visible Church and sacraments established by Christ? To that end, would it not be both prudent and necessary to include in this gospel clear references to the Church[65] and the sacraments?[66]

"There," thought John with a sigh of relief, "I believe that may be all I can handle right now. At least that much gives us some general ideas to follow. The rest will involve finer details. Those I can already begin thinking about, for example, which miracles of Jesus should we recount? Which symbols among the many possible ones used by Jesus would be the most effective in showing the true meaning of his life and death and resurrection? Dear Jesus, help me by your Holy Spirit to choose these wisely, so that you may shine forth in this gospel with all your glory as the Son of God and King of Kings!"

John was astonished when Prochorus and Polycarp showed up at his home early the next morning. He certainly had not expected them so soon or so early! As they explained, however, in a rather apologetic manner, they had become so excited about the prospect of helping him write a gospel that they just could not wait to learn whether he had been able to visualize any of the contents of the work. When he summarized for them the salient features of the material as they had developed in his mind, their enthusiasm grew by leaps and bounds.

Prochorus, with his experience of life among Jews as well as Greeks, was especially intrigued with the thought of featuring the perfect biblical number, seven, for Christ and Christianity in contrast with the imperfect number, six, for Pharisaic Judaism. He particularly liked the idea of seven signs and seven discourses, which in turn suggested the possibility of seven main titles[67] of Jesus and even of seven main acts[68] or episodes with which to structure the whole gospel, perhaps with a prologue and epilogue to round it out with a symmetrical beginning and end.

Not to be outdone, Polycarp added the interesting idea of employing such literary structures as concentric circles[69] and even chiasmus[70] as means of tying it all together. But both agreed that what was most needed first of all was for John to choose from his store of memories about Jesus those seven miracles, or signs, and those seven discourses and titles that would be most appropriate and meaningful. In the meantime, they could begin work on a possible prologue, featuring the three themes of light, love, and life that they all agreed to weave throughout the gospel.

"I'm glad you mentioned a prologue," remarked John, interrupting their excited chatter. "I think that's a good idea and an excellent way to begin the gospel. To me, the opening of Mark's gospel is perhaps too abrupt, though I understand the urgent circumstances in which he wrote. The other two gospels both begin with accounts of Jesus' birth and infancy, so there's no need to repeat that material. But a prologue that would quickly situate the whole story of Jesus Christ both in its divine-human setting as Son of God and in its historical setting as the Messiah of Israel and the fulfillment of all that was best in the Jewish Testament would certainly provide the gospel with a thought-provoking beginning.

"Along these lines, I believe we have a couple of models that may be helpful. One is that marvelous hymn in Paul's Letter to the Philippians,[71] the one he uses as a model of humility, beginning with references to Jesus' divine nature, equality with God, and preexistence with God. The other model is the personification of divine wisdom in the Jewish Scriptures, especially in the Books of Proverbs and Wisdom.[72] In my contemplation, I have often used such texts to help me understand who and what Jesus truly is, by passing from consideration of God's wisdom described as if it were a person to contemplation of his wisdom as indeed a divine person who became human like us and revealed himself to us as Jesus of Nazareth. Perhaps these thoughts, along with additional ideas from Genesis and Exodus, will assist you in drawing up the prologue in such a way that it will provide a fitting introduction to the entire gospel."

"Wait a minute," blurted Polycarp. "What additional ideas from Genesis and Exodus do you have in mind? If you tell us, it will make our work that much easier."

John could not but smile at his friend's consternation. He had intended to dwell on these things at a later date, but he could easily see that his friends were impatient to get started as soon as possible. "Very well," he surrendered. "What I had in mind from Genesis, as reflected in the personification of Wisdom, is the way in which divine wisdom is described as being with God in the beginning and indeed working with God to bring all things into existence.[73] And from Exodus, I love to see a parallel and in fact a prefiguration between the 'dwelling' of Yahweh with Israel in the famous desert tabernacle and Christ's dwelling with us in the 'tabernacle' of his human nature.[74] I hope that's not all too confusing for you, but to me it's full of meaning."

"Well, it *is* rather mystical," remarked Prochorus, "but I've been with you long enough to expect the mystical, and I can't imagine your gospel being anything but mystical. Polycarp and I don't have your years of contemplation to help us, but we'll do our best to understand what you're talking about and to help you put your thoughts into words that our fellow Christians can understand and translate into living. When we fail to comprehend your meaning, we'll just ask you and count on you to enlighten us."

"Oh! That reminds me," John quickly interjected, his memory obviously jogged by something Prochorus had said. "I do hope, in fact I insist, that this gospel will be couched in simple language[75] that anyone who knows Greek can understand. It's true that the thoughts may be profound, but the words ought to be simple. Why? Because that's the way I think and speak and am. I'm not learned and eloquent like Paul, and hence, as much as I admire him, I don't want to sound like him. But the main reason is that this gospel, like every gospel, is about Jesus, and however sublime his teaching was, he always used simple language so that everyone could understand him.[76] For example, what words could be simpler than light, love, and life, yet they contain a world of meaning that it takes a whole lifetime to comprehend. Such simplicity ought to be a basic characteristic of our gospel, don't you agree?"

"Indeed we do," chorused both Prochorus and Polycarp in unison, and then the latter added, "The more we talk, the more we begin to realize what a task we've undertaken, but our offer still stands. We'll do our level best to grasp whatever you tell us and to express it in simple but correct Greek for the glory of the Lord and for the spiritual good of all.'' With that, John's friends bade him farewell and set to work immediately on a prologue to the gospel along the lines that he had suggested.

When next they gathered a few days later, Prochorus and Polycarp were surprised and delighted to learn that John had already singled out not only the seven signs, titles, and discourses of Jesus but also seven nature symbols and seven biblical symbols to be woven into the gospel. That would surely expedite the work. There remained, however, the delicate task of arranging all of these in a general structure that would be both attractive and compelling. Polycarp reiterated his suggestion about the use of concentric circles and chiasmus, both of which were so popular at Ephesus, the crossroads of Eastern and Western cultures. John agreed that this would not detract from his cherished simplicity, but he preferred to leave the implementation of such structures to his companions. Meanwhile, he was eager to learn how they were progressing on the gospel's prologue.

''We've got to be honest,'' volunteered Prochorus. We've drawn up a prologue that, we feel, contains much of what we think you want in it. We also feel confident that it's expressed in simple but correct Greek. What bothers us is that it's a bit confusing. For example, it starts more or less as you recommended, ''In the beginning was the wisdom of God,'' but immediately we detected a source of confusion. The word for ''wisdom'' in Greek is *sophía*, which is feminine, but we're really talking about Jesus Christ, the wisdom of the Father, and of course Jesus was and is masculine. How, then, should we change the wording to avoid this confusion?''

John thought a moment, then asked, ''Well, as word rich as the Greek language is, don't we have a masculine word that would be the equivalent of the feminine word for wisdom?''

Prochorus and Polycarp exchanged mental question marks, then paused a moment in deep thought and, as if on cue, responded with the selfsame word: ''*lógos!*''[77] Then Polycarp explained why *lógos* would certainly fill the bill. ''First of all, it has a great variety of meanings, of which 'word' is the most basic. That in itself is appropriate because, as the Hebrew Scriptures describe it, God created all things by the power of his word.[78] But among other meanings is that of wisdom, especially the wisdom of God[79] as described and personalized in the Wisdom literature.''

"Wonderful!" exclaimed John. "Now, why don't we look over the entire prologue so that we can see how it reads and whether any changes need to be made. But before we begin, the thought of changes reminds me to insist from the outset that if anything needs to be added to this gospel after my death, you should feel free to add it.[80] I know you don't like to hear about my death, but I think of it daily and I want your agreement on this point in advance. All right? Good! Now let's check the prologue."

And so they did, this trio of like-minded friends, and when it was eventually finished the result was not only a perfect preface to the Gospel of John but also one of the most exquisite and profound statements ever written. To conclude our story, I can do no better than translate and explain (in endnotes) that magnificent prologue found in John 1:1-18, WFD, highlighting its key expressions with italics,[81] as follows:

In the beginning was[82] the *Word*,
   and the Word was with God[83]
   and the Word was God![84]
He was in the beginning with God.
All things came to be[85] through him,
   and without him came into being
   not one thing that came to be.
In him was *life,*[86] and his life
   was the *light* of humankind.[87]
His light shines in the darkness,
   and the darkness could neither
   take it in nor snuff it out.[88]

There came to be[89] a man,
   one who was sent from God,
   whose name was John.
He came for the sake of *witness,*[90]
   to testify about the light
   so that all might believe
   through him.
That man was not the light,
   but a witness to the light.

He was the genuine[91] light
   who enlightens every person
   that comes into the world.

He was in the world, and the world
   came into being through him,
   yet the world did not know[92] him.
He came among his own creation,
   and his very own people[93]
   did not accept him.
But to whoever did accept him,
   he gave authority to become
   children of God,[94]
Those who believe[95] in his name,
   who have been begotten,[96]
   not through human procreation,[97]
   nor out of natural desire,[98]
   nor out of a husband's will,[99]
   but rather of God.[100]

And the Word became *human*[101]
   and pitched his tent[102]
   in our midst.
And we gazed on his *glory,*[103]
   glory of the only-begotten
   from the Father,
   full of *love and truth.*[104]

John witnessed concerning him[105]
   and cried out, declaring:
"He is the one of whom I said,
   'The man who comes after me
   has been set above me
   because he was before me.' "

Out of his *fullness*[106] we have,
   every one of us, received
   gracious love upon love![107]
The Law was given through Moses.[108]
Love and truth have come to be
   through Jesus Christ.[109]
No one has ever seen God,
   but the only-begotten Son,[110]
   who is in the bosom
   of the Father,
   has *revealed*[111] him.

ANALYSIS OF JOHN'S GOSPEL

Having attempted to reconstruct in story form why and how I think John's Gospel came to be written, it is now time to present in outline form a brief analysis of that Gospel for our better visualization and understanding of this inspired work. Obviously, this analysis will be better comprehended if the reader is already familiar with the preceding story and, if possible, the notes as well. Unlike my previous analyses in this two-volume work, this one contains three sections: (1) an overview of John's Gospel, (2) an outline of its development, (3) a look at its theology.

I. Overview

A. General impression

Even a cursory reading of John's Gospel, especially in comparison with the Synoptic Gospels of Mark, "Matthew," and Luke, cannot but leave certain strong impressions on the reader, of which the following are a representative sampling:

1. This Gospel is beautifully simple in its language and straightforward presentation, but at the same time extremely profound in its thought content.

2. Whether by design or not, this is a deeply spiritual, even mystical, Gospel, which requires a great amount of study and prayerful reflection to grasp.

3. After reading the Synoptics and then John, it is patently evident that the author has made every attempt to avoid repeating what is already clear from the first three Gospels.

4. It is also apparent from the concrete details[112] that appear only in this Gospel that the author uses a tradition somewhat different from those of the Synoptics, yet one which seems to be that of a personal witness.

5. The central figure, Jesus Christ, is clearly presented in a way quite different from that of the Synoptics, one in which he explicitly emphasizes his divinity, royalty, and exaltation throughout his life, above all at his death and resurrection.[113]

6. The author seems to have a predilection for long discourses that generally begin with a dialogue and end with a monologue[114] on the part of Jesus.

7. Instead of the emphasis on Jesus' miracles and parables characteristic of the Synoptic Gospels, this Gospel seems to favor signs and symbols.

8. A comparison of the Gospel and the First Epistle of John singles out three major themes (light, life, and love), which seem to dominate both works.

B. Composition of the Fourth Gospel
   1. Circumstances of its writing:
      a) Tradition, objective scholarship, and careful analysis of the Gospel itself favor the city of Ephesus in western Asia Minor as the location and the last decade of the first century A.D. as the time of its writing.

      b) The particular circumstances at Ephesus in the 90s A.D. that seem to have led to the composition of this Gospel were the prevalence of religious syncretism, emperor worship under Domitian (81–96), incipient Gnosticism, and (perhaps to a lesser extent) the presence at Ephesus of devotees of John the Baptist and especially of Pharisaic Judaism.

      c) In addition to the foregoing, there may have been the desire on the part of Christians at Ephesus, especially John's closest friends,[115] to preserve more permanently for the future the Johannine tradition about Jesus Christ.

      d) After careful study of the interrelationship among the writings traditionally attributed to John, I favor the following scenario:
         (1) The writing of the First Epistle of John, possibly at the request of Bishop Timothy

         (2) The initial writing of the Gospel according to John, with the apostle providing the content and his two closest friends, Prochorus and Polycarp, planning and composing the almost complete work early in the 90s

         (3) The composition of the Apocalypse, or Book of Revelation, during the vicious persecution of Domition, which began in A.D. 95

(4) The completion of John's Gospel, especially with part or all of chapter 21, after John's death around the end of the first century

(5) The writing of the Second and Third Epistles (actually letters) of John, perhaps not by John the apostle but by the Presbyter[116]

2. Authorship

a) As is very well known in biblical circles, there has long been a dispute about the authorship of the works attributed to John, the son of Zebedee and apostle of Christ.

b) I submit that decisions on that authorship should not be made in the abstract, simply by comparing opinions about it from various authors, as is sometimes done, but rather by careful study of the works themselves and, above all, by testing one's opinion in a concrete scenario that accounts for what the works themselves contain.

c) So far, I have tried to supply this scenario for the Gospel (and to some extent, for the First Epistle) of John, but I will reserve my opinion on the authorship of the Apocalypse until I treat it in the next and final chapter.

3. Purposes

a) Primarily, to combat emperor worship, syncretistic religion, and incipient Gnosticism, in that order

b) Secondarily

(1) To win over devotees of John the Baptist and offset the influence of Pharisaic Judaism

(2) To preserve the Johannine tradition about Christ for future Christians

4. Sources

a) The kerygma of the Church, though in a somewhat different form from the other three Gospels[117]

b) A source independent of the Synoptics, probably the eyewitness, contemplative source of John the apostle himself *c)* There are indications, however, that the author of this Gospel is well aware not only of the three other Gospels[118] but also of the thought and writings of Paul.[119]

5. Characteristics

   a) As mentioned above, John's Gospel is noteworthy for a prevalence of symbols, particularly numerical, biblical, and natural.

      (1) Numerical symbols

         (a) Seven (perfection): signs (miracles), titles,[120] discourses, disciples,[121] acts, plus seven biblical and seven natural symbols, given below (Seven septets!)

         (b) Six (imperfection): water jars of Jewish purification and six Jewish feasts[122]

      (2) Biblical symbols[123] (seven): tabernacle or tent of dwelling, paschal lamb, manna in the desert, brazen serpent, bridegroom, shepherd and sheep, vine and branches

      (3) Natural symbols[124] (seven): light, water, wind, ripe fields, grain of wheat, way, woman in labor and giving birth

   b) Another basic characteristic of this Gospel is the use of long discourses (seven in all), which usually begin as a dialogue and end as a monologue.[125]

   c) Still another characteristic is the penchant for editorializing in such a way that it is sometimes difficult to know where the words of Jesus end and the editorials begin.[126]

   d) A fourth characteristic is the genius of John in seeming to omit some prominent events in the Synoptics but actually including them in a different and perhaps more natural setting.[127]

6. Structures: Of the various structures that John and his friends could have used, the two most prominent ones are those of concentric circles and chiasmus.

a) Concentric Circles:[128] used especially in the development of the three basic themes, the seven titles of Jesus, and in the discourse at the Last Supper

b) Chiasmus:[129] used, I believe, to form the basic structure of the entire Gospel, as will be seen in the following outline

II. Outline of John's Gospel

A. Organizing principles

1. On the righthand side, note the basic division, accepted by all, into the Book of Signs and the Book of Glory.

2. On the lefthand side, note the chiastic structure of seven acts (each including two scenes or episodes), plus a prologue and epilogue.

3. Within the body of the outline, note the following indications:

a) The seven signs (miracles) are indicated by S-1, etc., contained in parentheses.

b) The seven great discourses are indicated by D-1, etc., for example, D-1 with Nicodemus on baptism.

c) The seven titles occur in the introduction but are omitted from the outline to avoid clutter.

d) The seven biblical and seven natural symbols, as well as the seven disciples in the epilogue are also omitted to preserve some simplicity.

e) Finally, the six water jars of Jewish purification occur in Act I, chapter 2, while the six Jewish feasts are given in italics.

B. Chiastic outline of John's Gospel

 1. Prologue and introduction (ch. 1)
    a) Prologue: Incarnate Word—light, life, love
    b) Introduction: gathering of community (seven titles)

 2. Act I (ch. 2): Initial revelation of Jesus' glory
    a) Jesus' glory at Cana in Galilee (S-1) (light)
    b) Jesus' glory at Temple in Jerusalem (*Passover*)

 3. Act II (3:1–4:45): Revelation in Judea and Samaria
    a) D-1 with Nicodemus on water of life (baptism)
    b) D-2 with woman of Samaria on water of life (grace)

 4. Act III (4:46–6:71): Source of life, judge of dead
    a) Official's son (S-2), paralytic at Jerusalem (S-3),
        D-3 with Jewish leaders (*Pentecost?*)
    b) Feeding (S-4), walk on sea (S-5), D-4 on Eucharist
        (*Passover II*)

 5. Act IV (chs. 7–10): Light and life of world
    a) D-5 in Temple, conflict, light of blind (S-6) (*Booths*)
    b) D-6 on Good Shepherd, source of life (*Dedication*)

 6. Act V (chs. 11–12): Giver of life, destined for death
    a) Lazarus raised (S-7): Jesus, resurrection and life
    b) Sanhedrin plot, anointing, entry, hour of glory

 7. Act VI (chs. 13–17): Revelation of love in Jerusalem
    a) Washing of feet, betrayal and departure previewed
    b) D-7 at Last Supper, priestly prayer (*Passover III*)

 8. Act VII (chs. 18–20): Final revelation of glory
    a) Trials-denials, crucifixion-death-burial
    b) Empty tomb, appearances of the risen Christ

 9. Epilogue and conclusion (ch. 21)
    a) Epilogue: gathering of community (seven disciples),
        miraculous catch, breakfast, Peter-Shepherd
    b) Conclusion: Beloved Disciple, mortal-witness-author
        of the Gospel

CHIASMUS

BOOK OF SIGNS

BOOK OF GLORY

III. The Theology of John's Gospel

Since this Gospel is not only the most spiritual but also the most theological of the Gospels, I have thought it well to add this brief glimpse at its theological content, in two principal divisions, forming another septet.

A. Theology in the strict sense (study of God himself)

1. Jesus Christ: A preexistent being (Word, Wisdom), source of light, life, and love, who becomes a historical person, living, ministering, dying, and rising, all as the triumphant King and Son of God, identified with us to save us from sin and unite us with himself, filled with his light, life, love

2. The Father: Always the Creator, savior God of Israelite faith, but also the unique Father of Jesus and through him of all who accept Christ in faith, baptism, and a life of truth practiced in love

3. The Spirit: The gift of the Father and the Son as Paraclete (Comforter-Advocate), through whom we are filled with the light, life, and love of Christ and transformed into him in a spiritual life which is nothing less than heaven already begun on earth

B. Theology in the broad sense (other subjects regarding God)

1. Ecclesiology: The Church is a visible-invisible community, intimately united with Jesus, vivified by the Spirit, protected by Mary, with visible members, leaders and sacraments.

2. Mariology: In John 2:4 and 19:26, Jesus addresses Mary as woman (*gýnai*), not to belittle her but, in allusion to the first woman, Eve (Gen 2:22-23), to honor her as mother of all the redeemed, given to the Church (represented by John) as our mother, model, and mentor, notably in our spiritual life. (See also Rev 12.)

3. Soteriology and morality: As in Paul, justification and salvation come through faith and union with Christ through Church and sacraments, and morality is the living out of that union in truth that is practiced through love.

4. Eschatology: Realized eschatology is clear throughout the gospel, that is, Jesus is already in triumph all through his life but especially in his death and resurrection, and we al-

ready live his risen life today in preparation for and in earnest of the ultimate and eternal triumph when Christ will come again.

This concludes our brief analysis of John's Gospel. It may have been noticed that I have given no attention to two questions that have occasioned many discussions, namely, (1) whether the present order in the Gospel is the original one and (2) whether the story of Jesus and the adulteress in John 8:1-11 is authentic. Since these questions do not touch directly on our unique study of John, I have chosen to treat them in the notes.[130]

The story and analysis of the Gospel and First Epistle of John having been completed, there now remain only our reflections on those magnificent works with a view to their application to our personal and communal life.

REFLECTIONS ON JOHN'S GOSPEL AND OUR LIFE

The Gospel according to John, in its final conclusion, offers us this colorful hyperbole:[131] "There are also many other things that Jesus did which, if they were written down one by one, not even the entire world, I estimate, would have room enough for all the books that would need to be written" (John 21:25, WFD). Something very similar could be declared regarding books and articles about John himself and his writings. Their deep mystical thought provides material for innumerable studies, as evidenced by the multiplicity and variety of published works on Johannine literature.

In the interest of time and space, I must confine my reflections on John to a limited number of considerations that may be helpful in our spiritual life. Adhering to John's own emphases, both in his Gospel and in his First Epistle, I have chosen to restrict our reflections to the three great themes of light, life, and love as they are featured in those two great works and as they affect our own spiritual lives.

And while one could argue cogently for a different order of treatment among the three themes, I have decided to reflect on light, life, and love in that order because it seems to be suggested in the Genesis account of creation, in John's prologue, in the Gospel itself, and in our growth in the spiritual life.

The Theme of Light

With the possible exception of water as the symbol of life, there is probably no symbol more common and meaningful in the Scriptures than that of light. Perhaps that is one reason why the story of creation begins with the presence of water and the initial creation of light. And of course, the importance of light among the people of biblical times is readily understandable. Lacking the convenience of electricity, kerosene, and even candles, they were almost totally dependent on daylight for doing their work and living their lives. Olive oil lamps, which formed their common mode of illumination at night, offered little more than an eye-straining half-light that sufficed just to enable members of a household to find their way in the dark. Although the oil lamp is the traditional symbol of learning and wisdom, it is questionable just how much the learned and wise people of history were able to glean by its flickering light. Does not Jesus himself echo this reality when he declares, "The night is coming when no one can work" (John 9:4)?

We of the twentieth century can turn night into day with the flick of a switch. We can even carry portable light with us wherever we want to go. It is not easy, then, for us to appreciate the importance of light in the ancient world. Only when our electric light systems break down, for example, in a hurricane or thunderstorm, do we find it somewhat easy to identify with our ancient brothers and sisters in their dread of darkness and their esteem of light as the symbol of life, goodness, and above all, truth. Then we begin to realize why the Old Testament, especially the Prophetic literature, abounds with references to the world as enshrouded in the darkness of sin and ignorance as it awaits the light of the Messiah. In both "Matthew" and Luke,[132] but especially in John, Jesus is identified as that true light for which the world has been longing.

To quote all the passages referring to light in both the First Epistle of John and his Gospel would certainly lengthen our study beyond measure, so let me just indicate the principal texts and encourage the reader to invest some time in looking these up and reflecting upon them in their proper contexts for spiritual profit. After providing the references, I will then add some reflections that I hope will enhance our understanding of this very beautiful and salutary symbol.

The principal references to light in 1 John and John's Gospel are the following: 1 John 1:5-8; 2:8-11; John 1:4-9; 3:19-21; 5:35; 8:12; 9:3-5; 12:35-36, 46. In addition, there are the many references to revelation, especially to Christ as the revelation of the Father, as well as references to truth, faith, and sight, all of which are symbolized by or at least connected with light, as we see, for example, in the cure of the blind man in the ninth chapter of John.

Of all these references, however, perhaps none is so full of meaning as Jesus' bold statement in John 8:12, WFD: "I am the light of the world. The one who follows me will not walk in the darkness but will have the light of life!" Besides the obvious allusion to the light for which the darkened world has been waiting so long, are we justified in finding additional meaning in that text? I believe that we are. After all, what is the light of our world? The sun, of course! And what is the sun to our world and to us but the source of all our natural illumination, our warmth, even our energy! How very appropriate, then, that for the date of Jesus' birth, which unfortunately had not been preserved, the Church chose the mythical "birthday" of the sun, December 25,[133] when (according to Roman observation and reckoning) the days begin to get longer each year.

Of course, the human Jesus, like the people of his time, could hardly be expected to appreciate the complete role of the sun, for example, in the formation of oil and coal, but we in our scientific age do know about these things and therefore are able to derive from Jesus' reference to the sun all the rich meaning implied therein. Thus, it is most salutary to recognize Jesus as the indispensable source of the light of our truth, the warmth of our love, and the wealth of our energy. It is also essential for us to remember, in faith and patience, that even on the most cloudy of days the sun is still shining, and Christ, the light of the world, is still enlightening, warming, and energizing us.

In John 12:36, NAB, Jesus invites us, "While you have the light, believe in the light, so that you may become children of the light." What is meant by "children of the light"? It is another way of saying "people of the light," but with special emphasis on the simplicity and humility characteristic of children. It means that we belong to Christ, the light of the world; that he is at the very core of our being as the light of our life, that we are even possessed by the light. Just as a moth hovers around the light, so we hover around the light of Christ.

Not only that, but we are also called to mediate the light of Christ to the world about us, a world that is, unfortunately, still "sitting in darkness and the shadow of death."[134] In John 8:12, as we have seen, Jesus declares himself to be the light of the world, the sun of our lives.

In Matt 5:14-15, however, he asserts that we, his followers, are also the light of the world. Are he and we the light of the world in the same sense? Not at all! He is like the sun to our world, the source of all our illumination, warmth, and energy. We are not the source, like the sun, but instead we are called to be more like the moon, reflecting or, better still, radiating, the light of Christ to the world all around us. In reflection light and warmth only bounce off the surface, whereas in radiation they penetrate the surface, fill the interior, and emanate from the inside out. So must it be with the light of Christ. First, it must penetrate to the core of our being as the light of truth, the warmth of love, the wealth of energy, and then it must radiate from within us to all about us. Paul, in his own inimitable way, gives us a sublime description of this in 2 Cor 4:6, NAB: "For God who said, 'Let light shine out of darkness,' has shone in our hearts to bring to light the knowledge of the glory of God on the face of [Jesus] Christ."

In addition, parts of two different prayers may help to illustrate what we have been considering. The first one, which pertains to Christ as the light of the world, is the first verse of a hymn used for Compline, or Night Prayer, in the Liturgy of the Hours:[135]

> O Christ, you are the light and day
> Which drives away the night,
> The ever shining Sun of God
> And pledge of future light.

The second prayer, which touches on our responsibility in spreading the light of Christ, is that of the saintly and brilliant Cardinal Newman, entitled "Radiating Christ,"[136] of which I will quote only a small part:

> Shine through me, and be so in me
> That every soul I come in contact with
> May feel Your presence in my soul.
> Let them look up and see,
> No longer me, but only Jesus!

The Theme of Life

As I have already indicated, the theme of life and of water as the symbol of life is one of the most common and at the same time one of the richest in all of Scripture. In the very first chapter of Genesis, "the Spirit of God was hovering over the waters" (Gen 1:2, NIV) of initial creation, bringing order out of chaos and life of various kinds to fill the earth. And in the description of the formation of human beings in Gen 2:7, NIV, etc., we read that God "breathed into his [man's] nostrils the breath of life, and so man became a living being [or person]."

Our most basic instinct is that of self-preservation, insuring in normal persons the protection of human life. This is clearly reflected in Job 2:4, NAB, "All that a man has will he give for his life," as well as in Mark 8:37, NAB, "What could one give in exchange for his life?" Hence, the selfless love of the supreme sacrifice in John 15:13, NAB, "No one has greater love than this, to lay down one's life for one's friends."

It is not at all surprising, then, that there are even more references to life than to light in both Testaments, most notably in Genesis and Proverbs of the Old Testament and in John and 1 John of the New Testament. References in the latter two works are as follows: 1 John 1:1-2; 2:25; 3:14-16; John 1:4; 3:15-16, 36; 4:14, 36; 5:24-29, 39-40; 6:27-68 passim; 8:12; 10:10-17, 28; 11:25; 12:25, 50; 13:37-38; 14:6; 15:13; 17:2-3; 20:31. And that is not even counting the words "to live" and "living!"

In addition, there are in John's Gospel the remarkable number of references to water, the symbol of life, particularly in chapters three through seven, which include the following: Jesus' insistence with Nicodemus on baptism with water, his teaching about "living water" with the Samaritan woman at the well, his cure of the paralytic who had no one to help him into the water, his walking on the water of the Sea of Galilee, and his teaching on the "rivers of living water" in reference to the Spirit yet to be given.[137] Both in nature and in grace, water is truly "liquid life!"[138]

Besides the symbolism of water for life, let us not forget John's emphasis on sacraments, "carriers of divine life,"[139] especially the Holy Eucharist in the sixth chapter of John, where Jesus is indeed the "bread of life."[140] Then there are the life-giving miracles of the healing of the royal official's son at Cana in John 4:46-54, the healing of the paralytic in John 5:1-9, and above all the raising of Lazarus to life again in John 11:1-44.

Yes, the theme of life is pervasive throughout 1 John and John's Gospel and understandably so, for all life is sacred, especially human life, which, as we have seen from the creation accounts in Genesis, contains something of the Divine. And this sacredness pertains to human life from beginning to end of its individual and corporate existence. Hence in Isa 49:15, the implication seems clear that abortion as well as infanticide are unnatural and inconceivable, and in Luke 16:19-31 the neglect, let alone the killing, of poor Lazarus is enough to condemn the rich man to eternal punishment.

But having insisted that all life is sacred, we must now proceed to distinguish among different kinds of life. Not all kinds of life are equally sacred. Unfortunately, this is not always clear in our English language, where we have only the one word "life" for every possible state of living. In Greek, there are at least three words for life: *biós*, which stands for our lifespan; *psychě*, which pertains to our human or natural life; and *zōě*, which refers to supernatural, spiritual, eternal life, in fact divine life shared with us humans. Obviously, there is no comparison between our human life, precious as it is, and the life of God himself shared with us. And Jesus makes this abundantly clear in his categorical statement in John 12:25, WFD: "The one who loves his life [*psychě*] loses it, and the one who hates [loves less] his life [*psychě*] in this world will keep it for life [*zōě*] everlasting."

It is of this life of *zōě* that Jesus, the Good Shepherd, is speaking when he declares in John 10:10, WFD, "I came in order that they may have life [*zōě*] and have it to the full." When? After we die? Yes, but also right now! The life of grace, created and uncreated, the life of Christ, "the way, the truth, and the life" (John 14:6) within us, which is eternal life already begun for us.

Previously, I have spoken about "realized eschatology[141]" in the sense of Jesus' words and deeds throughout his human life as if he had already risen from the dead, but the more common meaning of "realized eschatology" is that used of all of us who already possess eternal life through Christ. For us, in a very true sense, the end time has already arrived. Christ, "the resurrection and the life" (John 11:25), already lives in us (John 14:21-23), and we need but to let him continue to live and grow in us through faith, trust, and love, the virtues that I like to refer to as those of "holding on."[142] But unfortunately, we are always tempted to "do what comes naturally," that is, to live according to the flesh, namely, the sinful inclinations of our natural life (*psychě*), as Paul describes so vividly in Gal 5:16-21 and Rom 8:5-8. For this reason, we need to practice the virtues that I like to call those of "letting go,"[143] namely humility, purity, and detachment from material concerns. But whether we are using the term "realized eschatology" in reference to Christ or ourselves, I cannot help thinking that John's obvious penchant for this kind of approach must have stemmed from the immediacy of his personal love for Christ, fostered not only during Jesus' public life but also during the following years through mystical contemplation. For John, the risen Christ was enlightening, living, and loving, not in some remote and abstract way but present and immediate, alive and lovable.

It has been well said that we are called to choose, not so much between good and evil as between life and death.[144] In other words, we are in a life-and-death situation not only for this earthly existence but for all eternity. How consoling to hear Jesus' words in John 6:57, NIV, "Just as the living Father sent me and I live because of the Father, so the one who feeds on me will live because of me," and in John 11:25, NIV, "He who believes in me will live, even though he dies; and whoever lives and believes in me will never die," as well as in John 14:19, "Because I live, you also will live."

The Theme of Love

Here we come to the very heart of John! For if the light of Christ's truth and the water of his superhuman life are central to John's thought, it is the surpassing, encompassing love of the incarnate Son of God that dominates everything the Beloved Disciple says, does, and writes. And this is as it should be, for does not "love make the world go round"?[145] It has even been demonstrated medically that love or lack of it can make all the difference between living and dying, especially in babies and young children. Indeed, in my own words, "to live is to love!"[146]

In Genesis, all of creation is the result of God's love, and after the beginning of light and life we see the early stages of human love in the formation of Adam and Eve and their union with each other in Gen 1:27-28; 2:18-24; 4:1-2. So also in the First Epistle of John, after God is shown to be light and life he is described at length as love itself in 1 John 3:1, 13-24; 4:7-21, especially 1 John 4:16, NAB: "God is love, and whoever remains in love remains in God and God in him."

In John's prologue, we again see that after the Word is described as light and life (John 1:3-9) he is shown to be the source of love and truth (John 1:14, 17). And this same pattern is carried on throughout the Gospel. Thus, the Book of Signs is primarily concerned with portraying Jesus as the light of revelation and truth and the source of life, not only for the ill and dying but even for the dead. Then the Book of Glory, featuring the tender discourse of Jesus at the Last Supper, is replete with expressions of love on Jesus' part and even a new commandment of love to guide us. How can anyone resist those touching assurances of Jesus in John 14:21, NAB, "Whoever loves me will be loved by my Father, and I will love him and reveal myself to him," and in John 14:23, NAB, "Whoever loves me will keep my word, and my Father will love him, and we will come to him and make our dwelling with him"? Notice first the light of revelation, then the indwelling of love!

A quick glance at the references to love in the Gospel reveals what has just been established, namely that the preponderance of emphasis on love comes in the Book of Glory. In the Book of Signs, the major mentions of love occur in John 3:16, 35; 5:20; 10:17; 11:3, 5, 36; 12:25; while in the Book of Glory, even a partial list would include the following: John 13:1, 23, 34-35; 14:15, 21, 23-28, 31; 15:9-19; 16:27; 17:23-27; 19:26; 20:2; 21:15-17, 20.

But as with life, so also with love, we need at this juncture to distinguish its different kinds lest we end in confusion over the very meaning of love. In English, word rich though our language certainly is, we have only the one word "love," which is stretched to cover every possible kind of love including much that does not even begin to qualify. In Greek, however, we use three different words: *érōs*, which indicates romantic, passionate, sexual love; *philía*, which is used for friendship, connoting a certain amount of true equality between friends; and *agápē*, which is specific for spiritual, supernatural, even divine love.

Of these three, the first is never used in the New Testament. That does not mean, of course, that such love is unworthy of a Christian but only that the inspired human authors did not find occasion to use the term. The second word, referring to friendship, is regularly used wherever the specific love of friendship is indicated. For example, Jesus uses it in John 15:13-15. But by and large, whenever the word love is used in the New Testament, it is almost always represented by the Greek term *agápē*.

In the epilogue of John's Gospel, John 21:15-17, there is an interesting contrast between Jesus' request for love (*agápē*) from Peter on the one hand and Peter's response in friendship (*philía*) on the other. Of course, they would most probably have spoken in Aramaic, where no such clear distinction would have been made, but evidently the author wanted to reveal Peter's reluctance to claim anything like a supernatural love for Jesus after his weak threefold denial of him during his trial.

In the institution, covenant, and sacrament of marriage, however, all three kinds of love have their proper and even necessary place: *érōs* in the union of married lovers in "one flesh" (Gen 2:24; Matt 19:5; Eph 5:31); *philía*, in their intimate relationship as friends, living together in good times and bad, respecting each other, and helping each other to fulfill their individual potential; and *agápē*, in their mutual, sacramental consecration in Christ and to Christ. The great mistake of so many married couples, and one that has led to a fifty percent incidence of divorce, is the unreasonable expectation of perfection in erotic love, not only early in marriage but also after many years, as if *érōs* were the only kind of love in marriage and were capable of endless growth throughout life. Love can and should grow all through married life, but not necessarily the love of *érōs*. After some years, the fires of passion are normally banked, but friendship (*philía*) and above all spiritual love (*agápē*) can and should be able to keep on growing for the rest of the couple's life.

When Jesus gives us his new commandment of love in John 13:14-15 and 15:12, a commandment that requires of us that we love one another as he has loved us, what does that mean? First of all, that we love one another in imitation of his selfless, unconditional love for us. After all, he loved us even when we crucified him. But the statement may well contain a further meaning, namely, that we are to love one another with the very same love with which Christ has loved us. He shares his unconditional love with us! So, whether we are married or not, we have the great privilege of loving with the very love that Christ has showered on us. We are, therefore, totally without excuse. Granted, some among us have been stunted in love by receiving too little during their formative period of life, and for this professional help may be required, but with or without it we still have at our disposal the very love of Christ with which he has so generously loved us.

No wonder Paul can exclaim in Rom 8:35, NIV, "Who shall separate us from the love of Christ?" In this love, we can and should continue to grow both in time and in eternity. What gratitude we owe "this tremendous lover"[147] of ours! And how, whether married or not, we should continuously plead with Jesus, who graced the marriage feast of Cana,[148] to constantly change our own weak and watery human love into the strong and rich wine of his divine love!

We have now reached the conclusion of our study of the Gospel and First Epistle of the Beloved Disciple, John. It will not be necessary to recapitulate all that we have had the opportunity to cover, but I would like briefly to apply our three themes of *light, life,* and *love* to our own personal and communal life. We have seen how those three great themes appear in that order in the early chapters of Genesis, in the prologue of John's Gospel and, indeed, in John's Gospel and First Epistle themselves. And this corresponds to the actual experience of the twelve apostles, as reflected in the Gospel. In the first two chapters of John, the apostles come to recognize Jesus as the *light* of truth and revelation of God. Then in John 3–12, they live with him and learn from him, not only that he is the "bread of life" (John 6:48-58) and has "the words of eternal life" (Peter in John 6:68) but that he has "come so that all might have *life* and have it to the full" (John 10:10) and that he is even "the resurrection and the life" (John 11:24). Finally, in John 13–21, they come to realize that "having loved his own in the world, he loves them to the end" (John 13:1), manifesting his love in his foot washing and final discourse, but above all in his self-sacrificing death and glorious resurrection. And even after his resurrection and ascension (John 20:17) he, together with the Father and the Spirit, will dwell with them in love (John 14:12-23).

Is this not the same process through which we ourselves are invited to go and grow in our relationship with Christ? First, we encounter him as the *light* of truth and revelation of God, to which our response should be, like that of the apostles, one of faith, trust, and obedience. Then, we receive *life* from him mainly through the companionship and communication of prayer, the reception of his Holy Word, as well as through the Church and sacraments, especially baptism and the Holy Eucharist. Finally, our relationship grows into one of genuine love, perhaps beginning with that of friendship (*philía*) but developing through his grace into one of deep, spiritual love (*agápē*) and indeed of that *loving union* (not just unity) for which Jesus prayed in his so-called priestly prayer of John 17.

I have wanted to reflect briefly on this application of the three main Johannine themes of light, life, and love to our own personal and communal spiritual life because, as we have seen, John's Gospel and First Epistle, reflecting his own experience and contemplation, follow the very same order.[149] Hence, it seems to me, considerations of this kind cannot but help both in the understanding of John and in our own progress in the spiritual life.

As we leave John's Gospel and First Epistle, then, we do so with a tranquil sense of fulfillment and even of discovery, the discovery, not just in theory but in fact, of Jesus Christ as the light, life, and love of our very being or, as he himself puts it in John 14:6, "the way,[150] the truth, and the life!"[151] Yes, he is our way of love, our light of truth, our water and bread of life! "Without the way there is no going, with out the truth there is no knowing, without the life there is no living."[151] He is our way without bending, our truth without ending, our life with out dying. May he be blessed forever!

NOTES

1. I have chosen to title this chapter "Ingenuous John and the Sublime Gospel" to call attention simultaneously to the acknowledged mystical nature of the Fourth Gospel and nevertheless its evident simplicity of expression.

The name John (Hebrew, *Yehohanan*; Greek, *Iōánnes*) means "Yahweh is gracious" and occurs in different forms in both the Old and New Testaments, e.g. John Hyrcanus (135–104 B.C.), one of the Hasmonean (Maccabean) rulers; John the Baptist; John the apostle-evangelist; and John Mark. In addition, under the alternate forms of *Hananiah* or *Hananías*, the name identifies a false prophet during the time of Jeremiah (Jer 27-28), a Jewish Christian in Jerusalem who is struck dead for lying to Peter and the apostles (Acts 5:1-11), a Jewish Christian of Damascus who receives Paul into the Church (Acts 9:10-19), and a Jewish high priest who opposed Paul in Jerusalem and in Caesarea (Acts 23:1-11; 24:1-23).

2. I have chosen as our opening Scripture text this profound, self-identifying statement of Jesus because it comes closest to the basic identification of him in the prologue and the entire Gospel of John as the light, love, and life of the world.

3. Ephesus in the final decade of the first century A.D. enjoyed the enviable reputation of being one of the four great cities of the Roman Empire along with Rome itself, Alexandria in Egypt, and Antioch of Syria. Her prominence stemmed from a combination of factors: (1) her commercial advantage as one of the principal ports on the eastern Aegean Sea, (2) her political advantage as the capital of the Roman province of Asia in western Asia Minor, (3) her religious advantage as the site of the famous temple of Diana or Artemis, and (4) her cultural advantage as the crossroads of Asian, Egyptian, and European influences.

Today, all of that prominence has long since vanished, mainly with the silt-ing up of her port, but in a special way Ephesus remains unique, as one of the only cities of the ancient world that has for years been undergoing excavation and restoration, thanks to her lack of habitation and to the generous dedication of Austrian archaeologists, so that one can again walk her streets and feel a sense of her past magnificence. For further information on Ephesus, see *Baedeker's Turkish Coast* (Englewood Cliffs, N.J.: Prentice-Hall 1987) 113–28; or *The Complete Guide to Ephesus* (Izmir, Turkey: Tigaret Matbaacilik, 1983).

4. The Magnesian Gate on the southeastern corner of the Hellenistic city wall was so named because it opened onto the road to the important ancient city of Magnesia. See *Baedeker's Turkish Coast*, 179–81.

5. The Curetes (in Greek, *kourêtes*) were legendary Cretan demigods who, at the urging of the mother-goddess Rhea, protected her newborn son, the god Zeus, from her husband and his father, the father-god Cronus, who regularly ate his offspring to avoid being supplanted by them. They saved Zeus by banging their bronze spears and shields so loudly that they drowned out the infant's cries. The Curetes were often identified, or at least confused, with the Corybantes, legendary priests of Cybele, the Asian mother-goddess, who worshiped her with loud, orgiastic dances. Since in syncretistic religion, Rhea came to be identified with Cybele, and Cybele in turn with Artemis, the patron-goddess of Ephesus, it is not surprising to find a college of Curetes situated on the Way of the Curetes at Ephesus. See, for example, *Harper's Dictionary of Classical Literature and Antiquities*, Harry Thurston Peck, ed. (New York: Cooper Square Publishers, 1962) 418, 442.

6. The Marble Road at Ephesus, which leads from the Way of the Curetes to the great theater, passes along the lower and greater of the city's two agoras, the very center of Ephesian life in the first century.

7. The great theater of Ephesus, begun under Claudius (A.D. 41–54) and finally completed under Trajan (98–117), seated some twenty-five thousand spectators and seems to have been the site of the silversmiths' riot against Paul in Acts 19:23-40.

8. The monumental road leading from the great theater to the port of Ephesus was called the Harbor Road in the time of Paul and John, but was later renamed the Arkadiane Way after Arcadius (377–408), the first Eastern emperor, who embellished it in magnificent fashion around A.D. 400, and thus it is designated today.

9. The famous Harbor of Ephesus, which was never situated on the Aegean Sea itself but rather on an artificial widening of the Cayster River that flowed into the Aegean, had to be ultimately abandoned because the technology of the time could not succeed in keeping natural erosion from filling it with silt. As a result, the site is today nothing but marshland, and Ephesus is now reached from the sea through the port of Kushadasi and a ten-mile bus trip.

10. Ephesus was rightly called the crossroads of pagan cults, not because it surpassed all other cities in the number of its temples and statues but rather because of its tendency to take the initiative in welcoming new deities and forms of worship from whatever direction and then proceeding to combine and identify them with other deities and forms of worship from other directions.

11. An odeon (or odeion) in ancient times differed from a theater both in

size and purpose, being much smaller and intended for recitals and lesser productions rather than the great plays and spectacles of the theater. While the odeon on the Way of the Curetes dates from the second century A.D., it would be incredible if a city of the size and importance of ancient Ephesus had no previous odeon.

12. Like the odeon, the famous Library of Celsus is of the second century, having been completed in A.D. 136 and dedicated to Governor Titus Julius Celsus Pelemainus by his son. However, it is difficult to imagine the famous Ephesus, located between the great libraries of Alexandria and Pergamum, without a prior library of her own.

13. Situated in the oldest part of ancient Ephesus, the Artemisium, or temple of Artemis, was roughly the size of an American football field and ornamented with two rows of columns numbering 127 altogether. Replacing an earlier temple destroyed by fire in 356 B.C., the one of John's time was in turn damaged by invading Goths about A.D. 260 and turned into a source of building materials during the Byzantine Empire. Today, all that remains of this famous temple is a small collection of stone pieces in a marshy swamp where the frogs seem to croak, "Great is Diana of the Ephesians!" *See* H. V. Morton, *In the Steps of St. Paul* (London: Rich and Cowan, 1936) 322.

14. Though derived from Greek, Cretan, Phrygian, and Aeolian or Anatolian mythology respectively, the goddesses Gaea, Rhea, Cybele, and Artemis were often identified with one another in syncretistic religion, all of them being linked in one way or another with the fertility of the earth.

15. The atmosphere of sexual immorality at Corinth, with its two ports, Isthmian Games, and temple of Aphrodite, was proverbial in the ancient world and has already been treated in connection with Paul's stay at Corinth and his Letters to the Corinthians in ch. 1 of this volume.

16. See *Harper's Dictionary of Classical Literature and Antiquities* 1106–07.

17. The cult of Serapis is an excellent example of syncretistic religion, for it actually resulted from the deliberate union of two Egyptian cults by Ptolemy I, called Soter (Savior or Preserver), the first Greek after Alexander the Great to rule Egypt (323–285 B.C.). In his desire to unite his Greek and Egyptian subjects, he decided to combine the cult of Osiris, the lord of the underworld or afterlife, with that of Apis, the bull-god of Memphis, under the single name of Serapis (Asar-Hapi, the Egyptian names of Osiris and Apis) and to promote the new cult by the construction of the colossal Serapeion (Serapeum) at Alexandria, the Greek center named after Alexander and marked with his reputed tomb. In the syncretistic process, Serapis came to be identified with Hades (or Pluto), the Greek god of the underworld; and Isis, sister and wife of Osiris, with Persephone, the abducted bride of Hades in the Elysinian Mysteries. In time, Serapis even came to be identified by the Greeks with Zeus himself and Isis with Hera, his sister and wife. In Asia Minor, however, the tendency was to identify Isis with Artemis, the goddess of Ephesus. *See* E. A. Wallis Budge, *The Gods of the Egyptians: Studies in Egyptian Mythology* (New York: Dover Publications, 1969) 2:195–201.

18. The term "syncretism" is derived from the Greek words *syn* (with, to-

gether) and either *kratismós* (power) or *kretismós* (Cretanism), the latter etymology referring to the Cretan tendency not only to unite different deities but also to form unlikely alliances against common foes. See *The Random House Dictionary of the English Language.*

19. The third and final Flavian emperor, Domitian (A.D. 81–96), was the younger brother and successor of Titus (79–81), the conqueror of Jerusalem, who in turn had succeeded his father, Vespasian (69–79), the first Flavian emperor and builder of the famous Flavian Amphitheater, popularly called the Colosseum, not because of its size but because of a colossal statue of Nero standing nearby. While both Vespasian and Titus were mostly good rulers as Roman emperors go, Domitian turned out to be an egocentric and paranoid tyrant, so like the infamous Nero that he was nicknamed *Nero Redivivus* (Nero Reborn). We will examine Domitian more fully when we study the Book of Revelation or Apocalypse in the following chapter.

20. The earliest temple honoring a Roman emperor seems to be the fairly well preserved temple of Augustus in the old city of Ancyra, present-day Ankara, the capital of Turkey. Its inscription, dating from A.D. 14, the year of Augustus' death, and beginning with the words *Index Rerum Gestarum Divi Augusti* (List of the Deeds of the Divine Augustus) is reproduced in *Harper's Dictionary of Classical Literature and Antiquities,* 171.

21. This expression, "Lord and God" (Greek *Kýrios kaì Theós* and Latin *Dominus et Deus*) may partially account for the unforgettable story of Doubting Thomas and his ultimate profession of faith, "My Lord and my God!" (*ho kýriós mou kaì ho theós mou*) in John 20:28.

22. *See* n. 5 above.

23. *See* my fairly extensive treatment of incipient Gnosticism in ch. 2, n. 64.

24. According to Eastern tradition, based somewhat on the apocryphal *Acts of John* by Prochorus (*pró-choros*, leader of the dance), this was the name of one of John's closest companions. If, however, he is identical with the Prochorus chosen as one of the first deacons along with Stephen and Philip in Acts 6:5, then he would not be a youth at this time as he is usually depicted. Rather, I would estimate his age at five to ten years younger than John, just as John was probably about ten years younger than Jesus. *See* Montague James, *The Apocryphal New Testament* (Oxford: Clarendon, 1972) 469; and Otto Meinardus, *St. John of Patmos and the Seven Churches of the Apocalypse* (Athens: Lycabettus Press, 1979) 1, 10.

25. Strong early testimony in the Church dating from St. Irenaeus (A.D. 120–202), a disciple of St. Polycarp before becoming bishop of Lyons, indicates that Polycarp (*polycarpós*, much fruit) was a disciple of John before becoming the bishop of Smyrna. According to the very reliable acts of his martyrdom, he was burned to death for his fidelity in the great stadium overlooking Smyrna (Izmir) in A.D. 156, at the age of eighty-six. That would put him in his twenties during the final decade of the first century. *See* "The Martyrdom of St. Polycarp," trans. Francis X. Glimm, *The Apostolic Fathers* (New York: Cima, 1947) 145–63; see also Irenaeus, *Against Heresies*, The Ante-Nicene Fathers, ed. Alex. Roberts and Jas. Donaldson (New York: Charles Scribner's Sons, 1926), 416.

It should also be noted here that some early writers, including Irenaeus, have Papias, later Bishop of Hierapolis, as personally acquainted with John, but the latter disavows this, according to Eusebius, who quotes from Papias' five books. *See* Eusebius, *History of the Church from Christ to Constantine* (New York: N.Y.U. Press, 1966) 149–50.

26. Most portraits of John show him as a beardless young man during the public life of Jesus. One of the few that portray him in his later years is a seventeenth century icon from the Byzantine Museum in Athens depicting John, white-bearded and largely bald, "dictating" the Fourth Gospel to Prochorus, young and beardless, an icon that is reproduced in Otto Meinardus, *St. John of Patmos*, opposite p. 1. In the early A.D. 90s, I picture John in his early eighties, but with the vigor of a man some twenty years younger. For more, *see* n. 34 below.

27. In the supposition that Prochorus was five to ten years younger than John, he would have been in his early or late seventies at this time.

28. As indicated in n. 25 above, Polycarp would have been in his 20's at this time and, somewhat like Timothy with Paul, would have been John's spiritual son, confidant, and heir.

29. Unanimous tradition holds that John survived all the other apostles by several years, until he finally passed away, according to Irenaeus, under the Emperor Trajan (A.D. 98–117). *See* Irenaeus, *Against Heresies*, 416; *see also* Eusebius, *History of the Church*, 128; Otto Meinardus, *St. John of Patmos*, 10.

30. Traditionally, the Beloved Disciple, mentioned in six places of the Fourth Gospel (13:23-26; 19:25-27; 20:2-10; 21:7, 20-23, 24), has been identified with John the son of Zebedee, and in spite of many arguments to the contrary, that identification still seems the most likely. *See* Raymond Brown, *The Gospel According to John*, vol. 1 (Garden City, N.Y.: Doubleday, 1966) xcii–xcviii.

31. In the Synoptic Gospels, Peter, James, and John are the only ones invited to accompany Jesus at the raising of Jairus' daughter (Mark 5:37; Luke 8:51), at the transfiguration (Mark 9:2; Matt 17:1; Luke 9:28), and at his prayer and agony in the Garden of Gethsemane (Mark 14:33; Matt 26:37), and, along with Andrew, at the healing of Peter's mother-in-law (Mark 1:29).

32. *See* John 19:25-27. That John took Mary with him to Ephesus, possibly after the beheading of his brother James in Jerusalem (Acts 12:2) is attested not only by various traditions but also by the existence at Ephesus of three important sites: (1) the Basilica of St. John, (2) the double Church of St. Mary, where at the Council of Ephesus in 431, Mary was declared *theótokos* (mother of God), and (3) the House of Mary (*Panaya Kapulu*, a Turkish corruption of the Greek-Latin *pân hagía-capella*, meaning "All Holy Chapel"), dating from the first century, described by the German mystic Katherine Emmerich (1774–1824) and rediscovered in 1891 by two Vincentian priests. Of these three places, probably the most important witness is the Church of St. Mary, because at that time it was not customary to dedicate a church to a saint except where he or she had lived and especially died. Just when Mary passed from this life into heaven is not known, but tradition and common sense indicate that John may have outlived her by at least twenty years.

33. Matt 10:8, NIV.

34. John's advanced age in the 90s is cited by some as a basic argument against his writing a gospel at this time, let alone an apocalypse. However, while I picture him in his early eighties during our time frame, I also imagine him as having the vigor of a person twenty years younger, for various reasons: (1) a lifetime of disciplined living, (2) an extraordinary energy, natural as well as supernatural, and (3) a spirit of serenity resulting from his total gift of self to Christ, his years with both Jesus and Mary, his habitual contemplation, and hence his total freedom from worry and anxiety. He had long ago completely overcome his natural impetuosity, which had earned him the nickname *Boanêrgés* (Son of Thunder, Mark 3:17), had impelled him to silence an "unauthorized" exorcist (Mark 9:38; Luke 9:49), had made him want to call down fire from heaven on the inhospitable Samaritans (Luke 9:54), and had moved him to seek one of the two first places in Jesus' kingdom (Mark 10:35-45; Matt 20:20-28). In fact, not only had he overcome his natural impetuosity but by the grace of God and the guidance of the Holy Spirit he had converted that energy into controlled zeal for Christ and his kingdom.

35. By "the one pastoral letter" here is indicated the First Epistle of John, which has many affinities with his Gospel, especially in their similarity of themes: light, love, and life. Which came first is disputed, but I have chosen to place the Epistle earlier than the Gospel and, in a sense, suggesting the themes for the Gospel. The additional note that the Epistle was written at the urging of Timothy is, of course, pure speculation, but it is not beyond the realm of possibility, considering Timothy's assumed reverence for John's apostolic and personal authority and John's respect for Timothy's ecclesial authority, as reflected in Paul's Pastoral Letters. Did John not govern the Church in Ephesus and indeed the whole Roman province of Asia? Many assume that he did, and some early literature may seem to confirm that view, but to me the greater likelikood is that he preferred to leave the administration in other hands, reserving the right, readily accorded him, to speak out and write in the role of bishop emeritus whenever the situation of the Church required it or its leadership requested it.

As for the Second and Third Epistles attributed to John, while there are some affinities with the First Epistle, I am following the opinion of many that the author, who refers to himself as the presbyter, may have been one John the Presbyter who is mentioned by Papias of Hierapolis and by Eusebius and who seems to have lived at the same time as John or somewhat later. *See* Eusebius, *History of the Church*, 150–51; *see also* Brown, *The Gospel According to John*, vol. 1, xc–xcii. At any rate, there is no comparison between the contents and flavor of 1 John and those of 2 and 3 John put together.

36. Note how 1 John begins with "The Word of life" (1:1-4), then moves on to God as light (1:5-10), then back to life (2:24-27), then on to God's love (3:1-3), the call to love one another (3:11-18), to the identification of God as love itself (4:7-21).

37. It should be noted that in 1 John the themes of light, love, and life are generally applied to God, while in the Gospel of John they are applied to Jesus Christ as the very embodiment or incarnation of God himself.

38. This legal expression which means "to stop voluntarily from presenting evidence pertinent to [a case at law] is used here as appropriate to the situation and familiar, I trust, to the reader. *Webster's Ninth New Collegiate Dictionary*, s.v. "rest."

39. The very fact that Galilee was commonly referred to, particularly by Judeans, as "Galilee of the Gentiles" on account of its proximity to and commerce with pagan lands, and the geographical fact that just across the Sea of Galilee was located the Decapolis, a collection of ten Greek cities, are sufficient to provide a reasonable assumption that Galileans, including the apostles and Jesus himself, were not ignorant of the international language of the day, Koine (Common Greek).

40. As indicated in n. 32 above, there may have been an interval of some twenty years after Mary's departure in which John quite probably used Greek almost exclusively, thus acquiring an even greater facility than previously.

41. According to Acts 19:1-7, there were disciples of the Baptist at Ephesus, twelve of whom Paul received into the Christian Church through the sacrament of baptism. How many other followers of Jesus' forerunner there were in Ephesus and its environs we can only guess, but that such a situation existed at the time would explain the obvious care with which the Fourth Gospel shows its respect for John the Baptist and also its determination to clarify his role as a witness and herald of the Messiah, Jesus.

42. Those who have studied the so-called Gospel of Matthew can easily note a similar apologetic, even a polemic, in the Fourth Gospel against the arguments and inroads of aggressive Pharisaic Judaism. When John recounts Jesus' running conflict with "the Jews," he is generally referring to the religious leaders of Judaism who, after the defeat of Israel and destruction of the Temple, were solely Pharisees and who, under Rabbi Gamaliel II some ten years previously, had proscribed Jewish Christians as *minim* (heretics), forbidding them entry into synagogues the world over. It is important to keep this in mind while reading John's Gospel, lest we subconsciously apply his references to "the Jews" to all Jews of that time or even of all time.

43. *See* volume 1 of *Human Authors of the New Testament*, ch. 2, for the underlying reasons leading to the writing of the so-called Gospel according to Matthew.

44. The reference here is to the powerful Epistle to the Hebrews, which traditionally was attributed to Paul but is now almost unanimously recognized as written by some anonymous author whom, with many others, I prefer to identify with the Apollos of Acts and I Corinthians for the simple reason that his rich Alexandrian background of Jewish belief and learning, together with Greek philosophy and rhetoric, would have ideally equipped him to write the masterful and moving Epistle to the Hebrews. *See* Acts 18:24–19:1 and 1 Cor 1–4.

45. In Eph 5:21-22, Paul uses the verb *hypotássomai*, from *hypo* (under), and *tássomai* (I arrange myself), from *tásso* (I order or arrange), applying it first to all his readers and then to wives in regard to their husbands. In the context, I think it clearly means "I defer to another for the sake of good order."

46. It is well known that, at the very time that John the apostle was still

living at Ephesus, it was Clement, the third successor of Peter as bishop of Rome and vicar of Christ, who settled the schism in the Church at Corinth by means of a very long letter. *See* "The Letter of Saint Clement of Rome to the Corinthians," trans. Francis Glimm, *The Apostolic Fathers*, 3–58.

47. *See* Mark 1:19-20; Matt 4:21-22; Luke 5:10-11.

48. *See* John 13:23.

49. *See* John 19:25-27.

50. That the Gospel of John is a uniquely spiritual work was recognized early by Clement of Alexandria (A.D. 150–215), who writes, "But John, the last of all, seeing that what was corporeal was set forth in the Gospels, on the entreaty of his intimate friends, and inspired by the Spirit, composed a spiritual Gospel." *See* Clement of Alexandria, *Fragments*, in The Ante-Nicene Fathers 2:580; also Paul-Marie de la Croix, *The Biblical Spirituality of St. John* (Staten Island, N.Y.: Alba, 1966); *see also* L. Wm. Countryman, *The Mystical Way in the Fourth Gospel: Crossing over into God* (Philadelphia: Fortress, 1987) 2–3.

51. This anticipation within the life of Jesus of what was to become evident only at his resurrection is well known as "realized eschatology," an expression popularized by the great English Scripture scholar, C. H. Dodd. This does not mean that there is nothing in this Gospel about the end time as still future, but what is emphasized by the term "realized eschatology" is that Jesus, in word and in deed, is already triumphant throughout his life, even and especially in his death by crucifixion, as seen for example in his threefold references to being "lifted up" in John 3:14; 8:28; and 12:32-33. Thus, in John's Gospel, as distinguished from the Synoptics, Jesus speaks of himself over and over again as divine, even as identified with Yahweh himself, for example in his several references to himself as "I AM" in John 8:24, 28, 58. *See* Brown, *The Gospel According to John*, vol. 1, pp. cxvi–cxxi.

52. As explained in *Human Authors of the New Testament*, vol 1, p. 36 and elsewhere, the kerygma, from *kēryx* (herald), is the public proclamation of the Church about Jesus Christ. It underlies all the Gospels and the main addresses in Acts and is generally considered to comprise four points: the baptism and witness by John the Baptist, the Galilean ministry, the journey to Jerusalem, and the saving events in Jerusalem.

53. John's Gospel contains six Jewish feasts, most of them celebrated by Jesus in Jerusalem, as a good observing Jew.

54. While the Synoptists emphasize Jesus' ministry in Galilee, clearly John focuses primarily on his ministry in Jerusalem, especially in terms of signs (miracles) and discourses, which formed a clear confrontation with Judaism.

55. John has several historical and geographical details that indicate the work of an eyewitness familiar with the time and place treated. The most famous instance is John's mention of the Sheep Pool with five porticoes, or covered walkways. This was usually dismissed as inaccurate or at least inattentive to detail until the Sheep Pool near the Crusader Church of St. Ann, just north of the temple area, was excavated and, sure enough, found to contain five porticoes, the fifth being across the middle. *See* Brown, *The Gospel According to John*, vol. 1, xlii–xliii.

56. The two reasons given for the difference between John and the Synoptics are, of course, practical and important, but a third reason could be added, namely that John uses a tradition different from that of the Synoptics. *See* Brown, *The Gospel According to John*, vol. 1, xliv–xlvii.

57. Examples of John's inclusion in a different manner of Synoptic episodes apparently omitted in the Fourth Gospel are Jesus' temptations (Mark 1:12-13; Matt 4:1-11; Luke 4:1-13; John 6:15, 26-35; 7:1-10); Peter's profession of faith in Jesus (Mark 8:27-29; Matt 16:13-16; Luke 9:18-20; John 6:66-69); Jesus' transfiguration (Mark 9:2-8; Matt 17:1-8; Luke 9:28-36; John 12:28-33); Jesus' prayer and agony in the garden (Mark 14:32-42; Matt 26:36-46; Luke 22:39-46; John 12:23-28).

58. See nn. 36 and 37 above. As we will see later in the analysis and outline, Christ as the light and life of the world is mainly the emphatic theme in John 1–13, and Christ as incarnate love demanding mutual love of us is the principal theme in John 13–21.

59. In John's Gospel, Jesus' miracles are never referred to as such but only as signs. This is highly significant, for it underlines the fact that just as the Synoptics differ among themselves in the use of Jesus' miracles (Mark employing them to show Jesus' power as messianic Son of God; "Matthew," to prepare for and introduce Jesus' discourses; and Luke, to exemplify Jesus' compassion as the universal Savior), so John recounts Jesus' miracles not so much as miracles, but as "works" of the Father and "signs," or symbols, of important truths, for example, the multiplication of the loaves and fishes and the walking on water as signs and symbols of the Holy Eucharist. And of all Jesus' miracles, John chooses only seven signs to fit in with his usual emphasis on the perfect number of seven.

60. An examination of John's Gospel reveals that the seven signs are often (but not always) followed by significant discourses, though sometimes the discourses are introduced without references to any particular sign. Altogether, there are seven main discourses in the Gospel of John.

61. Numbers in the Bible and in the ancient world generally were more often than not used symbolically. Probably the two most common positive numbers were seven and twelve with a relationship between the two. There are seven days in the week, possibly determined by the number of days in each of the four quarters of the moon, which comprise a lunar month. And there are twelve months in the year. Also, seven is the result of three plus four; twelve, the result of three times four. Thus, both the Old and New Testaments are understandably full of references to these two numbers in a positive way, for example, God rests on the seventh day after initial creation, thus sanctifying the seventh day as the Sabbath or day of rest. There are twelve tribes of Israel and twelve initial apostles. Quite naturally, then, seven and twelve became symbolic of perfection, wholeness, goodness, etc. Thus, for example, in John's Gospel there are seven signs, seven discourses, seven titles of Jesus, and apparently seven main acts altogether, as will be detailed in the analysis. *See* John L. McKenzie, *Dictionary of the Bible* (Milwaukee: Bruce, 1965), 620–21, 794.

62. Just as the number seven symbolized perfection in the ancient world, so the number six became the symbol of imperfection for the simple reason that it never reaches the perfect number of seven. Thus, in John's Gospel, the six waterpots of Jewish purification and the six Jewish feasts referred to during the public ministry of Jesus are clear reminders of the imperfection of the Jewish dispensation, which is shown being fulfilled and replaced by Christ and Christianity.

63. In John's highly symbolic Gospel, there are a number of symbols that seem to be drawn primarily from nature, perhaps adding up to seven altogether, as listed in the analysis.

64. There are also a number of symbols that seem to be drawn primarily from the Old Testament, perhaps also adding up to seven altogether, as listed in the analysis.

65. One might think that in a mystical gospel such as that of John, there would be little or nothing about the Church in its visible and institutional nature, but such is not the case. John is primarily concerned, it is true, with insisting on the hidden, invisible nature of the Church as a community intimately united with Christ as sheep to their shepherd (John 10:1-18) and branches to the vine (John 15:1-17), figures, incidentally, that reflect the union of Israel with Yahweh in Ps 80, but the community is not purely invisible, for it comprises a visible and discernible body of believers (e.g. John 6:66-68; 10:16; 13:35), with visible leadership (John 1:35-51; 17:1-26; 21:15-17), and visible sacraments, as seen in n. 66, below. *See* Brown, *The Gospel According to John*, vol. 1, cv–cxi.

66. It is surprising to discover in a mystical gospel like John's the many references to the sacraments of the Church, for example, to baptism in 3:3-7; Eucharist in 6:32-59; penance, or reconciliation, in 20:19-23. And, in addition to these explicit references, there are the implicit ones to confirmation in John 7:37-39, holy orders in John 13-17 passim, and possibly matrimony in John 2:1-11. For more, *see* Brown, *The Gospel According to John*, vol. 1, cxi-cxiv.

67. The seven titles of Jesus to which I refer occur, surprisingly enough, in the first chapter of John's Gospel, a clear indication, I believe, of the use of concentric circles, as will be explained further in n. 69 below.

68. In practice, a clear distinction should be made between acts and episodes. I do believe that John's Gospel divides naturally into seven acts, plus a prologue and an epilogue, but each act contains two scenes or episodes. See the outline of John's Gospel in this chapter for further clarification.

69. Contrary to our ordinary method of development, which proceeds from point 1 to point 2 and so on, writers in the time and area of the world in which John's Gospel was written were partial to a form of development known as concentric circles. In this structure, if I may refresh the reader's mind, the salient point or points are mentioned at the very beginning and then returned to with additional clarification or expansion throughout the piece. In our own day, this method is not infrequently followed in newspaper journalism, in which the first paragraph of an article contains the content in a nutshell, but the article continues to add details as it returns over and over again to the initial basic material. In John's Gospel, I think that this is done first with the basic

themes of light, life, and love in the prologue and with the seven titles of Jesus in ch. 1, both of these being developed in the rest of the Gospel. Another instance of concentric circles seems to be Jesus' discourse at the Last Supper.

70. Again, in contrast with our normal manner of development, the writers of that time and area of the world were very fond of using what has come to be known as chiasmus, from the Greek letter chi which looks like our capital X. However, only the lower part of the X is actually used, with a parallel between the first and last points, then the second and next to last points, and so on with the most emphatic point coming in the middle of the content, or at the top of the inverted V. This will be explained more fully when we take up structures in John's Gospel in the analysis section of this chapter.

71. The reference here, of course, is to Paul's famous *Carmen Christi* (Hymn of Christ) in Phil 2:5-11, which I have already presented in my own translation in ch. 1, "Passionate Paul and the Early Letters," pp. 56-57.

72. The reference is to Prov 8:22-36 and Wis 7:21-8:1. These are the most explicit and best examples of the personification of divine wisdom, though there are other and more implicit examples in Job 38-41 and Sir 24:1-31, as well as Bar 3:9-4:4.

73. The reference here is to Gen 1-2:4 in relation to the personification of wisdom in Prov 8:22-36, Wis 7:21-8:1, and John 1:1-5.

74. Here the reference is to Exod 40, the erection of the tabernacle, or tent of dwelling, in relation to John 1:14, NAB, "and made his dwelling among us" (literally, "and pitched his tent among us"). Another verse that should be considered in this regard is John 2:19, NAB, "Destroy this temple and in three days I will raise it up," after which John editorializes in John 2:21, "But he was speaking about the temple of his body."

75. Unquestionably, John's thought is couched in simple language, though with very profound meanings. What could be simpler than such words as light, life, and love, yet how profound their meaning! Contrast, for example, the Gospel of John with Paul's Letters, such as Romans, or with the First Epistle of Peter, which seems to owe its convoluted language to Silvanus, as we see in 1 Pet 5:12.

76. Some may object that, in Mark 4:10-12, Jesus seems to say that he preaches in parables precisely so that "those outside" may not understand. However, it must be remembered that, unlike "Matthew," Mark is not particularly concerned about being misunderstood, so he simply quotes (and maybe Jesus did also) the enigmatic statement of Yahweh in Isa 6:9-10, in which (as so often in the Old Testament) what will be the result of something is expressed as if it were the purpose. "Matthew," being well aware of this and concerned about misunderstandings regarding Jesus and the apostles, changes *hína* (so that) to *hóti* (because) in Matt 13:13.

77. It has been common among certain commentators to attribute John's use of the word *lógos* (word), from *légō* (I say), to the influence of Greek philosophy, but as I try to show in the story by the discussion on this word, the background is really the personification of divine wisdom in the Old Testament, and *lógos* is chosen primarily on account of its appropriateness as a masculine noun rather than *sophía* (wisdom), which is feminine.

78. *See* Gen 1:3, 6, 9, 14, 20, 24, 26.

79. *See* Kittel, ed., *Theological Dictionary of the New Testament* 4:132–33, 136; *see also* Joseph Thayer, *A Greek-English Lexicon of the New Testament* (New York: American Book Co., 1889) 381–82.

80. Whether John actually encouraged his collaborators to add to his gospel after his death is, of course, my own speculation, but it would help to explain ch. 21, particularly 21:20-25, which seems obviously to have been added after the death of John.

81. In italics also will be the Greek text, which will be faithfully presented in the following notes. The translation, or sometimes the paraphrase, will be given in quotation marks, with variations indicated in parentheses. Sometimes the translation or paraphrase in the notes may differ from my formal poetic one provided in the text, the reason being that the latter is to some extent limited by the requirements of the poetic form.

82. *En archê ên ho lógos.* "In the beginning was the Word." The opening words, *En archê*, "In the beginning," immediately evoke Genesis and personified wisdom, for Gen 1:1 begins in exactly the same way. *ên*, "was," the imperfect tense of *eimí*, "I am," is strongly contrasted with *egéneto*, "came to be, came into existence, became," the aorist (single action in past time) of *gínomai*, "I become," which will be used of creation, of John the Baptist, and of Jesus' human nature, all of which came into existence at a certain point in time. Hence, in the beginning of all things, including time, the Word was already in continuing existence; in fact, he already was in continuing existence from all eternity!

83. *kaì ho lógos ên pròs tòn theón*, "and the Word was in dynamic relationship with (the) God." The preposition, *pròs*, "to, toward, for, with," which I have translated simply as "with," means much more than that. It is a preposition of motion, of dynamic relationship, clearly expressing the dynamic relationship of the Word, or Son, with his Father!

Note the use of the article in *pròs tòn theón*, which indicates the person rather than the nature of God. In other words, the Word or Son as person was (always) in dynamic relationship with "the God," that is, "with his Father," with Yahweh Elohim, the only God, not only of Israel but of the entire universe!

84. *kaì theòs ên ho lógos*, "and God (or divine) was the Word." Note here the deliberate omission of the article, thereby expressing the divine nature rather than the persons in God. In other terms, the Word himself was (and is) actually divine, or more briefly, "the Word himself was God!" Verse 2 then closes off this description of the Word of God by repeating, *hoûtos ên en archê pròs tòn theón*, "he was in the beginning with (in dynamic relationship with) God," the Creator and Father of all.

85. *pánta di' autoû egéneto*, "all things came into being through him." Note here the verb *egéneto*, which I have already identified as the aorist or single action in past time of *gínomai*, "I become." Through the word, the wisdom of God, not just personified, but in person, all things in the universe came into being at the beginning of time! Or, to put it another way, as the prologue does in the two following lines, *kaì chōrìs autoû egéneto oudè hèn ho gégonen,*

"and without him there came to be not one single thing that has come into being."

I feel it necessary to mention here that some divide the sentences differently, construing "that (which) has come into being" with the following sentence. This is legitimate, of course, because in the ancient manuscripts, especially the uncial (capital letter) ones, there were no separations between paragraphs, sentences, or even words. However, to me the expression fits far more naturally with the foregoing both in thought and in poetic structure.

86. *en autô zōè ên,* "in him was life." Note once again the use of *ên,* the imperfect of *eimí,* "I am," indicating that in the Word or Wisdom or Son of God, life was always in continuing existence. The word *zōè,* used here for "life," is in contrast with such words as *biós* and *psychè,* both of which also signify life, but only on the natural level, whereas *zōè* refers to supernatural, spiritual, eternal, even divine life, which God and the Word always had but which, as we shall see, they have chosen to share with us in unselfish love.

87. *kaì hē zōè ên tò phôs tôn anthrōpōn,* "and the life (or his life) was the light of men (or human beings)." Here we have the identification of life and light with each other and their existence from all eternity in the Word, Wisdom, or Son of God. The Greek word *ánthrōpos,* "man," here used in the plural, always includes both male and female of the human species, whereas *anèp* means male or husband and *gynè* signifies female or wife.

88. *kaì tò phôs en tê skotía phaínei, kaì hē skotía autò ou katélaben.* "And the light is shining in the darkness, and the darkness has not received or accepted it, nor has it been able to extinguish it." Note the present tense of *phaínei,* indicating a continuing shining, without any interruption, past, present, or future. Note also that I have translated in the text and paraphrased in the notes two meanings of the same verb, *katélaben,* the aorist of single action (or many actions viewed as one) in past time of the verb *katalambánō,* "I receive, accept, take, overtake, seize, extinguish." From this variety of meanings, some of them even opposites, and from the penchant of Near Eastern writers, especially biblical writers, to intend more than one meaning, I feel justified in including the two opposite senses in the translation and in the notes.

89. *Egéneto ánthrōpos apestalménos parà theoû, ónoma autô Iōánnēs.* "There came into being a man sent from God, whose name (was) John." Note once again the use of *egéneto* in regard to created things and especially John the Baptist, in contrast with *ên,* which is used of the Word or Son because he always was.

90. *hoûtos êlthen eis martyrían, hína martyrésē perì toû phōtós, hína pántes pisteúsōsin di'autoû,* "he came for the sake of witnessing (or with the intention to witness), in order to testify concerning the light, so that all might believe through him." Note the identification in Greek of the words "witness" and "martyr," which is particularly important when speaking of John the Baptist because it was his martyrdom that constituted his ultimate witness.

And, just as the first part of the prologue about the Word and his relationship with the Father was completed with a clear if somewhat repetitive statement that he was in the beginning with God, so the segment on John the Baptist is also completed with a clear but somewhat repetitive statement, *ouk ên ekeî-*

nos tò phôs, all' hína martyrês̄ē perì toû phōtós, "that man (he) was not the light, but rather (came) to witness concerning the light." John himself will say much the same in John 1:19-28; 3:22-30.

91. *Ēn tò phôs tò alēthinón, hò phōtízei pánta ánthrōpon erchómenon eis tòn kósmon.* "That (or He) was the true light who enlightens every man (or person) coming (or who comes) into the world." I have chosen to translate *alēthinón* as "genuine" in the text because, coming from the Greek privative *a,* "not, nothing," and the verb *lanthánō,* "I am hidden," it really means "nothing hidden, authentic, genuine."

92. *en tô kósmō ēn, kaì ho kósmos di' autoû egéneto, kaì ho kósmos autòn ouk égnō,* "he was in the world, and the world came into being through him, and (yet) the world did not know him." The word *égnō,* the aorist or past tense of the verb *ginōskō,* "I know," refers to knowing in a personal, even a loving, way rather than an impersonal or scientific (or indifferent) way, which would be expressed rather by the verb *oîda,* "I know." There is approximately the same difference between *ginōskō* and *oîda* as between the Latin verbs *cognosco* and *scio.*

93. *eis tà ídia êlthen, kaì hoi ídioi autòn ou parélaben,* "he came into (or among) his own things (creation, domain), and his own (people) did not receive (or accept) him." Note the change from ta idia, "his own things," in the neuter gender, to *hoi ídioi,* "his own (people)," in the masculine gender. The former seems clearly to refer to creation or the world, while the latter probably embraces not only his own Jewish people but the entire human race.

94. *hósoi dè élabon autón, édōken autoîs exousían tékna theoû genésthai. . . .* "but whoever accepted him, he gave them authority to become children of God. . . ." The word *exousía,* "authority," is carefully distinguished from the word *dýnamis,* "power," in the New Testament. The former has the connotation of being ratified from above and lasting, hence Jesus gives authority to the apostles to make disciples of all the nations in Matt 28:18. The latter has the connotation of being more charismatic and transitory, hence the apostles receive power from above at Pentecost to speak in tongues, etc., as we see in Luke 24:49 and in Acts 1:8. Both are important, but translations should clearly reflect the precise word that is used because of the different connotations.

The expression *tékna theoû,* "children of God," refers to spiritual adoption by grace and the sacrament of baptism, so prominent in Paul (e.g., Rom 8:14-17), in Peter (1 Pet 1:1–2:10) and, of course, in John himself (John 3:3-7; 1 John 3:1-3).

95. *toîs pisteúousin eis tò ónoma autoû,* "to those who believe in his name (or in his revealed character)." Here, the necessity of faith is emphasized, to be followed by expressions focusing on the importance of the spiritual rebirth by baptism.

96. *hoì . . . egennḗthēsan,* "who . . . were begotten." Here, in my translation, I have dropped down and picked up the verb which in the Greek is held until the end of the sentence. Attention should also be called to the fact that the verb is from *gennáō,* "I beget," rather than from *tíktō,* "I give birth," possibly to emphasize that we are not just born again spiritually by baptism, but in Christ we are actually begotten of God the Father.

97. *ouk ex haimátōn*, "not from bloods," that is, not from the mingling of the blood of parents through sexual intercourse and human procreation. This expression, so strange to us, simply reflects the limited biological knowledge of the time in which this was written.

98. *oudè ek thelēmatos sarkòs*, "nor from (the) will (or desire) of the flesh (or of human nature)." For more on the meaning of the word *sárx*, "flesh," in Scripture, see n. 101 below.

99. *oudè ek thelēmatos andròs*, "nor from the will (or desire) of (a) man (or husband)." This reflects the common assumption of the time that whenever a husband desired to have relations with his wife, it was her duty to oblige him. His right was to initiate relations, hers was to respond without question or excuse.

100. *all' ek theoû*, "but rather from (or of) God." See my remarks about being begotten of God in n. 96.

101. *Kaì ho lógos sàrx egéneto.* "And the Word became flesh," that is, human in all our human weakness, sin alone excluded. Those who, out of a Greek philosophical background, take the word *sárx*, "flesh," to mean the body would naturally understand that the Word or Son took upon himself a human body but not a soul, which would be heresy. Keep in mind that in the Bible the expressions "flesh, person, spirit" describe our whole being in three dimensions: flesh describing our whole being in all our human weakness, subject to sickness, accident, death, temptation, sin; person (which is usually represented in Greek by either body or soul) describes our human nature primarily in our human dignity as endowed with intelligence, free will, and responsibility; and spirit describing our human nature as naturally oriented toward relationship and union with God. To translate these three dimensions as body, person, and soul in terms of Greek philosophy would result in distorting the meaning of the Scriptures with often ludicrous or even frightening results. For example, Paul in 1 Cor 5:5 does not condemn the incestuous man to death but to what we call excommunication for his own salvation.

102. *kaì eskēnōsen en hēmîn*, "and (he) pitched his tent (or dwelt) among us (or in our midst)." The verb *skēnóō*, "I pitch my tent," is the verbal form of the noun *skēnē*, "tent," (which is transliterated into "scene"). This is an obvious allusion to the tent or tabernacle of dwelling in Exod 40. For more along these lines, see my remarks about the annunciation (and incarnation) account in Luke in vol. 1 of this work, pp. 176 and 213.

103. *kaì etheasámetha tèn dóxan autoû, dóxan hōs monogenoûs parà patrós.* . . . "and we beheld (or gazed upon) his glory, glory of the only-begotten from the Father. . . ." The verb *etheasámetha*, "we beheld," is from *theáomai*, "I behold or gaze upon," from which we have the word "theater." And, as in theater, we do not simply see or look at, we gaze with all our attention and for a prolonged period of time. All of that is connoted here.

The word *dóxa*, "glory," from which we have the liturgical term "doxology," such as "Glory to the Father, etc.," is extremely important here, especially if this Gospel was intended to combat emperor worship. The glory of the Roman Empire, the emperor, and the army of Rome were basic in the thinking and life of Roman citizens. Hence, it was crucial to emphasize that this earthly glory was nothing in comparison with the surpassing glory of Jesus Christ, the Son of God, Lord of Lords, and King of Kings.

I chose not to translate the little Greek particle *hōs*, "as," that is, "as of the only-begotten" because while it is important and necessary in Greek, it is unnecessary and possibly misleading in English, for it can easily be construed in the sense of "as if," which would indicate that Christ is not truly the only-begotten (Son) of God.

104. *plērēs cháritos kaì alētheías*, "full of grace and truth." This is their generally understood meaning in Greek, but there is an obvious allusion here to the Old Testament praise of God's merciful love and fidelity to his promises (Hebrew: *hesed we'emeth*). It is for this reason and because love is one of the three main themes in John that I have chosen to translate *cháritos kaì alētheías* as "of love and truth." I have retained the meaning of "truth" rather than "fidelity" because, although the latter concept is obviously present, John emphasizes the light of truth in the prologue and throughout the gospel. If it did not interfere with the poetic form of the prologue, I would be inclined to use the longer and fuller expression "full of gracious love and faithful truth."

105. *Iōánnes martureî perì autoû kaì kékragen légōn, "Hoûtos ên hón eîpon, 'Ho opísō mou erchómenos émprosthén mou gégonen, hóti prōtós mou ên.' "* Here the translation that I have given in the text is, I believe, quite clear, but it may be helpful to point out the interesting play on words that shines through the Greek, "The one (or man) coming (or who comes) after (behind) me (in location) has begun to be (has been set) ahead of me (in dignity) because he was (existed) before me (in time)."

106. *hóti ek toû plērōmatos autoû hēmeîs pántes elábomen*, "for out of his fullness we have all received." The noun *plērōma*, "fullness," undoubtedly refers back to the adjective *plērēs*, "full," in v. 14. We have all received from the gracious love and faithful truth of which Jesus Christ, the Word, Wisdom, and Son of God was full. It may also, however, refer to the *plērōma*, "fullness," in Gnostic thought, which, as we have seen, Paul responded to in both Colossians and Ephesians, where Christ is shown as the fullness of God and the Church as the fullness of Christ.

107. *kaì chárin antì cháritos*. This is an enigmatic expression, and there are a wide variety of translations and explanations, mostly because of uncertainty about the exact meaning of *antí*, basically "against" in its usage here. As an example of the uncertainty, Maximilian Zerwick, brilliant New Testament Greek scholar that he was, seems to favor two different interpretations: that of substitution (New Testament grace in place of Old Testament grace) in *Biblical Greek*, trans. Jos. Smith (Rome: Biblical Institute Press, 1963) 31, par. 95; and that of succession (grace upon grace) in Max Zerwick and Mary Grosvenor, *A Grammatical Analysis of the Greek New Testament* (Rome: Biblical Institute Press, 1981) 287. I do not pretend to have the final word, but in keeping with what I have stated above, I have chosen to translate this enigmatic expression thus: "gracious love upon love."

108. *hóti ho nómos dià Mōüséōs edóthē* . . . , "for the *Law* was given through

Moses." Actually, it was, above all, the covenant that was given through Moses, while the Law was given through Moses as a primary means of keeping the covenant, the agreement establishing a bond of lasting relationship between Yahweh and Israel. *See* Exod 19-20 and my treatment of this in *To Live the Word, Inspired and Incarnate*, (Staten Island, N.Y.: Alba, 1985) 4-6, 71-72. Unfortunately, in the course of Israelite history, the Law outstripped the covenant in importance, so that at the time of Jesus' coming among us the Law, especially that of the Sabbath rest, was the all-important hallmark of an observing Jew. Perhaps it was for this reason that John omits mention here of the covenant.

109. *hē cháris kaì hē alētheia dià Iēsoû Christoû egéneto*. Here again, the controversy about exact meaning and translation continues, but in view of what has already been said, I have translated this passage thus: "Love and truth have come to be through Jesus Christ." Note also the use of the article *hē*, hence the emphasis on Christ as the source of *the* (complete) love and *the* (complete) truth.

110. *theòn oudeìs heóraken pōpote; monogenès theòs (huiós)*. "No one has ever seen God; (but) the only-begotten Son. . . ." The verb *heóraken* used here is in the perfect tense of *horáō* (I see, perceive, observe), less formal and intense than *theáomai*, "I gaze upon, behold" used above.

There is a textual problem concerning what I have chosen to translate "Son." The manuscript evidence is rather evenly divided between *theós*, "God," and *huiós*, "Son," but because of the greater affinity of the word "Son" with what immediately precedes and follows it in the sentence, I prefer it to the stranger expression, "the only-begotten God."

111. . . . *ho òn eis tòn kólpon toû patròs ekeînos exēgēsato*," ". . . who is in the bosom of the Father, he has revealed (him) (or made him known)." The expression "in the bosom of the Father" is another way of saying "nearest the heart of the Father" and is reminiscent of John's own privilege of resting on the bosom of Jesus at the Last Supper (John 13:23). The final term, *exēgēsato*, is in the aorist or past tense of *exēgéomai*, "I make known, reveal," (literally, "I lead out"). In my translation, I have favored the reading "revealed" especially because of the emphasis in the Gospel on Jesus' being the light, the revelation of God in the world.

112. As examples of these details that are unique to John's Gospel, let me mention a few that are singled out by Brown in his *Gospel According to John*, vol. 1, xlii: "In ch. iv John's references to the Samaritans, their theology, their practice of worshipping on Mt. Garizim, and the location of Jacob's well all seem to be accurate.

"In ch. v the very precise information about the pool of Bethesda is perfectly accurate as to name, location, and construction.

"The theological themes brought up in relation to Passover (ch. vi) and the Feast of Tabernacles (vii-viii) reflect an accurate knowledge of the festal ceremonies and of the synagogue readings associated with the feasts.

"Details about Jerusalem seem to be accurate, for example the reference to the Pool of Siloam (ix 7), to Solomon's Portico as a shelter in winter time (x 22-23), and to the stone pavement of Pilate's Praetorium (xix 13)."

113. In John's Gospel, the primary reason for the opposition of the Jewish religious leaders to Jesus is clearly his continuing claim to divinity, "because he not only broke the Sabbath but he also called God his own father, making himself equal to God" (John 5:18 NAB; *see also* John 8:58-59; 10:30-33, etc.).

114. John 5–10 is replete with discourse material that begins with a dialogue and ends with Jesus' monologue.

115. Clement of Alexandria (A.D. 150–215), in a fragment preserved by Eusebius (260–339), declares, "But John, the last of all, seeing that what was corporeal was set forth in the Gospels, on the entreaty of his intimate friends, and inspired by the Holy Spirit, composed a spiritual Gospel." *See* Clement of Alexandria, *Fragments*, in The Ante-Nicene Fathers 2:580.

116. Only in these two short letters does the anonymous author identify himself as the presbyter (2 John 1:1; 3 John 1:1). While there are affinities with 1 John, these do not seem sufficient to identify them as written by the same author. Philip of Side in Pamphylia, writing in the fifth century but using information from Papias in the second century by way of Eusebius in the fourth, states, "He (Papias) includes among the disciples Aristion and another John, whom he also called the Presbyter. According to him, some think that the latter John is the author of the two short Catholic Epistles published under John's name, on the ground that the Christians of the first age consider only the first [to be John's]." *See* Philip of Side, *Christian History*, quoted among "Fragments of Papias," *The Apostolic Fathers*, vol. 1 of The Fathers of the Church, 379.

117. The differences in John's use of the kerygma seem to be these: (1) John the Baptist himself describes his baptism of Jesus, (2) the Galilean ministry is greatly reduced in favor of a much larger Judean ministry, (3) there are several journeys from Galilee to Jerusalem, and (4) while the saving events in Jerusalem comprise the material in which John is closest to the Synoptics, there are significant differences, for example, the washing of feet and long discourse instead of the institution of the Eucharist, no explicit prayer and agony in the garden, prominence given to the trial before Pilate, different words of Jesus from the cross as well as different resurrection appearances, etc.

118. Indications of John's awareness of the Synoptics are these: (1) his mention, in common with Mark, of "two hundred denarii" of bread needed to feed the crowd (Mark 6:37; John 6:7) as well as "perfume made from real nard" worth some "three hundred denarii" used in the anointing of Jesus (Mark 14:3-5; John 12:3-4); (2) his emphasis with "Matthew" on Peter's Church authority (Matt 16:16-20; John 1:41-42; 6:68-69; 21:15-17); (3) greater parallels with Luke in the following examples (*a*) the miraculous catch of fish (Luke 5:4-9; John 21:5-11); (*b*) mention of figures like Lazarus, Martha and Mary, and the high priest Annas (Luke 3:2; 10:38-42; 16:19-31; John 11:1-44; 18:13; (*c*) similarities in the trials of Jesus (Luke 22:54-23:25; John 18:12-19:16); (*d*) similar details in resurrection appearances (Luke 24:12, 40; John 20:1-10, 19-29).

The above are all the things that a careful scholar observes, but in seeking ties between John and the Synoptists, I feel that we must go below the surface of such details to their hearts, their deep inner concerns. For example, who cannot recognize in John Mark and John the apostle kindred spirits in their mutual emphasis on the divinity of Christ? Who cannot sense the kinship of John, the evangelist of divine love, with "Matthew's" so-called Johannine segment, the poignant plea of Jesus, "Come to me, all you who labor and are burdened, and I will give you rest" (Matt 11:28, NAB)? And who, finally, is unable to see in the compassionate Luke John's kindred spirit, particularly in Jesus' loving relationship with Lazarus, Martha, and Mary, most notably in Jesus' beautiful assurance regarding the contemplative Mary that she had chosen the better part and would not be deprived of it (Luke 10:42)?

It must be borne in mind, however, that similarities in references and expressions and kinship of spirit do not of themselves prove acquaintance with another's writings. Yet it is inconceivable to me that John, living on as he did some fifteen to twenty years after the last Synoptic Gospel was written, and especially living in such a center as Ephesus, would not have been familiar with the other three Gospels and perhaps even possessed his very own copies.

119. In many ways, John has closer affinities with Paul than with his fellow evangelists. For example, both are primarily concerned with the inner, mystical portrait of Christ and Christianity, Christ and the individual Christian. Compare Jesus' parable of the vine and the branches (John 15) with his self-identification to Paul on the road to Damascus, "I am Jesus whom you are persecuting" (Acts 9:5), and Paul's landmark description of the Church as the Body of Christ in 1 Cor 12:12-31; Rom 12:3-9; Eph 4:1-6, 5:21-23. Or John's central teaching on divine love in 1 John 4:7-21 and John 15 with Paul's lyrical tribute to that love in such passages as 1 Cor 13 and Rom 8:35-39. Or, for that matter, are there not dramatic affinities between the Pauline hymns in Philippians, Colossians, and Ephesians on the one hand and the beautiful prologue of John's Gospel on the other? Can we not say that both of these great mystics provide us with unforgettable portraits of the all-encompassing role of the cosmic Christ?

120. The seven initial titles of Jesus, accorded him in the very first chapter of John's Gospel, and therefore clearly indicating the use of concentric circles here, are these: "Son of God, Lamb of God, Rabbi, Messiah, Prophet, King of Israel, and Son of Man." In subsequent chapters, these will be repeated and others added, for example, in ch. 3, "Son of God, Son of Man, and Bridegroom"; in ch. 4, "Prophet, Messiah, Savior"; in ch. 5, "Son of God, Judge, and Son of Man"; in ch. 6, "Prophet, King, Son of Man, God's Holy One"; in chs. 7-9, "Prophet, Messiah, I AM"; in ch. 10, "Good Shepherd" (with messianic and divine connotations), and "Son of God"; in ch. 11, "Messiah and Son of God"; in ch. 12, "Messiah, King, Son of Man"; in ch. 13, "Teacher, Lord, I AM, Son of Man"; in chs. 14-17, "Son of God, Advocate, and Friend"; in chs. 18-19, "I AM, King, Son of God, Paschal Lamb"; in ch. 20, "Rabbouni, Lord and God, Messiah, and Son of God"; in ch. 21, "Lord and Shepherd." (These will not be given in the outline.)

121. The seven disciples mentioned in ch. 21 are these: "Simon Peter, Thomas called Didymus, Nathaniel from Cana in Galilee, Zebedee's sons [James and John], and two others of his disciples" (John 21:2, NAB).

122. The six water jars of Jewish purification occur, of course, in the story

of the marraige feast at Cana in ch. 2, while the six Jewish feasts included in John's Gospel are these: three Passovers, the feast of Booths, the feast of Dedication (Hanukkah), and an unnamed feast, probably of the Covenant (Pentecost). These will be clearly shown in our outline, so there is no need of giving the references in John's Gospel here.

123. Between the biblical symbols and natural symbols in John's Gospel there is a certain amount of duplication, for example in the case of the two most important ones, the Good Shepherd and his sheep and the true vine and the branches, which are at the same time biblical and taken from nature. However, in my lists of biblical and natural symbols, I am avoiding such duplication, so that the biblical symbols here are listed as such and the natural symbols are generally not biblical.

The seven biblical symbols found in John, listed so far as possible in the order of their occurrence, are these: (1) the tabernacle (tent) of dwelling and Temple (Exod 40; 1 Kgs 8; John 1:14; 2:19-21); (2) the paschal lamb (Exod 12; John 1:29, 36; 19:36); (3) the brazen serpent (Num 21:4-9; John 3:14-15; 8:28; 12:32); (4) the bridegroom (Hos 2; Isa 54:4-10; 62:4-5; Jer 2:2; 3:20; Ezek 16; 23; John 3:27-30); (5) the manna in the desert or bread of life (Exod 16:12-35; Num 11:6-8; Deut 8:3, 16; Josh 5:12; Ps 78:24-25; John 6); (6) the shepherd and his sheep (Pss 23; 80; 95; Isa 40:10-11; Ezek 34; John 10; 21:15-19); (7) the vine and the branches (Ps 80; Isa 5; John 15). I have provided all the biblical references here because these symbols will not be included in the outline.

124. The seven natural symbols, that is, symbols derived primarily from nature rather than from the Bible or the history of Israel, are listed here as nearly as possible according to their order of occurrence in John's Gospel, as follows: (1) light (of truth) (John 1:4-5, 9; 8:12; 9:1-41; 12:35-36; 1 John 1:5-7); (2) water (of life) (John 3:5; 4:7-15; 7:37-39); (3) wind (of the Spirit) (John 3:8); (4) fields ripe for harvest (John 4:35-38); (5) the grain of wheat that dies (John 12:24-26); (6) the way (road, path, way of life) (John 14:6); (7) the woman in labor, giving birth, and rejoicing (John 16:20-22). (This list will not be included in the outline in order to keep it simple enough to understand readily.)

125. The list of seven major discourses of Jesus will be indicated in the outline as D-1, D-2, D-3, etc., but it may be helpful to the reader to mention them here as well, as follows: (1) Jesus' discourse with Nicodemus about birth from above through baptism (John 3:1-21); (2) Jesus' discourse with the Samaritan woman about the living water of grace (John 4:4-26); (3) Jesus' discourse with the Jewish leaders about his role as judge of the living and dead (John 5:1-47); (3) Jesus' discourse at the synagogue in Capernaum about himself as the bread of life in the Eucharist (John 6:1-71); (5) Jesus' discourse about himself as the light of the blind and of the world (John 7-10, particularly John 8:12-20; 9:1-41); (6) Jesus' discourse about himself as the Good Shepherd, come among us that we might have life and have it more abundantly (John 10:1-42); (7) Jesus' great discourse about love at the Last Supper (John 13-17).

A cursory glance at these seven great discourses will reveal that most, if not all, of them begin with a sign (miracle) or a dialogue or both and end in a monologue on the part of Jesus.

126. Perhaps the best example of editorializing is found in the very first great discourse, in which Jesus' monologue drifts into teaching about him in the third person, especially in the famous statement of John 3:16, NAB: "For God so loved the world that he gave his only Son, so that everyone who believes in him might not perish but might have eternal life."

127. *See* n. 57 above, where I have already treated this.

128. *See* n. 69 above for a fuller treatment of this point.

129. *See* n. 70 above for a general description of chiasmus. The importance of this structure, however, requires that I add further explanation to the information provided in that note.

Without consideration of possible structures such as chiasmus and concentric circles, we find ourselves confused and even somewhat dismayed by what seems to be a rather haphazard and repetitious development of thought in John's Gospel. An understanding of structures, however, provides us with a set of keys that open the door wide to greater understanding, acceptance, and enrichment.

I want to give full credit to Fr. Juan Alfaro, S.J., a Spanish Scripture scholar whom I met at MACC (the Mexican American Cultural Center) in San Antonio, Texas, during the summer of 1979, for suggesting the idea of a chiastic structure in John's Gospel as a means of penetrating its apparently confusing development. In *Jesus, The Light of the World: The Gospel of John* (San Antonio: MACC, 1977), Father Alfaro does an excellent job of applying the chiastic structure to John, with the central emphasis on Christ the light. At that time, I fully accepted his proposal but felt that the emphasis should include Christ the Life as well. And now, some dozen years later, I am of the opinion that the central teaching of John pictures Christ as the light, life, and love of the world. As I have previously indicated in n. 58 above, the themes of Christ the light and life of the world dominate the Book of Signs (John 1–12), while the theme of Christ the love of the world dominates the Book of Glory (John 13–21). See also Peter Ellis, *The Genius of John: A Composition-Critical Commentary on the Fourth Gospel* (Collegeville: The Liturgical Press, 1984) for a different chiastic approach to John, one based not on the number seven but on the number five (as in "Matthew"), with each of the five parts forming a chiastic structure of its own. Although I personally favor the seven-part chiasmus, particularly because of so many references to the number seven in the Gospel (in parallel with the Apocalypse?), I certainly admire Ellis' scholarship, both in his other works and in this one, and urge the reader to assess for himself or herself this alternate chiastic possibility.

130. Let us treat each of these two questions in order.

(1) While it is true that, geographically speaking, John 5 is far more logically followed by John 7 than John 6, the manuscript evidence does not at all support such a realignment, and with good reason. John's Gospel is written, not primarily according to geographical and historical principles, but according to theological, spiritual, and thematic principles. If we keep this in mind, geographical and historical considerations fade into the background and are no longer burning questions.

(2) The question about Jesus and the adulteress in John 8:1-11 is really three-fold: (*a*) Is this segment part of the original Gospel of John? (*b*) If not part of the original Gospel, is it part of the Johannine tradition? (*c*) Is it inspired and canonical? Let me answer each question as concisely as I can. (*a*) Its inclusion in the Gospel of John is not supported by the majority of ancient manuscripts, hence it is usually enclosed by brackets in our modern translations. (*b*) It is stylistically more Lukan than Johannine, and, in fact, some manuscripts place it after Luke 21:38, where it seems to fit much better than in its present location, in which it interrupts the festal dialogue and discourse of Jesus. (*c*) Since it was accepted by Jerome and included in the Vulgate, which has been used through the centuries by the Church as canonical Scripture, it is regarded as inspired and canonical today, in fact not only by Catholics but also by almost all Christians. For more information, *see* Brown, *The Gospel According to John*, vol. 1, 335--36.

131. Hyperbole, aptly defined in *Webster's Ninth New Collegiate Dictionary* as "extravagant exaggeration," was and is a favorite rhetorical mechanism for making a point. Prime examples in the Gospels are Jesus' statements about the camel passing through the eye of a needle (Mark 10:25) and the beam (of wood) located in the human eye (Matt 7:3-5). And any attempt to explain things by identifying the needle's eye as a gate in Jerusalem and the beam as one of light rather than wood not only lacks all historical and linguistic foundation but, above all, negates the very force of the hyperbole itself.

132. *See* Matt 4:15-16 and Luke 2:29-32.

133. *See* Claver Smith, "Christmas and its Cycle," NCE, 3: 656.

134. This traditional translation of the Hebrew Ps 107:10 in the King James Version and of the Greek and Latin Ps 106:10 in the Douay-Rheims is, to my mind, both more accurate and meaningful than the translation of "darkness and gloom" found in most modern English Bibles.

135. See *The Liturgy of the Hours* (New York: Catholic Book, 1975) 3:1266.

136. *See* Dicharry, *To Live the Word*, 255--56.

137. *See* John 7:37-39.

138. *See* O. A. Battista, *God's World and You* (Milwaukee: Bruce, 1957) 121.

139. George Maloney, *Breath of the Mystic* (Denville, N.J.: Dimension, 1974) 18.

140. John 6:35, 48-58.

141. *See* the analysis of John's Gospel in this chapter, specifically "The Theology of John's Gospel," pp. 162–63, "Eschatology"; *see also* n. 51 above.

142. *See* Dicharry, *To Live the Word*, 148–87.

143. *Ibid.*, 119–47.

144. *Ibid.*, 320; also see Deut 30:19-20.

145. *See* Dicharry, *To Live the Word*, 172.

146. *Ibid.*, 173, 183.

147. Francis Thompson, "The Hound of Heaven," ed. Wilfrid Meynell, *Collected Works of Francis Thompson* (Westminster, Md.: Newman, 1949) 1:108; *see also* Eugene Boylan, *This Tremendous Lover* (Westminster, Md.: Newman, 1948).

148. *See* John 2:1-11.

149. L. Wm. Countryman is so impressed with this order that in *The Mystical Way in the Fourth Gospel: Crossing Over into God* (Phila., PA: Fortress, 1987), he proposes that John actually wrote his Gospel in correspondence with the three ways of the mystical life. This is an intriguing theory, and even though it would be very difficult to demonstrate, nevertheless it does honor the mystical nature of the Fourth Gospel and avoids being caught up in the quicksand of biblical technicalities.

150. The expression "the way" (Hebrew, *derek*; Greek, *hodós*) is one of great frequency and importance in both Testaments. The simple reason for this is that in the ancient world there was a general lack of roads and road signs except for the famous Roman roads, which were few and far between and intended primarily for official use. Consequently, it was easy for travelers to lose their way, and they were always grateful for anything resembling a well-defined road or way. Hence, as with "water" and "light," the expression "road" or "way" became an important symbol in the ancient world, a symbol of sure direction and proper conduct in one's life, as in Ps 1:1. It is significant that Christians were first known as "followers of the way" (Acts 9:2; 16:17; 18:25-26; 19:9, 23; 22:4; 24:14, 22). For them this was not only a way of life but preeminently a way of love (Eph 5:2) and of salvation (John 14:6).

151. *See Thomas à Kempis, The Following of Christ* (New York: Catholic Book, 1941) bk. 3, ch. 56, par. 1, p. 381.

RECOMMENDED READING LIST

Brown, Raymond. *The Gospel According to John,* 2 vols., *Anchor Bible.* Garden City, N.Y.: Doubleday, 1966, 1970.

Countryman, L. Wm. *The Mystical Way in the Fourth Gospel: Crossing Over into God.* Philadelphia: Fortress, 1987.

Crane, Thomas. *The Message of Saint John: The Spiritual Teaching of the Beloved Disciple.* Staten Island, N.Y.: Alba, 1980.

Ellis, Peter. *The Genius of John: A Composition-Critical Commentary on the Fourth Gospel.* Collegeville: The Liturgical Press, 1984.

Taylor, Michael. *A Companion to John: Readings in Johannine Theology.* Staten Island, N.Y.: Alba, 1977. *John: The Different Gospel: A Reflective Commentary.* Staten Island, N.Y.: Alba, 1983.

QUESTIONS FOR REFLECTION AND DISCUSSION

1. What do you find most appealing in John and 1 John?

2. In general, how is John's Gospel different from and how is it similar to the other three Gospels?

3. How important a role does symbolism play in John's Gospel?
4. How important a role do the themes of light, life, and love play in John's Gospel and First Epistle?
5. Describe the structures of concentric circles and of chiasmus in relation to the Gospel of John.

THE ISLAND OF PATMOS

N

MT. ENDELOS

MT. KOMARA

MT. KONDROYOUNA

MT. VALHY

AEGEAN SEA

Ruins of the
Acropolis

Port and Town of Phōra (Skala)

To Samos

Cave of the
Apocalypse

Patmos
(Hora)

MT. ST. ELIAS

MT.
KYNOPS

To Leros and Kos

MT. PAKHEIA

4

Ingenious John and the Veiled Revelation[1]

THE STORY OF JOHN'S APOCALYPSE

King of Kings and Lord of Lords![2] (Rev 19:16)

Water! Blue, blue water! How beautiful, how meaningful, to be literally surrounded by the symbol of life[3] itself! What a lovely reminder of those wonderful years with the mother of Jesus in their home on a hillside near Ephesus[4] overlooking this same blue Aegean Sea! John, with his deep contemplative sense and love of symbolism, could, with a serene heart, give glory to God for the sight that met his gaze as he emerged from his cave.

A week earlier, however, when he had first arrived at the little Island of Patmos,[5] some seventy miles southwest of Ephesus, gratitude had been far from his mind and heart. Seasick from the voyage in a small boat, lonely without his friends, especially Prochorus and Polycarp,[6] and depressed over his condemnation to exile[7] by the governor of the Roman province of Asia, John, with his guard, had drifted into the small port in the heart of the island with the disturbing feeling that the mountains[8] rising to right and left were looming over him like the menacing wings of the Roman eagle. Cut off abruptly and indefinitely from all that was most near and dear to him and not knowing what to expect from the people of the island, the aged apostle[9] had tried desperately to resign himself without regrets or conditions to the holy will of God just as Jesus had done in the Garden of Gethsemane.[10]

What a pleasant surprise that the island's inhabitants had received him with compassion and concern! Simple shepherds, fishermen, and housewives, they had readily shared their simple fare and humble homes with him. In fact, they had tried to prevail on him to live in

View of Patmos from Mt. St. Elias.

The Temple of Augustus at Ancyra.

one of their houses, but he had declined with thanks. Both for their sakes, who had so little room for themselves, and for his sake, with his profound need of solitude, he had graciously turned down the invitation to live with them but had accepted the offer of a cave,[11] sometimes used by shepherds, halfway up the mountain to the left. Here he had quickly made himself at home and, as a matter of fact, was even beginning to enjoy his exile.

He could in time, John felt with relief, become so accustomed to his exile that he might not want to return to Ephesus if he were offered his freedom again. But wait! How could he possibly be content with forced inactivity when his beloved fellow Christians were under daily threat of persecution, torture, and death? How could a father abandon his children, a shepherd his sheep?[12] If ever there were a wolf threatening the flock of Christ, it was this monster of an emperor, Domitian,[13] commonly referred to as Nero Redivivus,[14] who was such a paranoid megalomaniac that he insisted on being called "Lord and God"[15] under threat of death. Poor innocent Christians! How could they possibly accede to that uncompromising demand for emperor worship and still remain true to Christ, their sole Lord and God? But what an overwhelming temptation, especially for Roman citizens, to retain life and friends, status and property, by the simple expedient of pretending to worship Domitian! What a dangerous situation! And how desperately in need of firm guidance and fatherly support must the Christian faithful find themselves in these terrible times![16]

What could John do to help his children, his flock? Obviously, he could not at will leave his exile to be with his own in their time of trial. He could and would, of course, pray his heart out for them and offer his own sufferings[17] for them. That would be the very least he could do. But was there not more he could do? Curiously, in his cave there was a natural writing niche.[18] Was that God's way of telling him that he ought to write something to encourage his flock in their time of trial? Was that not what blessed Paul had done so effectively during his imprisonments?[19] Would it not be helpful to write letters to the seven main Churches of the province of Asia? Sadly, they would hardly be very elegant[20] without the help of his beloved Prochorus and Polycarp, who had done such a masterful job on his pastoral letter and gospel. But given the crying needs of the Christians, even inelegant letters would be better than none, would they not?

"Yes," John thought to himself, "I'll write letters to the seven

Churches, particularly with warnings to correct abuses and with commendations wherever they're due. After all, unless the Churches are living in imitation of Christ, how can they survive a virulent anti-Christian persecution? But wait a minute! Don't these desperate times call for some kind of specific remedy in addition to letters? Think! Isn't there a kind of literature specially designed to support persecuted people without tipping off the persecutors and thus making life harder for the persecuted? Of course! Apocalyptic writing![21] What better example of underground or resistance literature is there than the apocalypses of the Jewish Testament, especially the Book of Daniel,[22] and those of the Jewish Apocrypha?[23] Perfect! Those works were composed in such a way, so full of symbols and visions, that their recipients were thoroughly encouraged in their time of persecution without fear that the persecuting authorities would recognize the antiestablishment nature of the writings.

"But can I write something like that? Can I, John[24] of Galilee, compose such a work without expert assistance, yet well enough that it will really fulfill its purpose? Perhaps more importantly, where will I get the material for this apocalypse? I wasn't allowed to bring any of my scrolls with me, so how can I do the research necessary? Well, maybe I shouldn't worry about that. After all, I've spent most of my life poring over the Scriptures,[25] the fathomless treasure of material for an apocalypse or any other writing. I can't claim to be able to quote what I need to from memory alone, but then I don't have to. I can just allude[26] to passages, figures, and symbols as they come to mind, and not worry about word-for-word quotations.

"Where, then, in the Scriptures should I try to find the imagery and symbolism that will encourage our Christians and confuse those who insist on being our enemies? First of all, from the apocalyptic literature, above all Daniel but also apocalyptic parts of Isaiah, Ezekiel, Joel, and Zechariah,[27] not to mention many other sections of the Bible, such as Genesis.[28] And let's not overlook Jesus' discourse on the end time[29] and Paul's Letters to the Thessalonians.[30] In fact, if I need to use anything from the apocalyptic literature of Israel beyond the Scriptures, I may as well feel free to incorporate that also.

"But what about visions? The apocalypses I've read, especially Daniel, have always featured visions, or at least purported visions,[31] as part of their very makeup. Well, that vision of Jesus when he was transfigured[32] on the mountain in Galilee has been enough to last me a whole lifetime. There's no reason why I can't use it in an apocalypse, at least if Jesus himself doesn't favor me with special visions for this purpose.

"Then again, there are the mystical visions[33] that he's granted me from time to time, visions somewhat like that beautiful one shown the deacon Stephen[34] just before his glorious martyrdom. It would be very helpful to our persecuted Christians if I can remind them, by means of these visions, of God in his serene glory, along with our risen Lord Jesus, surrounded by the whole heavenly court of angels and saints. They need to be able to look up in the midst of their trials, just as Stephen did in his, and see Jesus in triumph with the Father, now and definitively in the future. What a timely reminder of our Lord's assurance in his final discourse with us, 'In the world you will have trouble, but take courage, I have overcome the world!'[35]

"What would be particularly effective in these visions are appropriate hymns[36] sung by the heavenly choir, hymns that our beleaguered people can practically hear in all their grandeur. But where would I find these hymns? Let's see. First, I can always employ the words of some of the hymns used in our Christian liturgies.[37] I'm not sure how many I can remember, but with the help of the Holy Spirit and the advantage of solitude and silence, perhaps I'll be able to recall a number of the most pertinent and, if necessary, even use some of my own,[38] with which the Lord has inspired me from time to time, or with his help write new ones as needed.

"So far so good, but what about structures? How shall I put all this together so that it not only makes sense but also provides the support and encouragement that our good Christians so desperately need? This is where I wish my good friends, Prochorus and Polycarp, could be here to help me. But perhaps . . . perhaps they already have! They've already taught me about concentric circles[39] and chiasmus,[40] and they've even shown me how they could take my favorite symbol, the perfect number seven,[41] and blend it with these structures to form a coherent whole. Why can't I do the same thing in this apocalypse? At least I can try! In fact, the use of such structures can be one more way in which I can confuse the authorities. Yes, it may be somewhat perplexing also to our own people, but after our gospel [42] they are hopefully in a better position to grasp the development of thought involved.

"Uh-oh! I've just remembered something! I started out by thinking about writing letters to the seven Churches of Asia, and then I slipped into thoughts and plans about an apocalypse. Am I talking about two different projects or only one? And if only one, how do these two kinds of literature fit together? I honestly don't know, but maybe the Holy Spirit will enlighten me about it as I need to know. I do hope and pray that such enlightenment will come soon and in good measure, because I really need to get started on all this if I'm to have any hope of helping our Christians in the current crisis. As it is, whether or not I can find a secretary[43] on this primitive island, I'll probably have to write the work directly on papyrus or pergamum,[44] whatever I can obtain, without going through the normal process of using wax tablets and then transcribing to permanent materials. Of course, the end result will reveal all my lack of expertise[45] in Greek grammar, vocabulary, and style, but that can't be helped. The important thing is to finish this apocalypse as quickly as possible during this critical time for our Christians.''

With that realization of the need for ''patient urgency'' on his part, John, feeling at least ten years younger[46] and more useful than he had a week ago, decided to let his mind rest a while, confident that the Holy Spirit would be able to more than supply for his clearly recognized deficiencies. Besides, there was nothing like sleeping on a problem to find a solution. In complete peace and serenity, then, and with the great consolation of finding special meaning[47] in his exile, John took a light repast, supplied by the kind villagers, and then rested his weary head in the Lord just as he had reclined his head long ago on the Master's bosom.[48]

That night may have been, or at least seemed to be, one of the longest in John's long life. When he awoke ''on the Lord's day,''[49] his mind and heart were literally overflowing with ideas, images, symbols, directives, and even visions (or were they dreams?) that cried out to be incorporated into his apocalypse. He could even perceive with absolute clarity how his vision of Christ among the seven golden lampstands[50] would fit in admirably with his letters to the seven Churches of Asia, what those letters should contain, and how they should be constructed,[51] as well as how the rest of his apocalypse would fit together.[52] John was at once awed and exhilarated. But, above all, he was filled with love and gratitude toward his beloved Master, Lord, and friend, Jesus Christ.

''Dear Jesus, my loving Lord and gracious God,'' he prayed, ''once again you've shown me that you have not left me alone and orphaned.[53] Even in this godforsaken place you're still with me, always with me.[54] Thank you, dearest Lord, for your faithful presence, your gracious guidance, your gentle love. I'm still waiting for you to take me home to yourself,[55] to the Father, and to the Holy Spirit. I long to be with you again, with your holy mother, and with my fellow apostles. Haven't I lived long enough in this vestibule of life?[56] But if you want me to live longer and your Church needs me to help her through this current crisis, then, dear Jesus, I am completely at your disposal.[57] Use me as you will. And thank you for being with me to help me do what otherwise I could never accomplish: provide your Church with the kind of writing that may help to see her safely through these trying times. Your kindness always exceeds our needs!"

In the quiet days and weeks that followed, John worked, sometimes slowly and painfully, sometimes rapidly and even exuberantly, to fashion his apocalypse into a form that, in spite of its inferior Greek composition and deliberate obscurity, has retained its fascination throughout Church history and has achieved in our own day a level of veneration that is almost as mystifying[58] as the work itself.

We do not know if John was able to complete his project in time to help the Christians of Asia and elsewhere during the persecution of Domitian, that is, before the emperor's assassination[59] in A.D.96, but we do know that the Apocalypse, or Revelation of John, has served to offer hope and courage to harried Christians throughout the centuries, from the "classic" Roman persecutions[60] prior to Constantine down to our modern sophisticated forms of harassment that, according to Jesus' own words, will continue to characterize his Church until the end of time.[61]

ANALYSIS OF THE APOCALYPSE

Like the analysis of John's Gospel (and First Epistle), this brief analysis of the Apocalypse or Book of Revelation, will contain three sections: (1) an overview of the work, (2) an outline of its development, and (3) a look at its theology.

I. Overview

    A. General impression

        1. Probably of all the books of the New Testament, none leaves such strong impressions on the reader as does the Apocalypse. Very often these impressions are negative for

the simple reason that the reader may not be prepared by a knowledge of the ancient literary form of apocalyptic to understand the purpose and principal characteristics of this fascinating book.[62]

2. As with the first of our five authors, Mark, it was strongly recommended that his Gospel be read straight through to savor its sense of urgency, so also with our final work, the Apocalypse, one should make every effort to read it without interruption to feel its urgency. This similarity between Mark and the Apocalypse should not surprise us, for both seem to have been written with haste in an attempt to strengthen the Christian community against persecution or the threat thereof.

3. This is literally a fantastic book, being so filled with visions, symbols, heavenly hymns, and cosmic catastrophes as to boggle the mind.[63]

4. It seems to be a book of prophecy because it is always talking about the things that will come to pass in the future.[64]

5. Besides prophecy, there seems to be also a certain amount of epistolary literature[65] involved in the letters to the seven Churches of Asia.

6. Of the many symbols employed in the Apocalypse, there seem to be a number that are in common with the Gospel of John.[66]

7. There is a strong sense of dualism,[67] of cosmic conflict between good and evil, God and Satan, light and darkness, life and death, reward and punishment.

8. There also seems to be a dramatic two-story or split-level portrait throughout the work, with a periodic vision of heaven, apparently to reassure the reader that "God's in his heaven and all's right with the world."[68]

9. In these visions of heaven, there also seems to be an extraordinary collection of hymns,[69] more by far than in any other book of the New Testament.

B. Composition of the Apocalypse

  1. Circumstances of its writing

   a) Tradition, explicit declaration in the work itself, and indications from extrabiblical sources[70] seem to place the writing of the Apocalypse on the little island of Patmos in the Aegean Sea off the western coast of Asia Minor in the middle of the last decade of the first century A.D.[71]

b) The particular circumstances that seem to have occasioned the writing of the Apocalypse are the insistence on emperor worship by Domitian (A.D. 81–96), especially after various attempts at revolt and assassination, and a kind of general persecution of Christians on that basis, with particularly strong harassment against the Church in western Asia Minor, characterized by the exile of John to the Island of Patmos.

2. Authorship

a) The author identifies himself as John and describes himself in various ways, but not as an apostle,[72] which (along with other considerations) leads many if not most Scripture scholars to consider the name John here as pseudonymous and the actual authorship as anonymous.

b) However, such reliable early Christian writers as Sts. Justin Martyr (100–165), Irenaeus (140–202), and Hippolytus (170–235), along with Tertullian (160–220) and Origen (184–253), all attribute the Apocalypse to John the apostle.[73]

c) John's authorship of the Apocalypse seems to have gone unchallenged throughout the second and third centuries until St. Dionysius (Denis) of Alexandria (190–265) clearly questioned the Johannine authorship,[74] after which it has been widely debated until the present time. But was Dionysius' doubt about the Johannine authorship of the Apocalypse as objective as it appeared to be, or was it possibly influenced by his running clashes with the Gnostics and chiliasts,[75] or millenarians, both of whom used the Book of Revelation quite extensively?

d) It is widely contended among scholars today[76] that John could not possibly have authored both his Gospel and First Epistle on the one hand and the Apocalypse on the other because the differences in grammar, vocabulary, and style are simply too great.

(1) If by "author" is meant that John was solely and totally responsible for all three works, I would certainly have to agree.

(2) However, according to my scenario:

(a) John coauthored his Gospel and First Epistle with others, whom I identify rightly or wrongly as Prochorus and Polycarp, John providing the content and his two friends the arrangement, structures, and lucid Greek writing.

(b) John, deprived of the presence and help of his friends, but using ideas learned from them about structure, wrote the Apocalypse by himself (or at best with the help of a simple secretary), hence the comparatively poor Greek grammar, vocabulary, and style of the work.[77]

(c) In this way, both tradition and honest scholarship seem to be satisfied.

3. Purposes

a) As an apocalyptic work, that is, underground or resistance literature, to encourage Christians suffering persecution or the threat of it, without tipping off the persecutors.

(1) Hence, Christ is shown in triumph now and ultimately, as a reminder that he has already overcome the world,[78] including the seemingly invincible Roman Empire.

(2) Hence also, the work is deliberately couched in a multiplicity of visions, images, and symbols so that the persecuting authorities who might happen to see it would not realize that they are the negative part of the picture.

b) Also, to renew the seven Churches of the Roman province of Asia by correcting abuses and commending fidelity, all to ensure their ability with God's grace to withstand persecution from without and heresy or schism from within.

4. Sources

a) Some authors today delight in finding sources of the

symbolism of the Apocalypse in pagan mythology and astrology emanating out of the Near East, for example, from among the Parthians.[79]

b) Close examination, however, reveals that the symbols in question are derived primarily from the Bible, both Old and New Testament.[80]

c) If the pagan mythology and astrology have in any way influenced Jewish thought during and after the Babylonian Exile, then it has its effect on the Apocalypse only through the filter of the Bible itself.

5. Characteristics

a) The Apocalypse is indeed a fantastic book, full of visions, symbols, hymns, and catastrophes, but deliberately so, as part of the apocalyptic picture aimed at encouraging the persecuted without alerting the persecutors.

(1) Many of these symbols are numerical, particularly featuring the number seven,[81] the symbol of completeness and perfection. In fact, there seem to be at least seven septets in the very structure of the Apocalypse.

(a) In addition to and closely related to the number seven is that of twelve,[82] as in the tribes of Israel and the apostles.

(b) Another important numerical symbol is that of six, the number of incompleteness, imperfection, even evil, as, for example, in the name ''666''[83] of the beast in Rev 13:18.

(2) Most of the other symbols are borrowed from the Old Testament,[84] as is the case also in the Gospel of John. In fact many of these are common in the New Testament only to the Apocalypse and the Gospel (and 1 John).[85]

b) In addition to the avalanche of symbols in the Apocalypse, there is also a veritable cascade of Christological titles and descriptions, in fact, at least twenty of each![86]

c) While there is indeed prophecy in the Book of Revelation, it is subordinate to the primary emphasis, which is that of apocalyptic, that is, underground or resistance literature.

   (1) Even where there is genuine prophecy, one should remember that, as the Greek word itself, *prophētēs*[87] (one who speaks for another), indicates, biblical prophecy is not primarily predicting the future but speaking for God to his people about the present.

   (2) Where future predictions are involved, they are principally concerned with victory over the power of the Roman Empire[88] except in the final chapters,[89] where, as with apocalyptic generally, the ultimate triumph of God over Satan and the people of God over the forces of evil are clearly foreseen and prophesied.

d) The interesting two-story or split-level action of the Apocalypse is quite possibly influenced by Greek literature, especially drama.

   (1) Ephesus, like most Greek cities, had its great theater, which was one of the centers of Greek life and culture.

   (2) We have already seen in studying Paul that his references to being clothed with Christ[90] were quite possibly theatrical symbols.

   (3) Even the overall schema of the Apocalypse may involve Greek drama, for each of the seven septets or acts seems to comprise two parts, one the stage setting and the other the dramatic action.

   (4) In addition, the visions of the heavenly court are not unlike Greek stage settings.[92]

   (5) Finally, there may be a parallel with the *Iliad* of Homer, in which the decisive action of the Trojan War takes place not at the walls of Troy but at the summit of Mount Olympus, the abode of the gods.[93]

e) As in all apocalyptic literature, of course, there is a strong note of eschatology, of prophecy about the end time, in the final chapters of the Apocalypse.

   (1) Some authors see in this a theological contradiction with the "realized eschatology" of John's Gospel and argue from it against Johannine authorship of both.

(2) However, this is truly a misplaced argument, for the purpose and nature of the two works call for different emphases in eschatology. Besides, not all the eschatology in John's Gospel is "realized." Note, for example, the future eschatology of John 15:18–16:4.

6. Structures

a) As in John's Gospel, so also in the Apocalypse, the two principal structures are those of concentric circles and chiasmus,[94] particularly the latter.

b) The structure of concentric circles is involved primarily in the letters to the seven Churches of Asia.

(1) The first part of each letter refers back to some feature of the vision of Christ among the seven lampstands.

(2) The last part of each letter refers forward to some feature of the end time, that is, the heavenly Jerusalem and the restoration of the Genesis picture.

c) The structure of chiasmus is involved both in the letters to the Churches and in the overall arrangement of the Apocalypse.

(1) The letters to the Churches form a kind of spiritual and geographical[95] menorah, or Jewish seven-branched lampstand, with parallels between the letters to Ephesus and Laodicea, Smyrna and Philadelphia, Pergamum and Sardis, with the letter to Thyatira at the climactic peak.

(2) As will be seen in the outline, the entire Apocalypse is apparently divided into seven septets or acts in chiastic order, plus a prologue and an epilogue.

II. Outline of the Apocalypse

A. Organizing principles

1. As simple as John's Gospel at first appears and as complex as the Apocalypse seems by contrast, the actual development of the latter is easier to outline than that of the former.

2. One of the secrets, of course, is not to allow oneself to be so overwhelmed by the symbolism as to "miss the forest for the trees."

3. In general, note how the entire work is simply dominated by the number seven (three plus four) and the number twelve (three times four).

4. Note also, regarding the seven letters:

   a) How each letter follows a sevenfold pattern: (1) address, (2) description of Christ, (3) commendation, (4) reservation or condemnation, (5) warning or promise, (6) caution to heed the Spirit, and (7) reward of victory.

   b) Note, as mentioned earlier, how the beginning of each letter contains some element of the stylized vision of Christ in chapter 1.[96]

   c) In the same way, the end of each letter looks forward to some element of the heavenly Jerusalem and restored Genesis picture.[97]

5. Note in the Apocalypse as a whole:

   a) How it is divided into seven acts (each itself a septet) together with a prologue and an epilogue, comprising nine parts altogether.[98]

   b) How each act or septet is divided into two scenes, comprising a stage setting or scene and a dramatic action in seven parts.

   c) Note also that after the letters, all the acts dovetail with one another, each previous septet containing all seven parts of the one that follows, like circus elephants in a row.[99]

   d) Finally, note the chiastic arrangement shown on the lefthand side, with the prologue in parallel with the epilogue, Act I with Act VII, Act II with Act VI, Act III with Act V, and at the heart or peak is Act IV, showing the Church menaced by Satan out of hatred for Jesus Christ and his holy mother.[100]

   e) Because a completely detailed outline of the Apocalypse would be rather overwhelming and, above all, would tend to conceal the chiastic arrangement, I am reserving the details for the notes.

B. The Outline

  1. Prologue: title, salutation, initial praise[101] (1:1-8)

  2. Act I: the Church(es) on earth (1:9-3:22)

   a) Scene: vision of Christ and the lampstands[102] (1:9-20)

   b) Action: letters to the seven Churches[103] (2:1-3:22)

  3. Act II: the world judged by the Lamb (4:1-8:1)

   a) Scene: vision of God's heavenly court[104] (4:1-5:14)

   b) Action: the Lamb opens the seven seals[105] (6:1-8:1)

  4. Act III: the world and Church in agony (8:2-11:18)

   a) Scene: altars and prayers of the saints (8:2-6)

   f) Action: the seven trumpets[106] sounded (8:7-11:18)

  5. Act IV: Rome versus Christ and Church (11:19-15:4)

   a) Scene: the ark of the covenant[107] (11:19)

   b) Action: Mary/Church, seven signs[108] (12:1-15:4)

  6. Act V: the world in agony (15:5-16:21)

   a) Scene: the tent of witness (15:5-16:1)

   b) Action: the seven bowls[109] poured out (16:2-16)

  7. Act VI: "Babylon" (Rome) destroyed (16:17-19:5)

   a) Scene: an angel from the sanctuary (16:17-21)

   b) Action: the seven stages[110] of ruin (17:1-19:5)

  8. Act VII: the Church in heaven (19:6-22:5)

   a) Scene: the heavenly multitude (19:6-10)

   b) Action: the seven final scenes[111] (19:11-22:5)

  9. Epilogue: imprimaturs and blessings[112] (22:6-21)

CHIASMUS

III. Theology of the Apocalypse

Comparison of the theology of the Apocalypse with that of John and 1 John will reveal how much they have in common and how their differences are explainable by the diversity of the purpose and nature of the writings.

A. Theology in the strict sense (study of God himself)

  1. God the Father: The God of Israel but above all the Creator and Lord of the universe, enthroned in heaven amidst angels and saints and all creation in scenes reminiscent of the visions of Yahweh in Exod 24:9-11, Isa 6:1-4, and Ezek

1:4-28. His existence, transcendence, magnificence, control, and salvific intervention in the world are very clearly and vividly portrayed in Rev 4–5; 19–22.

2. Jesus Christ: The Son of God and Lamb of God who has been slain but is risen again, who alone can open the scrolls with the seven seals, who is one with the Church and already triumphant over the world. As already mentioned, he is depicted by the greatest number of titles and descriptions of the New Testament, for example, Witness, First-born, Ruler, Son of Man, First and Last, Son of God, Holy One, Amen, Source of Creation, Lion of Judah, Root of David, Lamb of God, Anointed One, Shepherd, Bridegroom, Word of God, King of Kings, Lord of Lords, Temple, Lamp, Alpha and Omega, Beginning and End, Morning Star, plus all the features in the vision of him among the seven golden lampstands.

3. The Holy Spirit: Not described or depicted, for example, as a dove or paraclete, but clearly indicated, especially at the beginning in the Spirit's word to the seven Churches (Rev 2–3) and at the end in the invitation of ''the Spirit and the Bride'' to come (Rev 22:17).

B. Theology in the broad sense (indirectly about God)

1. Ecclesiology

   a) The Church is identified with Christ in the vision of the lampstands and guided by the Spirit in the letters to the Churches; the hour of the Church is present and future, following the hour of Christ himself.

   b) The Church is the New Israel, surviving the destruction of Jerusalem in the past, the destruction of Rome in the near future, and all enemies throughout the future, culminating in the ultimate triumph of the Church, which is identified with Mary and united with Christ, the only Lord of Lords and King of Kings, already beginning his glorious reign, even in the midst of tribulation.

   c) The Church as the New or Heavenly Jerusalem, completely triumphant through Christ, is described in terms reminiscent of the Garden of Eden in Genesis, the dwelling of Yahweh with Israel in the tabernacle of Exodus and Numbers and the Temple of 1 Kings and Isaiah, as well as the New Israel of Ezek 40–48 and Zech 2; 12; 14.

2. Mariology: Mary is clearly the "woman clothed with the sun," giving birth to "a son, a male child who will rule all the nations with an iron scepter," and who is warred against by the great dragon in "the rest of her offspring" (Rev 12, NIV).

   a) Notice once again the use of "woman" in allusion to Eve, the first woman (Gen 2:23), as we have already seen in John 2:4 and 19:26.

   b) Notice also that this great vision of Mary, Christ, and the Church is the central one of the Apocalypse in the chiastic arrangement, the vision that begins to show the triumph of Christ and the Church over Satan warring against her through the Roman Empire.

   c) Finally, notice the specific sign or stage setting that introduces the vision of Mary, namely that of the ark of the covenant, in keeping with Luke's running allusion to David and the ark in 2 Sam 6, in his account of Mary's visitation (Luke 1:39-56), as already explained in Volume 1 under Luke's Gospel.

3. Morality and Spirituality: The ongoing existence of evil and sin in the world of humankind, the necessity of humility and purity, of faith and union with Christ, of patience and perseverance, of fulfillment of responsibility—these are all clear in the Apocalypse, while the letters to the Churches provide an excellent examination of conscience today, particularly concerning moral attitudes and habits of living.

4. Eschatology: In a sense, the entire Apocalypse is not only apocalyptic but eschatological. However, the final chapters are especially so, depicting the ultimate triumph of God through Christ over Satan and his forces of evil, in particular the persecuting Roman Empire, hence the triumph of the Church, the people and kingdom of God, the new and heavenly Jerusalem.

Having now completed our analysis of the Apocalypse, it remains for us to reflect upon its relevance and application to our life today, above all, to our moral and spiritual life. In particular, considering the amount of attention being devoted these days by evangelists and others to the supposed fulfillment in our time or in the near future of specific prophecies in the Book of Revelation, how are we to assess these? How in general can we use this marvelous book for our own spiritual benefit and that of others?

REFLECTIONS ON THE APOCALYPSE AND OUR LIFE

In our reflections on the Apocalypse, we will consider three subjects that seem particularly relevant to our life today, namely (1) the Apocalypse and the Church, (2) the Apocalypse and our own time, and (3) the Apocalypse and our own spiritual life.

The Apocalypse and the Church

That the Church is a primary concern in the Apocalypse is evident from the fact that the beginning, middle, and end of this extraordinary book all feature the Church and, most importantly, the Church in union with Jesus Christ. Thus, in the very first chapter, we find that marvelous vision of the glorified Christ in the midst of the seven golden lamp-stands (Rev 1:12-20). True, there is a special emphasis here on the seven individual Churches of the Roman province of Asia, but is not Jesus' union with them symbolic of his union with the entire Church? Is this imagery not reminiscent of Paul's figure of the Church as the body of Christ (1 Cor 12; Rom 12) and of Christ as the head of his body, the Church (Col 1:18; Eph 1:22-23; 4:1-16; 5:21-32)? Is it not, above all, reminiscent of that mystical union of Christ and the Church portrayed in Jesus' famous parable of the true vine and the branches in John 15:1-10?

But wait a minute! This Church and these individual Churches with which Christ is intimately united are far from being perfect! How can he possibly be regarded as truly one with them? Ah! That is what love does! That is all part of his divine-human condescension. Did he not also unite himself with our sinful human nature? "He who did not know sin, God made to be sin for our sakes, so that we might become the holiness of God in him" (2 Cor 5:21, WFD). In fact, did he not explicitly predict not only sin but scandals in his Church, for example, in the parable of the wheat and the weeds in Matt 13:24-30 as well as in the beginning of the ecclesial discourse (Matt 18:6-9)? It should not

The Great Theater at Pergamum.

surprise us, then, that from her very beginning and all through her history the Church has comprised both the good and the bad, the saint and the sinner, not only in her membership but alas! also in her leadership. In fact, when one stops to think about it, the scandals in the Church, in an ironic twist, help to confirm her divine origin and protection, for with this kind of leadership and membership any simply human institution would long ago have gone out of existence.

Not at all surprisingly, therefore, the letters to the Churches in the Apocalypse give them rather mixed reviews. The Church of Ephesus, the first one addressed, is indeed commended but also told, ''Yet I hold this against you: you have lost the love you had at first. Realize how far you have fallen. Repent and do the works you did at first'' (Rev 2:4-5, NAB). Then, after a totally positive letter to Smyrna, the Church at Pergamum is partly commended and partly condemned, the latter for having some members who follow the teaching of Balaam and some, called the Nicolaitans, [113] who follow the doctrine of a heresy.

Next, the church at Thyatira is generally commended, with the sole exception of tolerance toward ''the woman Jezebel, who calls herself a prophetess, who teaches and misleads my servants to play the harlot and to eat food sacrificed to idols" (Rev 2:20, NAB). But the Church at Sardis, except for a few faithful members (Rev 3:4), is condemned in no uncertain terms: "I know your works, that you have the reputation of being alive, but you are dead. Be watchful and strengthen what is left, which is going to die, for I have not found your works complete in the sight of my God" (Rev 3:1-2, NAB). Finally, after an unequivocal commendation of the Church at Philadelphia, Laodicea is forced to hear those familiar words of rejection in Rev 3:15-17, 19, NAB): "I know your works; I know that you are neither cold nor hot. I wish you were either cold or hot. So, because you are lukewarm, neither hot nor cold, I will spit you out of my mouth. For you say, 'I am rich and affluent and have no need of anything,' and yet do not realize that you are wretched, pitiable, poor, blind, and naked. . . . Those whom I love, I reprove and chastise. Be earnest, therefore, and repent." What a penetrating examination of conscience for us all! Is this not a reminder to all of us of the profound meaning of those enigmatic words of Jesus in Matt 12:38 and Luke 11:23, NAB. "Whoever is not with me is against me, and whoever does not gather with me scatters"? Which is quite a different statement, of course, from that clearly ecumenical declaration (spoken to John) in Mark 9:40, NAB, "For whoever is not against us is for us!"[114]

The one great consoling ingredient in the letter to the Church of Laodicea, besides the reminder that the Lord reproves and chastises those whom he loves (Rev 3:19), is that tender invitation which follows in Rev 3:20, NAB: "Behold, I stand at the door and knock. If anyone hears my voice and opens the door, I will enter his house and dine with him, and he with me." Does this beautiful invitation and assurance not remind us of similar words of Jesus in the discourse at the Last Supper, in John 14:23, NAB? Notice the close similarity: "Whoever loves me will keep my word and my Father will love him, and we will come to him and make our dwelling with him."

So much for the Church in its beginning, as reflected in the early chapters of the Apocalypse. It is directly in the middle of the work that we read the story of her pursuit and persecution by Satan, symbolized by the great dragon of Rev 12, through the Roman Empire, particularly the two persecuting emperors of John's time, namely Nero and Domitian, represented by the two beasts of Rev 13.

But along with persecution comes the beginning of the liberation of the Church through our Savior, the Lamb of God, who is already triumphant in heaven and will also be triumphant on earth (Rev 14).

And so, to return to the heart of the Apocalypse, we first have the preparatory sign in Rev 11:19 of the ark of the covenant, symbol of Mary in Luke 1:39-56, then the great sign of

> a woman clothed with the sun, with the moon at her feet, and on her head a crown of twelve stars. She was with child and wailed aloud in pain[115] as she labored to give birth. . . . She gave birth to a son, a male child, destined to rule all the nations with an iron rod.[116] Her child was caught up to God and his throne.[117] The woman herself fled into the desert where she had a place[118] prepared by God, that there she might be taken care of for twelve hundred and sixty days.[119] . . . Then the dragon became angry with the woman and went off to wage war against the rest of her offspring, those who keep God's commandments and bear witness to Jesus (Rev 12:1-2, 5-6, 17, NAB).

It is significant that immediately after the above we read, "It [the dragon] took its position on the sand of the sea" (Rev 12:18, NAB), after which we learn about the two beasts, one from the sea, the other from the land (Rev 13), which seem to represent the Roman Empire or, more specifically, Nero and Domitian, the two great persecutors of Christianity in John's time. The overall lesson from all this, I believe, is that as Jesus was persecuted, so the Church can expect to be persecuted,[120] as was now happening at the hands of the Roman Empire.

After the fall of Babylon or Rome, there is mention of a first resurrection and a thousand-year reign with Christ. What is the meaning of this? Certainly not, as the chiliasts[121] would have it, a reign of all earthly delights with Christ here on earth. Possibly it refers to a kind of resurrection from the dead on the part of the Church with the temporary cessation of persecutions, followed by a thousand-year period of comparative peace. The "thousand-year reign" probably refers to the entire period of time between the fall of the Roman Empire and the final triumph of Christ and the Church following a brief onslaught by Satan and those under his influence.

Could the "thousand-year reign" perhaps refer to the roughly thousand years between the fall of the Roman Empire and the breakup of Christendom mainly through the Protestant Reformation? It could be tempting to some Catholics to follow this interpretation, but besides a number of other considerations such as the Eastern schism, this kind of understanding is drawn from the Apocalypse as a supposed book of prophecy rather than as an actual book of apocalyptic.

What, then, is the meaning of that mysterious reference to "the first resurrection"? It is difficult, of course, to say for sure, but it could refer to baptism as a rising with Christ to new life (Rom 6:1-11), or, perhaps more in keeping with the context, it may refer to the martyrdom and resurrection at death[122] of Christians, after which they reign with Christ in heaven for a long period (symbolized by the thousand years) until the final triumph of Christ and the Church in the "second resurrection" at the end of time. Or, given the tendency of biblical writers, especially John, to have more than one meaning in mind for a given passage, the fullness of meaning of this mysterious part of the Apocalypse may embrace both of these possibilities.

At the end of time, according to the Apocalypse, the triumph of the Church will be complete, like and with the triumph of Christ himself. This is depicted in the final chapters of the book, where we find the magnificent panorama of the "new heaven and new earth"[123] and the Church as the bride of Christ[124] and the new Jerusalem coming down from heaven.[125] Now, does this mean an actual, visible, tangible, triumphant reign of the Church with Christ here on earth, or is the new Jerusalem another way of referring to what we call "the Church triumphant" in heaven? Unfortunately, the picture is not clear, and so we must simply remain one with Christ in the faith and patience of the saints and thus be ready for whatever form the triumph of the Church will actually take.

But when will these events of the *éschaton*, or end time, occur? Or, more relevantly for us, are we perhaps in the midst of that end time right now, as so many preachers are proclaiming these days? That will be the subject of our next reflection.

The Apocalypse and Our Own Time

Are we by any chance living in the "last days" of our history, our civilization, our planet? Many[126] today are so declaring, especially as we approach the end of the second millennium after Christ. Very much the same thing happened, history tells us, at the end of the first millennium. What then should be our attitude toward these proclamations of prophecies fulfilled, these declamations of doom?

Well, first of all, I hesitate to say anything about what should be our attitude, for fear of indulging in a form of mind control. That having been said, however, it seems to me that the following reflections are worthy of consideration.

In the first place, if the sense of impending doom is based on the entire Apocalypse understood as a book of prophecy,[127] then the very foundation of this approach is faulty for the simple reason that it ignores the literary form of apocalyptic according to which the Apocalypse is written. If, however, it is based only on the final chapters[128] of the Book of Revelation, then there may be some validity to the contention that we are in the *éschaton*. For example, if this is not the period in which Satan has been "released from prison" for a while "to deceive the nations at the four corners of the earth" (Rev 20:7-8), what other time would qualify? Have not more people lost their lives in war, oppression,[129] and violence than at any previous time in history? Are we not seeing the wholesale slaughter of unborn children[130] as well as widespread child abuse, both violent and sexual? Are we not witnessing an epidemic breakdown in morality, ethics, and character, as well as the unchecked incidence of addictions of various kinds? And, finally, are we not aware that various cults, including Satanism itself, have captured the minds of many, especially the young,[131] who comprise our future?

Going beyond the Apocalypse for confirmation, if we are not living in the time of the great apostasy of 2 Thess 2:3, what else can we call it? This is the first time in human history that there is a world movement based on the idea that there is no God! No, not Nazism, for as inhuman as that was, it was a national, not a world movement. Rather I refer to atheistic communism, which, in its history of domination since 1917, has enslaved the minds and wills of many millions, even billions, of human beings.

But is not communism disgraced as ineffectual and on the wane throughout the world? No, not quite. In Europe, yes, and to some extent in the Soviet Union and elsewhere, but it still rules over a billion Chinese, not to mention the suffering people of Cuba. And even where it has been rejected, for example in eastern Europe, careful studies reveal that the crucial opposition has found its motivation not primarily in economic or even political freedom but in religion, especially Catholicism.[132]

Speaking of apostasy, however, we cannot afford to confine our attention to the formal atheism of communism and ignore the more subtle apostasy and practical atheism of so many all over the world, and notably in our own country, who choose to live as if God did not exist. It is about this that Ps 14, NIV, declares, ''The fool says in his heart, 'There is no God!' '' Of course he knows that God exists, but for all practical purposes, to him God is irrelevant.[133]

But, viewing the Bible as a whole, there may be another indication that we are reaching the *éschaton,* or end time. According to some scholars,[134] salvation history began some two thousand years before Christ with the call of Abraham. Is it unreasonable to speculate that it may well end some two thousand years after Christ, thus underlining the fact that Jesus Christ is the very center of salvation history? At least it is worth considering.

Ultimately, however, while there may be indications in Scripture and beyond that we may be in or at least nearing the end time, we must admit that God has not chosen to let us know clearly when the *éschaton* will occur. About this even Jesus himself, as the Son of Man, denied having knowledge of when the things he was predicting would come to pass. ''But of that day or hour, no one knows, neither the angels in heaven, nor the Son, but only the Father'' (Mark 13:32), after which he reminds his apostles and us what our proper attitude ought to be. ''Be watchful! Be alert! You do not know when the time will come. . . . What I say to you, I say to all: 'Watch!' '' (Mark 13:33, 37).

The Apocalypse and Our Spiritual Life

Our reflections about the meaning of the Apocalypse for the Church and about the time of the *éschaton* have been interesting, but how relevant is this mysterious book to our spiritual life? What can we learn from it that will be helpful in our striving to live in love and union with Christ, in continuing his life and ministry to others in the world today? A great deal indeed! However, concerns about time and space suggest that we limit our reflections to certain key ones that touch the very heart of the spiritual life.

The first is that of *love for and union with Jesus Christ,* a union that he himself desires to be truly spiritual (not just emotional or intellectual), personal (not just communal or corporate), and intimate (not just superficial or formal). We see references to this kind of union from beginning to end of the Apocalypse. For example, in Rev 1:5-6, NAB, we read, ''To him who loves us and has freed us from our sins by his blood, who has made us into a kingdom, priests[135] for his God and

Father, to him be glory and power forever and ever. Amen.'' Then there follow those firm but gentle appeals to the seven Churches of Asia, at the end of which he offers, not only to the Church of Laodicea but to all the Churches and indeed to all of us, that tender invitation in Rev 1:19-21, NIV: ''Those whom I love I rebuke and discipline. So be earnest and repent. Here I am! I stand at the door and knock. If anyone hears my voice and opens the door, I will go in and eat with him, and he with me.''

Throughout the Apocalypse occur those fourteen[136] magnificent hymns, which, when carefully examined, reveal a depth of meaning and breadth of teaching that can provide food for a lifetime of contemplation. Consider, for example, the beautiful hymn of those ''who have come out of the great tribulation'' and ''have washed their robes in the blood of the Lamb'' in Rev 7:15-17, NIV:

> They are before the throne of God
> and serve him day and night in his temple:
> and he who sits on the throne will spread
> his tent[137] over them.
> Never again will they hunger;
> never again will they thirst.
> The sun will not beat upon them,
> nor any scorching heat.
> For the Lamb at the center of the throne
> will be their shepherd;[138]
> he will lead them to springs of living water.
> And God will wipe away every tear from their eyes.

Or, as another memorable example, let us look at the end of the final hymn, that of the ''great multitude, like the roar of rushing waters and like peals of thunder,'' which is found in Rev 19:6-8, NIV:

> Hallelujah!
> For our Lord God Almighty reigns.
> Let us rejoice and be glad
> and give him glory!
> For the wedding[139] of the Lamb has come,
> and his bride has made herself ready.
> Fine linen, bright and clean,
> was given her to wear.

The fine linen, it is added, ''stands for the righteous acts of the saints.'' Then, in chapter 21, notice these inspired and inspiring passages: ''Behold, God's dwelling[140] is with the human race. He will dwell with them and they will be his people, and God himself will always be with them.[141] He will wipe every tear from their eyes, and there shall be no more death or mourning, wailing or pain, for the old order has passed away. . . . Behold I make all things new!" (Rev 21:3-5, NAB). Then, this gem, which follows almost immediately in Rev 21:6-7, NIV: "It is done! I am the Alpha and the Omega, the Beginning and the End. To him who is thirsty I will give to drink without cost from the spring of the water of life.[142] He who overcomes will inherit all this, and I will be his God and he will be my son."[143] And in the magnificent description of the Church as the New Jerusalem, we read this lyrical passage: "I did not see a temple in the city, because the Lord God Almighty and the Lamb are its temple.[144] The city does not need the sun or the moon to shine on it for the glory of God gives it light, and the Lamb is its lamp.[145] . . . On no day will its gates ever be shut, for there will be no night there" (Rev 21:22-23, 25, NIV).

In the final chapter, there are a number of passages that cumulatively impart the overwhelming realization of Christ's tender love and desire for union with us, for example:

> Behold, I am coming soon! My reward is with me, and I will give to everyone according to what he has done. I am the Alpha and the Omega, the First and the Last, the Beginning and the End. . . . I am the Root and the Offspring of David, and the bright Morning Star (Rev 22:12-13, 16, NIV).
>
> The Spirit and the bride say, "Come!"[146] And let him who hears say, "Come!" Whoever is thirsty, let him come; and whoever wishes, let him take the free gift of the water of life[147] (Rev 22:17, NIV).
>
> He who testifies to these things says, "Yes, I am coming soon." Amen. Come, Lord Jesus! The grace of the Lord Jesus be with God's people. Amen (Rev 22:20-21, NIV).

In connection with the intimate union with Jesus Christ to which we are called, our picture would not be complete if it did not mention his holy mother who, as we can see so clearly from that central twelfth chapter, has a crucial role in our salvation and sanctification, not only as the physical mother of our Savior, but also as the mother, model, and mentor of "the rest of her offspring" (Rev 12:17, NIV), that is, all of us, whom she guides and protects as the Help of Christians and Refuge of Sinners;[148] above all, inculcating in us the three indispensable virtues that she exemplifies in her threefold responses to the angel at the annunciation, namely, humility (Luke 1:29), purity (Luke 1:34), and selfless love (Luke 1:38). The combination of the three "woman" passages in John 2:4; 19:26; and Rev 12:1-2, 4-6, 13-17, so reminiscent of the original woman, Eve, mother of the human race in Gen 2:23; 3:20, are moving in their cumulative effect.

Our second reflection should be on *the precious value of suffering*,[149] which is reflected in the Apocalypse over and over again. In fact, basic to the entire book is that it is a great privilege to suffer and even to give our life for the sake of Jesus. Those who do so are the intimate friends of Jesus who have washed their robes in the blood of the Lamb and follow him wherever he goes (Rev 14:1-5).

This is so important because our most basic instinct of self-preservation, the cultural climate in which we live, often even popular Christian preachers, all urge us to avoid suffering at all cost. Yet both Scripture and tradition make it absolutely clear that Jesus saved us from our sins not by his preaching, teaching, and miracles but by his suffering, death, and resurrection. Recall those words of Jesus in what might be called John's equivalent of the agony in the garden (John 12:23-26, NAB): "The hour has come for the Son of Man to be glorified. Amen, amen, I say to you, unless a grain of wheat falls to the ground and dies, it remains just a grain of wheat, but if it dies, it produces much fruit. Whoever loves his life loses it, and whoever hates his life in this world will preserve it for eternal life. Whoever serves me must follow[150] me, and where I am, there also will my servant be. The Father will honor whoever serves me."

And so, in keeping with this precious value of suffering, especially in the supreme sacrifice, that of life itself, we hear those inspiring words in Rev 14:13, NAB: "Blessed are the dead who die in the Lord from now on. Yes, . . . let them find rest from their labors, for their works accompany them."

Our third and final reflection is closely related to the foregoing one, namely the importance, even the necessity, in the spiritual life of *abandonment to the will of God* in imitation of Jesus and the saints. In fact, until we learn to abandon ourselves without anxiety about anything, we are hardly living a Christian life, let alone a deeply spiritual one.

If we truly believe that God, our heavenly Father, who knows all things and can do all things, is our own personal "daddy," according to the full meaning of the term *abba*[151] used by Jesus with particular appropriateness in the Garden of Gethsemane (Mark 14:36), then how can we do anything less than abandon ourselves to his holy will? If God is indeed love itself (1 John 4:8, 16), how can we possibly allow ourselves to be worried and anxious about anything instead of doing what we can (which is ultimately very little) and then leaving everything in God's providential care? In the beautiful words of 1 Pet 5:7, NIV, "Cast all your anxiety on him because he cares for you."

It has been well observed that the besetting sin of Americans (and most people generally) is anxiety,[152] which is at the basis of most, if not all, neuroses.[153] Only when we truly and completely abandon ourselves to God can we be really free. Then, in fact, we can not only live in freedom but even with abandon, like a little child[154] or like a butterfly.[155]

In the Apocalypse this truth is taught so often that it would take us far afield if we attempted to list, still less quote, all the places where it is inculcated. Suffice it to point out that this seems to be the underlying reason for the frequent visions of heaven, where God is in control and all the blessed live without fear or anxiety, in total freedom, joy, and glory.

One of the great secrets of the spiritual life is that with total abandonment we can accomplish so much more for God and for others. We have only so much energy, and what we expend in worry we cannot expend in work. It follows, then, that if we live without anxiety, we can accomplish a great deal more for the glory of God, the good of others, and our own sanctification. Is this not what Jesus had in mind when he exhorted us all to live without worry in the Sermon on the Mount (Matt 6:25-34)?

These are only a few of the many teachings in the Apocalypse that provide food for reflection with important applications to our spiritual life. Others, I trust, will suggest themselves to the reader, and I can only urge him or her to take time out for these reflections.

GENERAL CONCLUSION

We have now arrived at the end of our stories, analyses, and reflections on the five main human authors of the New Testament, whom I like to think of informally and privately as "Five Alive!" It has been a long and, at times, difficult journey. One obvious reason for this, as I am sure the reader is well aware, has been my preoccupation with documentation and background information in the notes. Here I have deliberately placed a great deal of additional content for the sake of those desirous of checking sources and delving more deeply, without distracting and burdening those readers who are not so inclined.

Appropriately, we have concluded our study with that mysterious and enriching book called the Apocalypse. I say "appropriately" because this very special book brings a sense of completeness not only to the New Testament but to the entire Bible. If the Acts of Apostles is the first Church history, the Apocalypse is the first theology of Church history. And if Genesis commences with the beginning of all things, so the Apocalypse concludes with the ending of all things and, I might add, a number of allusions back to the beginnings in Genesis. May our study of the whole Bible, notably the Apocalypse, increase our union with God, our creator, redeemer, and sanctifier!

NOTES

1. I have chosen to use the title "Ingenious John and the Veiled Revelation" for this treatment of the Apocalypse for three reasons: (1) to identify John the apostle and evangelist as the author of this work, (2) to indicate the ingenious quality of that authorship, and (3) to show why the work is so difficult to understand, namely because it is deliberately written in a veiled or hidden fashion. Further explanation of (1) and (3) will be given in the analysis section of this chapter. For reasons that will be evident later, I will normally use the term derived from Greek, "Apocalypse," in preference to that derived from Latin, "Revelation."

2. I have chosen this dual title of the Word because it so aptly describes him in his conquering, triumphant role, and at the same time it directly opposes emperor worship and the Domitian persecution occasioned thereby.

3. *See* the considerations on water as the symbol of life in ch. 3, "Ingenuous John and the Sublime Gospel," pp. 166–69, "The Theme of Life."

4. Panaya Kapulu is the Turkish name for All Holy Chapel, the purported home of Mary and John at Ephesus, seen in a vision and described by the German mystic Catherine Emmerich, rediscovered in the late nineteenth century by two Vincentian priests and restored for veneration and pilgrimages by the archbishop of Izmir, with an access road constructed by the Turkish government.

5. Patmos, the expressed and traditional site of the exile of John, the author of the Apocalypse (Rev 1:9) is one of the smaller islands in the Dodecanese Chain of Greek Isles in the Aegean Sea. Approximately ten miles long and six miles wide, Patmos is volcanic, rather bare and rocky, but because of its connection with John and the Apocalypse, it is today a favorite pilgrimage site in this area. *See* Otto Meinardus, *St. John of Patmos and the Seven Churches of the Apocalypse* (Athens: Lycabettus Press, 1979) 13.

6. *See* the role of Prochorus and Polycarp in the writing of John and 1 John, as described in the story section, "Ingenuous John and the Sublime Gospel," ch. 3.

7. In Rev 1:9, NAB, John lists the reason for his exile as "because I proclaimed God's word and gave testimony to Jesus." However, since Christian missionaries had been doing that for some sixty years (Acts 2:9) without being exiled, the real occasion must have had something to do with proclaiming Jesus as the true "Lord and God" rather than the emperor, Domitian.

It is difficult for us to feel the trauma of exile as a regular form of punishment in the Roman Empire. The Romans used prisons and jails either as detention centers for those awaiting trial or as places of execution by beheading or by starvation. As the equivalent of our prison system of confinement for a period of time or for life, they used exile, which generally involved three things: (1) confiscation of one's home, land, and goods by the state; (2) enslavement of one's family and sometimes near relatives; and (3) transportation, alone and unattended, for a definite amount of time or, more often, for life to a small, uninhabited or sparsely inhabited island. For many, it was a fate worse than death, and as a matter of fact, many chose suicide rather than exile or committed suicide during it.

8. Interestingly, there are seven low mountains or high hills on Patmos of which the two most noteworthy, according to current nomenclature, are Mount St. Elias to the left or southwest of the port and town of Skala and Mount Komara to the right or northeast. John in the Apocalypse makes explicit mention of the "seven hills on which the woman (Babylon, i.e., Rome) rests" (Rev 17:9).

9. The author of the Apocalypse identifies himself in Rev 1:1, 4, 9 as John, a servant, messenger, and prophet of Jesus as well as brother and fellow sufferer to those whom he addresses. Nowhere does he positively identify himself with John the son of Zebedee and apostle of Jesus, but for reasons I will detail in the next part, the analysis, I am willing to run counter to what is probably now the majority of biblical experts by identifying the author with John the Beloved Disciple, apostle, and evangelist.

The date of the Apocalypse is usually placed around A.D. 95, during or just before the first general persecution of Christians, attributed to the emperor, Domitian. John's age at this time, according to my estimates, would have been around eighty-five. However, as I explain in the text and notes of John's Gospel, I envision his being at lest ten years younger in outlook and energy, thanks to a simple lifestyle, close association with Jesus and Mary, and the total gift of himself without anxiety to the providence of God. Therefore, though aged in years, John was still energetic, driven by the love of Christ (2 Cor 5:14), and quite capable of creating a work like the Apocalypse.

10. *See* Mark 14:32-42; Matt 26:36-46; Luke 22:39-46; and John's equivalent in John 12:27-28.

11. The cave that is venerated today as the site of the composition of the Apocalypse is now enclosed in the famous Monastery of the Apocalypse about halfway up Mount St. Elias.

12. *See* John 10:11-17.

13. Titus Flavius Domitianus, the younger son of Vespasian and younger brother of Titus, the two Roman emperors of the Flavian House who preceded him in power, was born in A.D. 51 and at the age of thirty became Roman emperor after the untimely death of Titus, reigning from A.D. 81 to 96.

14. Even from the beginning of his reign, Domitian did not compare with Vespasian and Titus in character, personality, and popularity, but it was not until the failed conspiracies of Lucius Antonius and others that he became as paranoid and cruel, even to his family and household, as Herod the Great and Nero. *See* Suetonius (Gaius Suetonius Tranquillus), *The Twelve Caesars*, trans. Robert Graves (Baltimore: Penguin Books, 1961), 295-309. Among authors who ridiculed Domitian as "Nero Redivivus," though without explicitly using that particular expression, were Juvenal in his fourth *Satire*, line 38, and Pliny in his *Panegyrics*, no. 53, par. 3-4. The former may be found in the volume entitled *Juvenal and Persius*, trans. G. G. Ramsay in the Loeb Classical Library (Cambridge Mass.: Harvard University Press, 1950) 60-61. The latter is in the volume entitled *Pliny: Letters and Panegyrics* II, trans. Betty Radice (Cambridge, Mass.: Harvard University Press, 1969) 442--43.

15. This insistence on being addressed as "Lord and God" is universally attested to, for example, *see* Suetonius, 304.

16. It has been questioned by some historians and Scripture scholars whether there was any persecution at all initiated by Domitian, since there seems to be no mention of such in Suetonius and Dio Cassius. In reply, I would like to point out that the two historians mentioned, unlike Tacitus, show no real interest in Nero's persecution of Christians in Rome. Also, it should be noted that while there may not have been a formal worldwide persecution decreed by Domitian himself, this would not at all contraindicate a virulent persecution in Asia Minor, where emperor worship was at its height. In any case, even the threat of persecution, which was surely real enough, would have been sufficient to call for the writing of an apocalypse.

17. Like St. Paul suffering for his flock. *See* Col 1:24.

18. This is referred to as a "rocky bookstand" in Meinardus, *St. John of Patmos*, 16, with a photograph on p. 17.

19. *See* Paul's Letters to the Philippians and Philemon, the Colossians and "Ephesians," as well as 2 Timothy.

20. As will be shown in the analysis, the Greek of the Apocalypse is generally regarded as the worst of the entire New Testament, which may well constitute a good argument for the Johannine authorship of Revelation.

21. Apocalyptic writing, which may or may not contain genuine prophecy, is in itself a distinct literary form, best described, as I indicate in the story, as underground or resistance literature, written to encourage the persecuted without alerting the persecutors. A great disservice is done, then, when the Apocalypse of John and other apocalyptic literature are interpreted as books of prophecy pure and simple instead of apocalyptic writings, as they actually are.

22. The Book of Daniel is the original and only book of apocalyptic litera-

ture in the Old Testament. Written in or about 165 B.C. during the persecution of the Jews by Antiochus Epiphanes, the Seleucid (Greek) king of Syria, it purports to tell about one Daniel (otherwise unknown in the Jewish Testament) who supposedly lived in Mesopotamia under Babylonian and Persian rulers (three centuries previously) and who, by means of (apparent) visions and prophecies, clearly predicted the destruction of Antiochus and his kingdom, thereby greatly encouraging the persecuted Jews without tipping off their persecutors.

23. During Roman domination of Israel, beginning with the capture of Jerusalem by Pompey in 63 B.C.and culminating in the destruction of Jerusalem and the Temple in A.D. 70, a number of apocryphal (that is, noninspired) apocalypses appeared, such as the *Books of Enoch*, the *Testaments of the Twelve Patriarchs*, the *Sybilline Oracles*, the *Assumption of Moses*, the *Books of Baruch*, and the *Fourth Book of Esdras. See* John L. McKenzie, *Dictionary of the Bible*, (Milwaukee: Bruce, 1965) 43–44.

24. It is assumed by many that John the apostle and evangelist could not possibly have written the Apocalypse. This negative attitude stems from the idea that John, like the rest of the apostles, with the possible exception of Matthew and Judas Iscariot, was totally unlettered throughout his life. The truth is that, like other Jewish children, John undoubtedly learned to read Hebrew and Aramaic at synagogue school in preparation for his Bar Mitzvah, or coming of age, as a Jewish male at the age of thirteen. In addition, in Galilee of the Gentiles, John would probably have grown up with some knowledge of Koine (Common) Greek, the international language of the day. Decades later, as we find him at this time, he would certainly have had a much greater knowledge of all three languages. However, the fact that Greek was a second language may well be reflected in the comparatively poor quality of Greek in the Apocalypse.

25. Especially during the quiet years with Mary, it is understandable that John spent a great deal of time with her in studying the Jewish Testament, probably in Hebrew, which is also reflected in the fact that references in the Book of Revelation seem to be more commonly to the Hebrew Old Testament than to the Greek translation.

26. The Old Testament references just mentioned are normally in the form of allusions rather than quotations, indicating perhaps that the author is not in possession of the texts themselves to which he so often refers.

27. The apocalyptic parts of the prophets indicated are Isa 24–27 and elsewhere passim; Ezek 37–47 and elsewhere passim; and almost all of Joel and Zechariah.

28. Rev 22:1-5 shows clear allusions to the early chapters of Genesis, especially Gen 2:8-14.

29. *See* Mark 13, Matt 24, and Luke 21.

30. *See* especially 1 Thess 4:13–5:3 and 2 Thess 2:1-12.

31. It is characteristic of apocalyptic literature to include "revelations" gained from purported visions apparently received much earlier but applicable to the time in which and for which the apocalypse is written. Whether the

visions in John's Apocalypse are constructed "out of the whole cloth," or whether, given his privileged relationship with Christ, these were genuine visions, private revelations, I am not prepared to say and prefer to leave it an open question. Either possibility is valid in the inspired writing of Sacred Scripture.

32. Cf. the description of Jesus transfigured in Mark 9:2-8; Matt 17:1-8; Luke 9:28-36 with the vision of Jesus in Rev 1:9-20.

33. As indicated in n. 31 above, the mystical John may well have been the privileged recipient of genuine visions from time to time, as needed not so much by John himself as by the Church. It must be remembered, however, that visions and other so-called mystical phenomena are not a necessary part of mysticism itself, which rather describes a state of self-giving to God, living by his life, and praying the prayer of passive contemplation.

34. *See* Acts 7:55-56.

35. *See* John 16:33, WFD.

36. The Apocalypse seems to contain no fewer than fourteen hymns, twice the perfect biblical number of seven. What is their source? That would be difficult to determine. As I have speculated in the text, some may be from Christian liturgies, some from John's prior composition, some written to fit the apocalyptic scenario. *See* Robert Coleman, *Songs of Heaven* (Old Tappan, N.J.: Revell, 1980).

37. Then as now, it was both natural and supernatural for Christians to compose hymns and other music for their celebrations of the sacred liturgy. How many of these found their way into the New Testament, for example, in the writings of Paul and John, is a matter of much speculation.

38. To those who would discount the possibility of John's composing hymns at his advanced age, or even earlier, I would offer the reminder that, according to everyone's assessment, John was a mystic, and historically, mystics have been prime candidates as poets. In our own day, for example, just note the large body of poetry that has emanated from the mystical mind and pen of Thomas Merton.

39. As already noted in the study of John's Gospel, the structure of concentric circles, which was a favorite in the ancient world, tended to go right to the heart of the matter and then return to it over and over, adding details and clarifying the picture. Some of the apparent repetition in the Apocalypse may be due to this structure. Perhaps even more clearly, the initial vision of Christ in the midst of the seven golden lampstands, details of which appear again in the letters to the Churches, may provide an example of this kind of structure. Simply described, this structure is best visualized by imagining a pebble dropped into water, resulting in ever-widening circles.

40. Again, as we have seen in studying the Gospel of John, chiasmus, or a chiastic arrangement, was a favorite type of structure in the ancient world. For example, in a frame of seven points, the first and last would be in parallel, as would be the second and sixth, as well as the third and fifth, with the fourth comprising the peak of the pyramid (the bottom of the Greek letter chi, which looks like our X). In other words, the emphatic point is the one that comes,

surprisingly to us, right in the middle. I believe that we have seen a clear case of this in the Gospel, and in the analysis we will see perhaps an even clearer case in the Apocalypse of John.

41. The number seven symbolized perfection, apparently because each week (seven days) constituted one quarter of the moon's phases in the lunar month. Hence, God is pictured as resting on the seventh day of creation. In John's Gospel, we have discovered at least seven septets or combinations of seven and, if anything, the same number will be emphasized even more in the Apocalypse. I might add at this point that, especially in the Apocalypse, the number twelve is second only to seven in importance. In fact, the two are related, for seven is the result of three plus four, while twelve is derived from three times four. Hence, in the Apocalypse in various ways, both the twelve tribes of Israel and the twelve apostles are prominent.

42. I picture John as referring to "our gospel" because he is well aware of the work of Prochorus and Polycarp in the arrangement of his material into the actual written work that we now identify as the Gospel of John. This is, of course, only speculation on my part, but based partly on tradition and partly on a literary comparison of the Gospel, the First Epistle, and the Apocalypse of John.

43. As is well known in scholarly circles, it was normal for writers in ancient times to use one or more secretaries or amanuenses, who would first write on wax tablets and then transcribe onto papyrus or parchment. The different writing styles and the various amounts of freedom accorded to different secretaries were sometimes enough to explain variations in the compositions attributed to the same author. A careful comparison of John's Gospel and First Epistle with his Apocalypse reveals many similarities in content and form but also such significant literary differences that different secretaries alone would hardly explain the diversity. Hence, my recourse to the possibility that John wrote the first two works with the help of his coauthors, but composed the Apocalypse on his own and out of his own rather deficient knowledge of the Greek language.

44. Papyrus is a paper-like material formed from the stalk of the papyrus plant, which grows along the Nile in Egypt. In the ancient world, it was the writing material of choice until the development of parchment. When Egypt, fearful that the library at Pergamum, one of the seven cities of the Apocalypse, might one day surpass the famous library of Alexandria, refused to send any more papyrus there, the inventive people of Pergamum developed the use of animal skin (usually sheep or goats) into what we now know as parchment. The word parchment itself comes from *pergamum* by way of the French *parchemin*. Until the ultimate invention of paper from wood pulp or cloth, parchment became preferable even to papyrus because of its greater survivability under any and all weather conditions.

45. In addition to John's inferior knowledge of Greek, a second explanation for the poor quality and downright errors of grammar, vocabulary, and style in the Apocalypse may be attributable to the possibility that in the need of getting his Apocalypse to the beleaguered Christians as soon as possible,

John may have felt it necessary to omit the intermediate step of writing initially on wax tablets and then transcribing onto papyrus or parchment.

46. While John, as I have speculated before, was normally of a disposition and energy that would characterize one ten years younger than his chronological age, the very excitement of his new writing project would have caused him, quite possibly, to feel an extra ten years younger, in other words, about sixty-five years old.

47. Also contributing to John's exhilaration would have been the discovery of special meaning in his prolonged life and even in his traumatic exile. Victor Frankl, the developer of logotherapy and author of the famous little work, *Man's Search for Meaning: An Introduction to Logotherapy*, trans. Ilse Lasch (Boston: Beacon, 1963), learned in the Nazi holocaust the truth of Friedrich Nietzsche's saying that "he who has a why to live can endure almost any how!" *See* the preface of *Man's Search for Meaning*, xiii.

48. *See* John 13:23.

49. Rev 1:10; *see also* Dicharry, "The Lord's Day," NCE 8:990–91. Not only does this earliest mention of the Lord's Day, together with references to the first day of the week in Acts 20:7 and 1 Cor 16:2 as well as in early Christian literature, clearly show the early change of the Christian Sabbath from Saturday to Sunday, but it also suggests a wealth of meanings that have been largely lost or ignored, for example, (1) the resurrection, which established Jesus as Lord and Christ; (2) Christ's oneness with Yahweh, Creator and Lord of the earth; (3) the "day of the Lord," a day of judgment and salvation; (4) the unique and universal lordship of Christ; and (5) his fullness as Lord and head of his body, the Church.

50. *See* Rev 1:12-13, 20. Notice the proper translation of *lychnía*, "lampstand," rather than "candlestick" or "candelabra," for there were no candles in those days. The lampstands, of course, symbolize the seven Churches of Asia, to which John addresses the seven letters. Notice that together they form a kind of menorah, or Jewish seven-branched lampstand. Given the order of the letters, there is even a kind of chiastic arrangement here, the whole forming a somewhat imperfect geographical menorah, beginning with Ephesus and ending with Laodicea.

51. There is a very intricate structure in the letters, each of them containing a seven-point formula, the beginning of which looks back to the vision of Christ in Rev 1:9-20 and the end of which looks forward to the heavenly Jerusalem and the restored bliss of the Garden of Eden in Genesis (Rev 21:9–22:5).

52. As will be seen in the outline of the Apocalypse, there is a grand chiastic arrangement in seven septets or acts, each containing two scenes, one of dramatic setting and the other of dramatic action. Moreover, after the first act these seven septets dovetail with one another, that is, the seventh of the preceding septet contains all seven of the following septet. I visualize this as somewhat like a line of circus elephants, each one's trunk grasping the tail of the preceding one.

53. *See* John 14:18.

54. *See* John 14:23; 16:32; Rev 3:20; Matt 28:20.

55. John must have found himself in the same kind of ambivalence as Paul expresses in Phil 1:21-26, namely torn between dying and being with the Lord or continuing to live in order to serve others, especially the faithful. Perhaps there is a more personal meaning than the one ordinarily given for the epilogue of the Apocalypse, which emphasizes Jesus' coming, notably in the plaintive plea of Rev 22:20, NAB, etc. "Amen! Come, Lord Jesus!"

56. Could it be that the long delay in John's passing over to the eternal life of heaven had something to do with his development of "realized eschatology," his characteristic emphasis on eternal life as already begun in this life?

57. This total self-abandonment John may have learned, not only from Jesus' conformity to his Father's will in the Garden of Gethsemane and on the cross of Calvary but also from Mary whose fiat in Luke 1:38 must have continued all her life, including her sojourn at Ephesus with John.

58. The popularity of the Apocalypse today is mystifying when one considers the difficulty of understanding it, but not when one is aware of the wholesale misinterpretation of the work, seeing in it a book full of prophecies, many of which are viewed as being fulfilled in our own time, the (fateful?) final decade of the second millennium. The reason why I have consistently referred to the last book of the New Testament (and the whole Bible) as the "Apocalypse" rather than the "Book of Revelation" is precisely to remind us all that it is not a book of prophecy as such but rather a book of apocalyptic, of resistance or underground literature. There is, of course, some prophecy, above all concerning the destruction of the Roman Empire in the short term and, in the long term, the triumph of the Church as the heavenly Jerusalem.

59. As Domitian became more and more paranoid and murderous, putting people to death on the slightest pretext, a number of conspiracies were formed to terminate his reign, but all were unsuccessful until his own wife, Domitia, along with a number of his friends and freedmen, arranged his assassination on September 18, A.D. 96. So exultant were the senate and people of Rome (*senatus populusque Romanus*) that Domitian was posthumously stripped of all honors and all his decrees annulled. That meant that any persecution he may have initiated was forthwith terminated and John was free to return to Ephesus.

60. The so-called classic Roman persecutions of Christians are generally listed as ten in number, designated by the name of the Roman emperor during whose reign they occurred: Domitian (81–96), Trajan (98–117), Hadrian (117–38), Antoninus Pius (138–61), Marcus Aurelius (161–80), Commodus (180–92), Septimius Severus (193–211), Decius (249–51), Valerian (253–60), and Diocletian (284–305). It should be noted, however, that there is no unanimity on this listing. For example, sometimes Nero is added and either Domitian or Hadrian omitted, for although the persecution of Nero was confined to the city of Rome, it was one of the fiercest ever and may have caused more martyrdoms than any other persecution with the possible exceptions of those of Decius and Diocletian.

61. *See* John 15:18-27, in parallel with the eschatological discourse of Jesus

in Mark 13, Matt 24, and Luke 21. What is especially meaningful about this passage in John on the world's hatred is that it immediately follows and contrasts sharply with Jesus' teaching about his union with his Church (John 15:1-8), his new love-commandment (John 15:9-13), and his special relationship of friendship with his apostles (John 15:13-17).

62. We owe it to God and to his holy Word to interpret this fascinating book not according to our natural inclinations, for example, toward the exotic and spectacular, but according to the literary form in which it was inspired and written. Anything less, it seems to me, would be an abuse of Sacred Scripture, which is a sacrilege.

63. It is imperative that we not allow ourselves to be so engrossed in the individual symbolic details that we may "miss the forest for the trees" by failing to grasp the overall purpose, nature, and meaning of the book.

64. It is precisely by interpreting this work as a book of prophecy, pure and simple, instead of as a book of apocalyptic that contains some prophecy, that one tends to misinterpret and distort this precious writing.

65. There is indeed epistolary literature in this book, but it is different from the letters of Paul and the General Epistles in that all seven letters, albeit to seven different Churches, should be read together and understood as a septet, all according to a similar formula and with connections backward and forward in the book as a whole, according to explanations to be given later.

66. To list just a few, the following are found in the New Testament only in Johannine literature: Christ as the Lamb of God, the Good Shepherd, the Word of God, the King, the Light, the Temple, etc.

67. There is indeed dualism in the Apocalypse, in the basic struggle between God and Satan, good and evil, light and darkness, life and death. A similar dualism exists also in the Gospel of John, though not as clearly. But I must confess that I have deliberately played down this aspect both of the Gospel and the Apocalypse because of the tendency of some scholars to overemphasize it, drawing the conclusion therefrom that both works, especially the Apocalypse, are heavily influenced by Eastern mythology, for example, that of the ancient Persians.

68. This familiar quotation is from Robert Browning, "Pippa Passes" in the *Poetical Works of Robert Browning*, ed. Geoffrey Cumberlege (London: Oxford University Press, 1953), 171.

69. There are some fourteen hymns altogether, far more than in any other New Testament book, and six of them are used regularly as canticles in Vespers, or Evening Prayer, in the Liturgy of the Hours, official prayers of the Church.

70. The evidence involved here is found in the statements of early Christian writers (to be detailed under authorship), in the explicit statement of the author in Rev 1:9, and in background information from descriptions of the reign of Domitian by such famous historians as Suetonius and Pliny, descriptions that lend plausibility to the generally accepted circumstances indicated here.

71. On the date and place of the writing of the Apocalypse, there is almost

universal agreement among scholars, though it must be admitted that there are a few who consider the entire setting part of what they regard as the pseudonymous authorship of the work.

72. John does refer to himself as a servant of Jesus, witness to the Word of God, and a prophet with a special message (Rev 1:1-3). The fact that he does not call himself an apostle can hardly be used against Johannine authorship, not only because arguments from silence are weak indeed, but also because the very name John at that time and place was sufficient to identify the apostle without further indications.

73. These attributions can be found in the following works: Justin Martyr, *Dialogue with Trypho* in the Ante-Nicene Fathers, eds. Alexander Roberts and James Donaldson (New York: Charles Scribner's Sons, 1886), 1:240; Irenaeus, *Against Heresies, ibid.* 1:491; Hippolytus, *Appendix: On the Twelve Apostles, ibid.* 5:255; Tertullian, *The Instructions of Commodianus, ibid.* 4:211; Origen, *De Principiis, ibid.* 4:375.

74. Dionysius' questioning of Johannine authorship of the Apocalypse can be found in Dionysius the Great, "Extant Fragments," *ibid.* 6:82-84.

75. It must be remembered that Gnosticism was particularly strong in Egypt, as evidenced by the discovery of the *Nag Hammadi* or *Chenoboskion* documents there, and also that St. Dionysius was deeply embroiled in controversy with the millenarians or chiliasts (from Latin and Greek terms for one thousand respectively), who insisted on interpreting the thousand-year reign of Christ in the Apocalypse (Rev 20:1-6) as referring to a visible rule of the glorified Christ here on earth for a thousand years, with all kinds of natural pleasures available. Actually, it is curious that there was almost precisely a thousand years between the fall of the Roman Empire and the beginning of the breakup of united Christendom, but the exact significance of the "thousand-year reign" is open to interpretation.

76. There is no general agreement today on whether John the apostle wrote any of the works attributed to him, although there seems to be more of a tendency to consider the possibility of his writing the Apocalypse than the Gospel. Perhaps Patrick Sena best summarizes this tendency when he writes, "Some have said that since the writing of the Apocalypse is so different from the Gospel of John and since we get the impression that the apostles were fishermen and probably had little education, it just might be that the Apocalypse was written by the apostle, but the Gospel and Letters by someone else." *See* Patrick Sena, *The Apocalypse: Biblical Revelation Explained* (Staten Island, N.Y.: Alba, 1983) 27-28.

77. For a thorough study of the Greek grammar, vocabulary, and style in the Apocalypse, I refer the reader to the excellent work of G. Mussies, *The Morphology of Koine Greek as Used in the Apocalypse of St. John: A Study in Bilingualism* (Leiden, The Netherlands: E. J. Brill, 1971).

78. See John 16:33.

79. *See*, for example, Gilles Quispel, *The Secret Book of Revelation* (New York: McGraw-Hill, 1979), which states in its introduction, p. 5, "The fundamental idea in the Apocalypse is that the East will one day dominate the whole of

the world again. The Parthians will bring about the downfall of Rome, but the final and decisive victory is Israel's. . . . It is an elaboration of a folk tale about the second coming of Nero from Parthia. Originally it was anything but Christian. . . . Jewish Christianity and a pagan folk tale are thus the two keys to the interpretation of this book.''

80. While many of the biblical books are alluded to in the Apocalypse, the principal ones that provide most of the symbolism of the Apocalypse are the Old Testament books of Isaiah, Ezekiel, Daniel, Joel, and Zechariah, and in the New Testament the eschatological discourse of Jesus in Mark 13, Matt 24, and Luke 21, as well as Paul's Eschatological Letters, 1 and 2 Thessalonians. This can easily be confirmed by recourse to a good reference Bible such as the Jerusalem Bible.

81. As already explained when treating John's Gospel, the number seven seems to have derived its sacredness from the fact that each of the four quarters of the moon in the lunar month consists of seven days, hence it was natural to depict creation as comprising a week, with the work consuming six days and God resting on the seventh. One of the most obvious connections between the Gospel of John and the Apocalypse is their common and pervasive emphasis on the number seven.

82. The number twelve is represented in the Apocalypse in the twelve tribes of Israel and the twelve apostles, for example, symbolized by the twelve stars surrounding the woman in Rev 12:1 and the twelve courses of stones, twelve gates, and twelve guarding angels in the heavenly Jerusalem of Rev 21:9-21, in addition to the multiples of twelve in the twenty-four elders of Rev 4:4, etc. and the 144,000 sealed in Rev 7:1-8. Twelve, of course, is related to seven as four times three are related to four plus three.

83. The number ''666'' is significant in two ways: (1) The number six repeated three times indicates the epitome of imperfection or evil just as the word ''holy'' repeated three times symbolizes the epitome of holiness in Isa 6:3; (2) according to the system of *gematria*, in which the letters of the Greek or Hebrew alphabet were also used as numbers (since Arabic numerals were a later invention and Roman numerals too cumbersome for ordinary usage), ''666'' probably translates into Kaisar Neron or Caesar Nero, in recognition of the common nickname of Domitian as Nero Redivivus.

84. *See* n. 80 above.

85. *See* n. 66 above.

86. *See* ''The Theology of the Apocalypse,'' p. 214.

87. The Greek noun *prophētēs*, from which we derive our English word ''prophet,'' comes from the verb *phēmí* (I speak) and the preposition *pró* (for or on behalf of). Clearly, then, it is not primarily concerned with the prediction of distant future events.

88. That the Roman Empire is marked for destruction is clear from a number of indications, of which I will list only two: (1) The ''seven heads'' of the beast in Rev 17:9 represent seven hills upon which the woman sits, and (2) ch. 18 describes the fall of Babylon, a symbolic name for Rome as we see in 1 Pet 5:13. The use of Babylon as a symbolic name for Rome probably had

a threefold rationale: (1) It was a means of hiding the place of origin of 1 Peter and the subject of the Apocalypse from the Roman authorities; (2) it served to draw a parallel between the decadence of ancient Babylon and current Rome; and (3) it called attention to the parallel between the Babylonian destruction of the first Temple (that of Solomon) and the Roman destruction of the second (that of Zorobabel).

89. In the final chapters, following the destruction of Babylon (Rome), we have the rejoicing over her fall, the invitation to the wedding feast, the triumph of the King of Kings, the thousand-year reign (of united Christendom?), the final onslaught of Satan, his total defeat, and the ultimate triumph of God, Christ, and the Church. In our reflections, we will discuss the possible relevance of these final chapters for our own time.

90. *See* Gal 3:27 and Rom 13:14.

91. *See* the outline, which follows.

92. In the great theater at Ephesus, on which John may have modeled the heavenly scene, there was a *skēnē*, or stage (from the Greek word for tent, whence our stage scenery), in front of which was a *proskēnion*, or forestage (orchestra), and to the sides of which were two *paraskēnia*, or sidestages. With this knowledge it may be easier to visualize the descriptions in Rev 4–5 and similar scenes. *See* J. W. Bowman, ''Revelation, the Book of,'' *Interpreter's Dictionary of the Bible* (Nashville: Abingdon, 1962) 4:63.

93. Just as the real action of the Trojan War takes place at Mount Olympus, where Zeus tends to favor the Greeks or Trojans according to the intercessions of gods and goddesses who favor one side or the other, so also the real action of the Apocalypse takes place in heaven, where God is in complete control and always open to the intercession of the saints for the suffering Church on earth.

94. The structures of concentric circles and chiasmus are described more in detail in the next section, the outline, for which the reader will be prepared by an explanation of the organizing principles, including these structures.

95. The very locations of the seven Churches of the Roman province of Asia form a kind of menorah, albeit an irregular one, in a chiastic arrangement, as will be explained more fully in the next section. An additional point of information, however, is that generally speaking those Churches that are commended in the letters, for example, Smyrna, Thyatira, and Philadelphia, are the sites of flourishing cities today, while those Churches that are condemned, for example, Ephesus, Sardis, and Laodicea, are the sites of ruins today. The sole exception seems to be Pergamum, which receives ''mixed reviews'' and is largely mixed today, with an abandoned acropolis and asclepium (high city and health city), but which otherwise is a flourishing town.

96. Thus, for example, in the letter to Ephesus, Jesus is described as ''the one who holds the seven stars in his right hand and walks in the midst of the seven gold lampstands'' (Rev 2:1, NAB), which of course refers back to details of the vision of Christ in Rev 1:12-13, 16. And so these flashbacks to the vision of Christ continue in the other six letters.

97. Thus, for example, at the end of the first letter, the Church of Ephesus

is told, "To the victor, I will give the right to eat from the tree of life that is in the garden of God" (Rev 2:7, NAB), which refers forward to details of the final triumph in Rev 22:2. And so it goes with the other six letters.

98. Cf. this outline with the nine-part outline of the Gospel of John in chapter 3, "Ingenuous John and the Sublime Gospel," p. 161.

99. The imagery here is of circus elephants following one another in a line, with each elephant having its trunk wrapped around the tail of the preceding one. In this dovetailing feature, the Apocalypse differs from the Gospel of John.

100. For more on the central vision of Mary, Christ, and the Church in the Apocalypse, see the treatment on Mariology in the following section, "*The Theology of the Apocalypse.*"

101. The "initial praise" of Rev 1:4-9 is quite remarkable, clearly recalling the great covenant at Sinai in Exod 19 and the comparison of the new covenant to it in 1 Pet 2:9-10.

102. In the great mystical vision of Christ amid the seven golden lampstands, one cannot help thinking of the transfiguration of Jesus, witnessed by John, in Mark 9:2-8; Matt 17:1-8; Luke 9:28-36; and John's equivalent in John 12:28-33, as well as the great parable of Jesus concerning the vine and the branches, describing his union with the Church, in John 15:1-10.

103. In these letters, there seems to be a deliberate fusion of the roles of the risen Christ and the Holy Spirit, for each letter contains what the Spirit says to each Church, but at the same time reference is made to Christ speaking to each Church. Note too that it is the "angel" of each Church that is addressed. According to many if not most commentators, the angel is the administrative and pastoral leader, whether bishop, priest, or deacon.

The first septet, the letters to the Churches, seems to follow this geographical and chiastic order:

```
                      4. Thyatira
        3. Pergamum   (mixed)    5. Sardis
    2. Smyrna         (good)       6. Philadelphia
1. Ephesus            (bad)          7. Laodicea
```

104. It should be noted here that the "four living creatures" of the heavenly vision in Rev 4:6-9, which refer back to the visions of Ezekiel and Isaiah in Ezek 1:5-20 and Isa 6:1-4, do not describe the four evangelists. The attribution to them is not biblical and was made only later by the Fathers of the Church. Here, in the Apocalypse, as in Ezekiel and Isaiah, the reference seems to be to all living creation: the lion representing wild animals, the ox domesticated animals, the eagle the bird kingdom, and the man the human kingdom.

105. The second septet, the seven *seals* of the great scroll, seems to depict the trying conditions on earth as contrasted with the serenity of heaven, conditions that have been very clearly foretold in the eschatological discourse (Mark 13; Matt 24; Luke 21) of Jesus, who is at once the "lion of the tribe of Judah" (Rev 5:5) and the sacrificial Lamb of God "that seemed to have been slain" (Rev 5:6) and risen again, and who alone can open the seals to the sound of a magnificent threefold hymn of praise. The seven seals are apparently as fol-

lows: (1) the white horse of conquest, (2) the red horse of war and violence, (3) the black horse of famine, (4) the pale green horse of plague and death, (5) the persecution and martyrdom of the just, (6) earthquake and other natural catastrophes, all the "ordinary" sufferings of humankind to be expected through the centuries, but only "the beginning of labor pains" (Mark 13:8; Matt 24:8). Then after a heartening vision of the elect, both Jews and Gentiles, who triumph over persecution, (7) the seventh seal is opened, containing the seven trumpets.

106. After a preliminary vision of the saints offering the incense of their intercessory prayers, the seven *trumpets* of eschatological (end time) catastrophes are blown, thus: (1) the first trumpet of hail and fire mixed with blood, (2) the second trumpet of a burning mountain (volcano?) falling into the sea, (3) the third trumpet of a falling star (meteor or asteroid?) causing great destruction, (4) darkening of the stars and moon. After three warning woes, (5) the blowing of the fifth trumpet of a diabolical locust plague like that in Joel 1–2, either locusts like an army or an army like locusts, (6) the sixth trumpet of plagues of fire, smoke, and sulphur (caused by earthquakes and volcanoes?). Then, after the eating of the small scroll of tribulations (Ezek 3:1-3), and the death and rising of the two witnesses (olive trees or lampstands, Zech 4:11-14), (7) the seventh trumpet is blown, containing the seven signs, which follow. Who are the two witnesses? In Zechariah, they seem to be the priest Joshua and the governor Zorobabel, but in the Apocalypse the identification is more difficult. Perhaps the most common opinion focuses on Peter and Paul, but there is no certitude about it.

107. After another vision of heaven and another triumphant hymn, then a special vision of the ark of the covenant, symbol of Mary in Luke 1:39-56, the seven *signs* appear as follows: (1) the woman clothed with the sun and giving birth to the son who will rule the nations (Mary and Jesus), (2) the great dragon (Satan), (3) the beast from the sea (probably the Roman Empire under Nero), (4) the beast from the land (probably Domitian, "Nero Redivivus") (5) the Lamb and the virgins, (6) angels and the Son of Man harvesting the earth, then (7) seven angels with the seven bowls of God's wrath.

108. On Mary, Jesus, and the Church, see the following section on the theology of the Apocalypse, the treatment on Mariology under "Theology in the Broad Sense."

109. After a preliminary vision of the heavenly tent, or tabernacle of witness or testimony, the seven *bowls* of God's wrath are poured out on those deserving them, as follows: (1) The first bowl is poured on the earth, causing a plague of festering sores; (2) the second bowl is poured on the sea, causing it to turn to blood; (3) the third bowl is poured out on the rivers and springs, causing them also to turn to blood; (4) the fourth bowl is poured on the sun, causing it to scorch people; (5) the fifth bowl is poured out on the throne of the beast (Domitian), causing darkness and pain on the blasphemers; (6) the sixth bowl is poured on the great river Euphrates (location of Babylon, symbol of Rome), drying up its water in preparation for invasion by the kings of the East and the coming battle of Armageddon; (7) finally, the seventh bowl

of God's wrath is poured out, containing the seven stages of the destruction of Babylon the Great, symbol of Rome. If these bowls of God's wrath remind the reader of the ten plagues with which God vanquished Egypt in the Book of Exodus and forced the Pharaoh to let his people go, there is a reason. Scholars generally agree that there is a host of conscious allusions in this section of the Apocalypse to the plagues of Egypt, and understandably so, for in the same way as the Pharaoh and Egyptian Empire were the great enemies of Israel at one time, so Domitian and the Roman Empire were the great enemies of the Church in the time of John.

110. After a preliminary hearing of the voice from the Temple saying, ''It is done!'' (Rev 16:17), then the accompanying signs of lightning, thunder, and earthquakes, the great city and empire of Babylon (Rome) is described in seven *stages*: (1) the depravity of Babylon deserving punishment; (2) the baleful influence of Babylon throughout the earth deserving punishment; (3) the fall of Babylon, that is, of the Roman Empire (see Isa 21; Jer 50–51; Ezek 27–28); (4) mourning over Babylon (Rome) by all the earth; (5) the final ruin of Babylon, symbolizing the Roman Empire; (6) a heavenly hymn rejoicing over the Fall of Babylon or Rome; (7) finally, the seventh stage containing all of the following septet, the triumph of God, Christ, and the Church.

111. After a preliminary vision of the heavenly multitude praising God over his victory, the establishment of his reign, and the marriage feast of the Lamb, we now see the final seven *scenes*: (1) the conquering rider on the white horse, the ''King of Kings and Lord of Lords'' (Rev 19:16); (2) invitation to the great feast on the enemies of God; (3) the thousand-year reign of Christ and his own; (4) final defeat of Satan and triumph of God; (5) the new heaven and new earth; (6) the Church triumphant as the New Jerusalem; (7) the restoration of the bliss in the Garden of Eden.

112. The epilogue contains final approvals of the book, blessings on those who heed its contents, and promises of coming soon.

113. According to Irenaeus, *Against Heresies*, in the Ante-Nicene Fathers, 1:352, ''The Nicolaitanes (*sic*) are the followers of that Nicolas who was one of the seven first ordained to the diaconate by the apostles. [This is disputed by other primitive authorities.] They lead lives of unrestrained indulgence. The character of these men is very plainly pointed out in the Apocalypse of John, when they are represented as teaching that it is a matter of indifference to practice adultery, and to eat things sacrificed to idols.''

114. The great difference, of course, is that in the former statement Jesus is speaking about those who are supposed to be his followers, whereas in the latter statement he refers to those who are not members, at least not full members, of his following, his Church.

115. It is objected by some that the woman in the vision cannot be Mary because in the virgin birth of Jesus, she would have had no labor pains. According to Gen 3:16, labor pains are the punishment of Eve as a result of original sin, from which Mary was preserved in view of Jesus' future redemption of our human race from sin. However, such a contention fails to recognize the literary figure of *etiology* employed in all three punishments, namely that

of the serpent, Eve, and Adam. Etiology is a reference to something familiar to the hearer and reader to remind them of an important event or truth. There is no more reason to think that before or without the "original sin" of Adam and Eve, women would have given birth totally free of pain than to believe that serpents did not always slither on the ground and that those who till the soil did not often experience the frustration of hard labor resulting in poor crops. Though Mary conceived Jesus virginally and miraculously, there is no reason to believe that Jesus' birth was not in the normal fashion and, given the anatomy of women, some pain at least was normal and expected.

116. The allusion here is to Ps 2:9, describing the universal reign of the Messiah. The expression, "iron rod," does not connote ruling with cruelty, but rather with authority and power, since iron at that time was greatly admired as both stronger and more effective than bronze.

117. The expression "caught up to God and his throne" is probably a reference to Jesus' resurrection and ascension.

118. The "place prepared by God" may refer to Mary's protection by John at Ephesus, away from possible danger to her life from the Jews, or perhaps even to her assumption into heaven, which may have taken place either at Jerusalem or, more probably, Ephesus.

119. Twelve hundred and sixty days is the sum of three and a half lunar years of 360 days each, the approximate time of the great persecution of the Jews under Antiochus Epiphanes in Dan 7:25, with which, here and particularly in regard to various beasts, the Apocalypse is in parallel.

120. See John 15:18–16:4.

121. The term "chiliast" comes from the Greek word for the number thousand, namely *chiliás*, which is simply another word for "millenarian" (from the Latin word for "thousand," *mille*), that is, one who awaits a thousand year reign on earth with Christ, enjoying all kinds of natural delights.

122. On the possibility of our personal resurrection occurring at the moment of our death, see ch. 2, "Prolific Paul and the Later Letters," under "Paul's Vision of Our Bodily Resurrection," p. 121. See also my book, *To Live the Word, Inspired and Incarnate*, (Staten Island, N.Y.: Alba, 1985) app. A: "Resurrection and the Last Things," 403–14.

123. See Rev 21:1.

124. See Rev 21:9; also see Eph 5:21-33.

125. See Rev 21:2, 9-27; also see Isa 66:7-24.

126. Among so many evangelists stressing this theme, it is difficult to single out any particular ones, but two that come immediately to mind are the prestigious Billy Graham in, *Approaching Hoofbeats: The Four Horsemen of the Apocalypse* (New York: Avon Books, 1985), and of course Hal Lindsey, in his various books, such as *The Late Great Planet Earth* (Grand Rapids: Zondervan, 1976) as well as *There's a New World Coming: A Prophetic Odyssey* (Santa Ana, Calif.: Vision, 1975), which is really a prophetic interpretation of the Apocalypse.

127. It is true that the term "prophecy" is referred to at the beginning and end of the Apocalypse, in Rev 1:3 and 22:10, 19, but that does not turn this book of apocalyptic literature into a book of prophecy.

128. By final chapters, I am referring to Rev 20–22.

129. By oppression, I have in mind especially the horribly inhuman exterminations of the Nazi death camps and the almost equally inhuman enslavement of the communist gulags, or labor camps, in Siberia and elsewhere in the communist world, notably in China during the "cultural revolution."

130. There is a growing tendency today for politicians to evade their responsibility by claiming to be personally opposed to abortion but to recognize each one's right of choice in a pluralistic society like ours, yet how can there be a choice when an innocent life is at stake? Or what parity is there between the right to privacy, which is the basis of the Supreme Court decision permitting abortion, and someone's right to life?

131. This statement about the young is in no way intended to deny that there are many, many young people (and others) who have, by God's grace, managed not only to avoid all the addictions of our society but even to become crusaders for a better life and culture.

132. It is recognized by careful commentators and historians that such developments as the Solidarity union movement in Poland and the Pope's triumphant visit to his native Poland have had a central role in throwing off the yoke of communism, not just in Poland but in all of Eastern Europe, and even of breaking the grip of communism on the Soviet Union itself, particularly in Catholic areas such as Lithuania, Armenia, and the Ukraine.

133. Part of the problem is that many have grown up with an image of God as someone we turn to in time of need, and in our so-called affluent society a great number of people, especially "self-made" people, no longer feel any need beyond themselves, and hence tend to regard God as irrelevant.

134. Scholars generally place the time of Abraham somewhere between 2000 and 1500 B.C., and then consider it earlier or later in that timespan, depending on whether they accept a fifteenth- or thirteenth-century date for the Exodus. An additional consideration may be, however, the date of the destruction of Sodom and Gomorrah in Gen 19, which is usually fixed by geologists and archaeologists from 2000 to 1900 B.C.

135. There seems to be a clear allusion here to the covenant at Sinai in Exod 19:6 and to baptism in 1 Pet 2:9.

136. These hymns are often listed as fourteen in number, for example, in Coleman, *Songs of Heaven*, but a study of the hymns themselves suggests that their enumeration depends on how one groups smaller segments into larger songs.

137. The expression "will spread his tent" from *skēnóō* (I pitch, spread my tent, I dwell, live) recalls the tent of dwelling or tabernacle in the desert (Exod 40) as well as the incarnation or enfleshing of the Word in John 1:14.

138. The reference to the Lamb as Shepherd has obvious allusions, not only to the many references to shepherding in the Old Testament, especially Ps 23 and Ezek 34, but above all to the parable of the Good Shepherd in John 10.

139. The reference to the wedding of the Lamb suggests allusions to Yahweh as the bridegroom in the Old Testament, particularly in Hos 2; Isa 54 and 62; Jer 2:2; 3:20; and Ezek 16 and 23, but especially to Christ as the bridegroom in Matt 22:1-14; 25:1-13; John 3:29; and Eph 5:21-33.

140. *See* n. 139 above; *see also* John 14:23.

141. *See* Isa 7:14; Matt 1:23; 28:20; John 14:18.

142. *See* Isa 55:1-3; John 4:10; 7:37-39, etc.

143. *See* 2 Sam 7:14; Gal 4:4-7; Rom 8:14-17; Jn 1:12-13; 1 John 3:1-3.

144. *See* John 2:19-21.

145. *See* John 1:3-5, 9; 8:12; 9:5.

146. This seems to be a reference to the *parousía* or second coming of Christ (Mark 13:26, Matt 25:30; Luke 21:27).

147. *See* n. 142 above.

148. These are two favorites among the many titles of Mary in the Litany of the Blessed Virgin Mary. The former title was popularized especially by the lovable St. John Bosco.

149. *See* my reflections on suffering in ch. 1, "Passionate Paul and the Early Letters," under "Paul the Mystic," p. 40, and "Paul the Missionary," p. 51; *see also* my treatment of this important subject of suffering in my book *To Live the Word*, 266–72.

150. This seems to be John's equivalent of the well-known declaration of Jesus, "Whoever wishes to come after me must deny himself, take up his cross, and follow me" (Mark 8:34, NAB; Matt 16:24; Luke 9:23).

151. As adopted children of God, we are invited to address him with the same familiar term used by Jesus himself, as we see in Gal 4:4-7 and Rom 8:14-17.

152. According to *Time* magazine, March 31, 1961, "Anxiety seems to be the dominant fact and is threatening to become the dominant cliché of modern life."

153. And according to the *Dictionary of Behavioral Sciences*, ed. Benjamin Wolman (New York: Van Nostrand Reinhold, 1973) 253, "Anxiety is the chief characteristic of neuroses."

154. Recall Jesus' profound statement, "Amen, I say to you, unless you change and become like little children, you will not enter the kingdom of the heavens" (Matt 18:3, WFD).

155. The reference here is to the freedom of the butterfly, symbol of resurrection, to fly at will, in contrast to the limitations of the caterpillar before it became a butterfly.

RECOMMENDED READING LIST

Collins, Adela. *Crisis and Catharsis: The Power of the Apocalypse*. Philadelphia: Westminster, 1984.

Corsini, Eugenio. *The Apocalypse: The Perennial Revelation of Jesus Christ*. Wilmington, Del.: Michael Glazier, 1983.

Fiorenza, Elisabeth. *The Book of Revelation: Justice and Judgment*. Philadelphia: Fortress, 1985.

Ford, J. Massyngberde. *Revelation: Introduction, Translation, and Commentary, Anchor Bible*. Garden City, N.Y.: Doubleday, 1975.

Sena, Patrick. *The Apocalypse: Biblical Revelation Explained*. Staten Island, N.Y.: Alba, 1983.

QUESTIONS FOR REFLECTION AND DISCUSSION

1. What seems to be the historical setting for the writing of the Apocalypse, or Book of Revelation?

2. What is the literary form of the Apocalypse, and how does this affect its interpretation?

3. How are Christ, Mary, and the Church portrayed in the Apocalypse?

4. Can you describe the principal structures involved in the writing of the Apocalypse?

5. What, if any, relevance does the Apocalypse have for you and for the Church in today's world?

Index

REMARKS: This subject index is at the same time selective and comprehensive; selective because an index of each and every subject touched on in this volume, let alone all proper names and scripture references, would be far too unwieldy, but comprehensive because, unlike many indices, references are also made to the endnotes, where subjects are expanded for the sake of greater clarification and explanation as well as documentation without burdening the main text, especially the story part. For economy of time and space, all references are to page numbers, including the endnotes.